MEDIEVAL NONSENSE

FORDHAM SERIES IN MEDIEVAL STUDIES

Mary C. Erler and Franklin T. Harkins, series editors

MEDIEVAL NONSENSE

*Signifying Nothing
in Fourteenth-Century England*

JORDAN KIRK

FORDHAM UNIVERSITY PRESS

New York   2021

Copyright © 2021 Fordham University Press

All rights reserved. No part of this publication may be reproduced, stored in a retrieval system, or transmitted in any form or by any means—electronic, mechanical, photocopy, recording, or any other—except for brief quotations in printed reviews, without the prior permission of the publisher.

Fordham University Press has no responsibility for the persistence or accuracy of URLs for external or third-party Internet websites referred to in this publication and does not guarantee that any content on such websites is, or will remain, accurate or appropriate.

Fordham University Press also publishes its books in a variety of electronic formats. Some content that appears in print may not be available in electronic books.

Visit us online at www.fordhampress.com.

Library of Congress Cataloging-in-Publication Data

Names: Kirk, Jordan, author.
Title: Medieval nonsense : signifying nothing in fourteenth-century England / Jordan Kirk.
Other titles: Fordham series in medieval studies.
Description: New York : Fordham University Press, 2021. | Series: Fordham series in medieval studies | Includes bibliographical references and index.
Identifiers: LCCN 2021005881 | ISBN 9780823294466 (hardback) | ISBN 9780823294473 (paperback) | ISBN 9780823294480 (epub)
Subjects: LCSH: English literature—Old English, ca. 450–1100—History and criticism. | Nonsense literature, English—History and criticism. | Philosophy, Medieval.
Classification: LCC PR255 .K53 2021 | DDC 820.9/001—dc23
LC record available at https://lccn.loc.gov/2021005881

Printed in the United States of America

23 22 21   5 4 3 2 1

First edition

Bu, ba, buf.
—Logica "Cum sit nostra"

Rum, ram, ruf.
—Chaucer

CONTENTS

The Wind in the Shell: Prolegomena to the Study
of Medieval Nonsignification / 1

1 Priscian, Boethius, and Augustine on *Vox Sola* / 27

2 Walter Burley on *Suppositio Materialis* / 52

3 The *Cloud of Unknowing* on the *Litil Worde of O Silable* / 76

4 *St. Erkenwald* on the *Caracter* / 98

Acknowledgments / 127

Notes / 129

Bibliography / 157

Index / 183

MEDIEVAL NONSENSE

THE WIND IN THE SHELL:
PROLEGOMENA TO THE STUDY
OF MEDIEVAL NONSIGNIFICATION

The theory of signification in the West began as a theory of the oracular.[1] The word *semeion* (sign) first emerged in the realm of divination, as a technical term referring to the enigmas of the mantic utterance.[2] The sound that emerges from the mouth of the oracle would seem to signify something; but just what it would signify remains altogether unclear. And likewise—given certain states of mind, or at certain ritually determined times and places, or indeed *sub specie aeternitatis*—with the sounds of the trees and waters, the configuration of the creases in the palm, or the path a bird takes across the sky.[3] A sound, inscription, or gesture seems to point beyond itself—but toward what? When you try to divine something from these appearances, you get nothing more than riddles.

The originary object of linguistic study is thus not what communicates a meaning but what defies all efforts to make sense of it. Indeed, historically speaking it is only belatedly that the category of *semeion* will come to include signs whose meaning is anything other than obscure. Moreover, the ancient scientists of language were familiar with certain sounds, inscriptions, and gestures that are refractory to interpretation not because they are ambiguous or abstruse but simply because they are devoid of any meaning whatsoever. Neither did they fail to notice that what presents itself in these strange signs, their own mere matter or empty form, is no less present in even the most meaningful signs. For there is a nonsignifying element in every signification, and it is not some extralinguistic substrate on which language would happen to rely but rather what survives, within the scarcely linguistic realm of our various communications, of language itself. In this residue—the bare voice, ductus, or flection—the animal with language, the human being, comes face-to-face with what it is. And yet it is all but impossible to keep the attention there, as anyone who tries it will be able to attest, for when the mind encounters a void of meaning it tends either to turn away from it immediately or, if that strategy fails, to project fabricated significations onto it and then busy itself with them instead of with it. Knowing this, certain technicians of the word have created apparatuses to capture our attention and train it on the meaningless site of all possible meanings.

I began writing this book when, some years ago, I first read the work of a great translator of the fourteenth century, an Englishman who had gathered obscene jokes, character studies, reports of visionary experience, and liturgies of the cult of Love from his own observation as well as from rumors that had reached him from even the most distant lands, and then wove them together into texts that our own speech and writing remain patterned after more than six hundred years later. Scattered throughout the works of the poet whom Virginia Woolf would one day call "the great originator of this still-continuing conversation or argument or song" was a series of words that I could not make any sense of and that no glossary or commentary could help me with.[4] For they seemed to be written in an idiom made up only of syllables:

> buf

he had written in one place,

> rum ram ruf

in another, and

> cok cok

in still another; not to mention

> cokkow cokkow cokkow

and

> kek kek kokkow quek quek

and, perhaps most enigmatically of all,

> awak . . . awak.[5]

I could not figure out how to read these words, if that is what they are; nor, by the same token, could I figure out how to stop reading them. And so I began to inquire into the question of nonsignification, and in particular into how it might have made itself available for thinking, contemplation, and experiment at the time and place in which this poet, Geoffrey Chaucer, had written them down.

TREGETRIE

Chaucer was in the habit of recording his dreams—if they were not rather revelations, hallucinations, or prophecies, not to speak of flights of fancy.[6] In the report of a dream that he says he had on December 10 of an unspecified year, he claims to have beheld a strange sight. This particular apparition was not, perhaps, quite as wondrous as some of the other sights he saw that same night: a vast desert, an ice mountain, a talking bird, a goddess holding court, a wicker labyrinth spinning in thin air. Not as wondrous, indeed, as the mere fact of seeing anything at all. But it stopped him in his tracks. It was a windmill, and it was being placed under a walnut shell.[7]

The vision arose in a very particular place—midway between the heavens, the earth, and the sea, wherever that might be—that Chaucer called the *hous of Fame*, which means the "realm of language itself."[8] His discovery or positing of this obscure place, fanciful as it might be, is also something more: the solution of an ostensible problem in the physics of sound. It is easily observable that noises do not remain where they arise, that as soon as they become audible in one place they are already becoming fainter there and starting to become audible somewhere else. Where, then, are all the noises going? In response to such a line of questioning, the poet asserts, on the uncompromisingly ironic authority of his book learning and of his quasi-transcendent stultification, that just as heavy objects naturally tend toward the lowest place possible, sounds are naturally drawn toward their own most proper place, and that somewhere in the universe there is a point at which they all collect.[9] That point will be known henceforth as the *hous of Fame*. Moreover, as the various squeaks, thuds, grumbles, and enunciations of all the world arrive in this zone—utterly removed now from the contexts in which they might once have been meaningful—they are bestowed, in a kind of universal inverse ekphrasis, with a certain visibility: they seem to take on the forms of the beings that made them.[10] Thus it is that the unimaginably loud clamor of the realm of language itself discloses itself to the eyes of the dreamer who arrives there as a land of mountains and valleys and architectural constructions in which living beings abide.

Among these beings of every description, Chaucer encounters a host of wonder-workers: sorcerers, natural scientists, tricksters. These he lists in passing, pausing only in the case of one of them. The figure who arrests his attention is a *tregetour*—a sleight-of-hand artist—by the name of Colin, to whom the following five lines are devoted:

> Ther saugh I Colle tregetour
> Upon a table of sycamour
> Pleye an uncouth thyng to telle—
> Y saugh him carien a wynd-melle
> Under a walsh-note shale.[11]
>
> [There I saw Colin the tregetour
> Perform, on a sycamore table,
> A thing that is strange to recount:
> I saw him put a windmill
> Under a walnut shell.]

If the significance of this passage has never, perhaps, been altogether clear, so much is perfectly in keeping with its own indications: for what Chaucer beheld is, as he says, *uncouth to telle*. This specification could mean a number of things—that the act of placing a windmill under a walnut shell is unfamiliar, or marvelous, or outrageous, or occult—but in fact the poet is using the word *uncouth* here in the etymological sense of *unknown*, so that *uncouth to telle* means *unknown with respect to its being discussed*.¹² Accordingly, any speech that says "I saw" such a thing—and the poet says it twice here—can only be the production, and perhaps the transmission, of an ignorance of that same thing. The full measure of this declaration should be taken: this passage will give rise to nothing else than an unknowing of what it discusses. But we do not need to throw up our hands before the specter of ineffability; the poet, for his part, certainly does not. For if the thing beheld cannot be known in the telling, there is nothing to prevent that ignorance itself from being known—and known with precision. What is opened by this passage is a question: What sort of unknowing is produced by the report of the placement of a windmill under a walnut shell?

Chaucer does not neglect to provide the means of answering this question. In his list of the various kinds of charmers, illusionists, and practitioners of *magyke naturel* to be found in the palace of Fame—a list in which the passage in question terminates—he has just set up a rudimentary taxonomy of the possible ways of bringing about a wondrous phenomenon. Tregetry, the specific means employed in the matter of the windmill and the shell, seems to be distinguished on the one hand from sorcery and on the other from natural science. This shell game, whatever else it will prove to have been, is something accomplished neither by mere spontaneous force of nature nor by supernatural spell but by means of the application of a technical skill. What is more, this technical skill can itself be identified without difficulty. In the late fourteenth century, the word *tregetrie* could refer to various kinds of prestidigitation, but Chaucer makes explicit that he is using it here in the literal sense of trajection, throwing across—that is, juggling.¹³ What allows for a windmill to be placed under a walnut shell is a variety of juggling: a movement from hand to hand, a circulation of objects such that they are constantly in motion without ever arriving anywhere other than where they started, but also without ever remaining in their place of origin. Tregetry is a peculiar mode of suspended transmission, characteristic of clubs tossed in the air or shells shifted around on a tabletop, in which the transfer does not exhaust itself in delivering its object across some gap but rather retains it within the configuration of its own unceasing circulation—that is, within the gap itself.

When Colin the tregetour's operation is described in such a fashion, it is impossible not to recognize in it the basic gesture of the *House of Fame* as a whole. For the passage in question comes only after a series of variations on the theme of transmission: a self-conscious translation of Virgil, various invocations of poetic and other lineages, a quasi-scientific account of the transfer of sound through space, ostentatious displays of metaphorization, and so forth. In each case, whatever transfer might be expected to take place—from idiom to idiom, generation to generation, location to location, or image to image—is turned back on itself to circulate in a void, inoperative. This gesture becomes most spectacularly visible in the poem's famous final pages, in which Chaucer evokes a wicker house whirling in the air about its own axis, resounding with the clamor of a constant communication of news, and then breaks off his description, leaving the poem "unfinished," seemingly just when he is about to disclose the crucial bit of news around whose discovery the whole text would have seemed to be organized. The work that the poet is carrying out answers to the same description as the placement of a windmill under a walnut shell, in short, and if both the one and the other are *uncouth to telle*, it is because they consist precisely in stripping the communicative function from a means of communication.

So much is legible in the epithet *tregetour*, and it is no less legible in the particular sleight-of-hand artistry in which Colin engages. For the walnut shell that he manipulates cannot be said to be unfamiliar. In the much-discussed integumental model of interpretation that is a basic presupposition of medieval literary theory, a text is likened to a nut whose shell, the mere letter, is to be cracked open in order that the kernel of signification it conceals might be revealed.[14] Alain de Lille, Bernardus Silvestris, Bede, Fulgentius, Jerome, and Plautus—to give only a small fraction of the possible names—had all put the matter this way; and Chaucer and his contemporaries recurred to the figure with frequency. But, as is only fitting in the context of the *House of Fame*, here it appears only in the form of its own disfigurement, as a shell containing no nut to speak of, but, unthinkably, something else entirely: a windmill.

This disfigurement is a reenvisioning of the integumental model for the purposes of tregetry. It develops out of the observation that, if a shell can contain a nut, it can also (and for the same reason) be empty of any nut. Tregetry takes advantage of the fact that the sound-shape of a word can exist without any meaning's inhering within it, that there can be a full-fledged word in the absence of sense. For this emptiness makes possible a certain maneuver. It means that a shell is capable of sheltering not only a kernel of meaning but other things as well, or at any rate one other thing in particular. And, like the shell in which it is placed, this particular thing will not be selected at random. For the windmill, too, was a familiar linguistic figure in Chaucer's time and place: "the clacking of the windmill," it has been observed in another context, "was commonly used to convey empty garrulity."[15] In this manner the force of the figure seems at first simply to be redoubled: what is found within the mere noise of a shell without a kernel would just be more noise. But the noise of a windmill is of course not just any noise but that of the very apparatus whose exemplary purpose (not least in Chaucer's own "Reeve's Tale") is the crushing of kernels in particular. Sheltered impossibly within the emptiness of the word the poet beholds not just an absence of meaning but a technology for its pulverization. It is not merely the case, then, that there are words that do not signify; there are also words that might serve as the site of an engineered destruction of signification generally.

But it cannot yet be said with certainty that such a destruction is actually taking place. The windmill in question, after all, might not be a real machine in working order; indeed, the fact that it can be placed under a walnut shell might seem to suggest that it is nothing but a trinket or figurine. In such a case, however, it is not clear what would be *uncouth to telle* about its placement there. Moreover, there is good reason to think that the windmill is in fact in operation. For not the least part of the racket emitted by a windmill is that produced by the part of the apparatus that actually grinds the kernels themselves: the millstone. And it is precisely to the sound of stone that the realm of Fame is repeatedly likened: as when—after making an oath by Saint Peter, of all things—the dreamer declares that this sound is "lyk betynge of the see . . . ayen the roches holowe" (like the beating of the sea against a hollow in the rocks); or when he compares the *gret noyse* of the whirling wicker house to the "rowtynge of the ston / That from th'engyn ys leten gon" (the roaring of the stone that has been thrown from a machine: a catapult, no doubt, though other readings remain possible); or again, quasi-analogically, when the sound that makes up whatever appears in the realm of Fame is said to travel there the way a ripple moves across the surface of a body of water when a stone, in particular, has been thrown into it; or yet again when the *tydynges* that are Fame's *prima materia* are enumerated by reference to the pulverized form of stone ("moo tydynges . . . then greynes be of sondes"; more tidings than there are grains of sand).[16] So insistently does Chaucer return to the figure of rock in the *House of Fame* that a reader could perhaps be forgiven for taking as a paronomasia his affirmation that the writers of old arrayed in the memory palace of Fame are as numerous "as ben on trees rokes nestes" (as there are rooks' nests on trees).[17] Indeed, it can be observed that the dream vision's most memorable images and axioms emerge from the multiplicative fragmentation of the semantic kernel of the word *roke*, whose various senses in Middle English include not only "stone" and "rook" but also "castle" and "distaff" and "mist": think of its castle built upon a rock of ice, of the "femynyne creature" within it spinning out her tales, of the radical dictum it introduces that "every thing ys wyst / though hit be kevered with the myst" (everything is known / though it be covered with the mist).[18] In short, the sound of the realm of language itself is a specifically petrological sound, and the figures into which that sound is made visible by inverse ekphrasis are no less petrological.[19]

What resounds in "thise rokkes or thise milnestones," as the synecdoche is elaborated in the *Troilus*, is in short the millstone housed within the windmill beneath Colin's walnut shell.[20] Its racket—the clamor of the inanimate—has no meaning; it is the sound of the pulverization of meaning itself. But this "empty garrulity" is also the announcement aloud, in the mode of betokening, of the existence of a perhaps unsuspected phenomenon. For if the millstone is grinding, that means that the sails of the apparatus are turning, and that in turn means that the abyss within the empty shell of the mere letter is not an inert void but a dynamic zone traversed by meteorological forces. There must be a wind that blows, of its own accord, through the hollows of the word. Chaucer's vision of the placement of a windmill in a walnut shell is thus *uncouth to telle*—to recapitulate in a single unwieldy formula everything that has been said so far—in the precise sense that it is the beholding, by inverse ekphrasis, of a word found within the realm of language itself that shelters an emptiness traversed by a spontaneous energy that can be harnessed to power an apparatus designed to pulverize signification.

The *House of Fame* is a device engineered to transmit this word. It is the *récit visionnaire* of a mind-technician whose practice is said to consist in maintaining an unsurfeited sorrow over his books, keeping the ironic vigil of his astonishment, the doors of his senses sealed, always "also domb as any stoon" (as mute as a stone: but how mute is that, again?).[21] This contemplative practice or engineering of awareness is undertaken in order that the practitioner might enter such a dream-state as will allow him or her to encounter the being of language as such, which resounds as visibility in the emptiness of the mantric word given over to the inoperativity of transmission.[22] The record of this encounter—the literary work—is an apparatus designed to bring about a like encounter in those who come across it, begin fiddling with it, and find that they cannot put it down. It functions not by transmitting some particular information, opinion, or instruction but by being constructed in such a manner that when we, whoever we might be, search it for such a kernel of meaning, we will have at last no choice—if we do not first grasp at our own projections of solid form into the void it shelters—but to come face-to-face with our inability to find anything at all. By transmitting nothing in such a manner, the work makes possible the spontaneous arising across time and space of the empty awareness of the bare fact that anything occurs at all. The poems that make up the Chaucerian corpus are generated, as it were holographically, from the empty words with whose preservation they have been entrusted and in which they are contained *in nuce*. It is in their moments of sheer uninterpretability that Chaucer's works make known most unmistakably the nature of the poet's practice.

To identify the essence of Chaucer's poetics as "tregetry" in this sense—that is, as what Giorgio Agamben calls *experimentum vocis*, the experience and experiment of the bare vocalization—is to rejoin an important line of current scholarly research.[23] For Chaucerians have been bringing to light, over the course of the past decade, the extent to which the poet was preoccupied with exactly this matter.[24] Peter Travis, in his *Disseminal Chaucer*, sums up the matter with characteristic perspicacity: "Chaucer was absolutely fascinated by noise throughout his career, and by the possible significance, political and otherwise, of sounds that are traditionally understood to be devoid of meaning. . . . [The poet] explores the essence of history via his experimental interrogations of the semiotics of noise, even as he explores with equal intensity the resistance of noise to our understanding."[25] Likewise, D. Vance Smith writes: "One terminus of [Chaucer's] writing [is] the hubbub of English noise, the noise that he will celebrate in the midst of a minisumma of rhetorical art in the "Nun's Priest's Tale," the 'out' and 'harrow' of the rural landscape and the sounds of angry rebels in 1381.... The scene of English noise is always there, and occasionally Chaucer stops briefly to listen to it, to show how its noise is the all-too-often disparaged echo chamber of his poetic invention."[26]

But such suggestions, just because they are so well founded, should also come as something of a surprise. For it might have seemed that medieval literature, not to speak of medieval thought and culture generally, could be characterized by a thoroughgoing commitment to the kernel of meaning as over against the shell of the mere letter. That was of course the strongly stated position of the "Robertsonians" in the last century; but even when their detractors objected most forcefully that medieval literary works could not, in fact, be reduced to allegories of Christian teachings, they did so on the basis of the fact—which it would be foolish indeed to contest—that other meanings can be ascribed to them just as convincingly. The various schools of thought that have dominated medieval literary study hold in common, notwithstanding their marked differences, a presupposition that what matters in a given medieval text is what it signifies, if not in a mode of allegory at least in one of intention, representation, evidentiation, or symptomatization.

It may be that this presupposition is warranted, and that if—as both the foregoing commentary and the scholars just cited suggest—what matters in a text of Chaucer's is something else altogether, not its meaning but its noise, it is because there is something exceptional about this particular poet. Here it would be tempting to invoke the category of genius, or at least to point toward a Borgesian possibility of anachronistic reading, in order to skirt the difficulties involved in the recognition that Chaucer can be said to anticipate the poets who will come five and six hundred years after him. For it is not simply that a concern with nonsignification seems not quite medieval: it also seems positively—even suspiciously—modern.

REINE SPRACHE

In 1916, Walter Benjamin sent an unfinished essay to Gershom Scholem under the title "On Language as Such and on the Language of Man." In it, the young philosopher set out to expose the "invalidity and emptiness" of what he called "the bourgeois conception of language." According to such a conception—whose putative self-evidence shows no sign, a century on, of having diminished—language would be a tool by which "man is communicating factual subject matter to other men ... through the word by which he denotes a thing."[27] A signifying system, it would be made up of words that are, by their very nature, carriers of meaning. In order for a word to count as a word, it would have to signify something to someone, and only when such a signification is present could there be language at all. In the absence of signification, there might be raw noise, random marks, unmotivated gestures; there might be human beings relating to one another, dumbly, in passion, aggression, or indifference; there might be various sorts of things existing in the world—but there would not be language.

As Benjamin saw it, this bourgeois conception of language is "intrinsically false."[28] However much human beings might indeed seem to speak to one another in order to communicate, the true nature of language must be sought elsewhere. Benjamin is not of course suggesting that language is simply random noise. He is rather pointing toward an ultimate linguistic dimension where meaning is held in suspension: a pure language (*reine Sprache*) that communicates nothing at all and to no one. This dimension is the bare possibility of signification, sheltered within meaningful speech but not itself meaningful. To be in language is sooner or later to encounter this dimension, where pure communicability will bring about the undoing of all communication. For, as he will write five years later, in the celebrated essay on "The Task of the Translator": "In this pure language—which no longer means or expresses anything but is, as expressionless [*ausdruckslos*] and creative Word, that which is meant in all languages—all information, all sense, and all intention finally encounter a stratum in which they are destined to be extinguished."[29]

But in neither of these essays, which have been central to the continental philosophy of language of the last one hundred years, does Benjamin give an example of such a word. Indeed, he appears to leave unspecified when, exactly, this extinguishing of sense is meant to take place—in what circumstances we could expect to come up against the "expressionless and creative word" itself. It might well be imagined that this word will arrive only in some endlessly deferred future, a time always still to come when all the various languages will be rapt into the final pleroma. Or that what he is talking about belongs exclusively to the past, an Adamic utterance long since forgotten and without the possibility of recovery. Or again, that the expressionlessness of the word is something that obtains now, at this very moment, but merely as a kind of "permanent disjunction which inhabits all languages as such."[30] Whatever their differences, each of these possibilities amounts to the same thing: the expressionless word, whether relegated to the future, to the past, or to the shadow of the present, would be something of which there could never be found a proper instance, here and now.

But there is another possibility. For Benjamin did not neglect, after all, to provide an example of the expressionless word. In the "protocol" or report of a hashish experiment from 1930, he notes that his trance—apparently, in this respect, unlike certain others—was "not very rich" in what he calls *großen Prägungen* (great coinages).[31] Only one such coinage is he able to retrieve from it: *Haupelzwerg*, a made-up word in which (it would seem) an invented prefix has been attached to a root that means *dwarf*. Benjamin has very little to say about this invention, only that he "tried"—that is, was unable—"to explain it to the others." Nonetheless, its characteristics can be discerned without difficulty: a coinage, it is "creative"; unfamiliar and inexplicable, it is "expressionless"; but, appearing as it does in the protocol, it is also just another word among the thousands of others recorded there. It can be written, evidently; nothing would stop a person from speaking it aloud; although it will not be found in any *Wörterbuch*, it is nonetheless unmistakably a word in German (and not, say, Russian or Japanese); as such, it gives every indication that it is susceptible of grammatical analysis, insofar as any speaker of that language could identify it as belonging to a particular part of speech; neither would anything prevent its being included in a line of verse, where one might consider it in the light, for example, of its syllabic quantity or of its capacities for assonance or rhyme; and so forth.

Benjamin has nothing more to say about *Haupelzwerg*, in the hashish protocol, than the few sentences just cited. But he knew well that a detailed description of just such a word—of its nature, status, and effects—had been made some decades before, in Knut Hamsun's *Hunger*. I am referring to that passage in the novel that Roman Jakobson, praising the precision and comprehensiveness of its linguistic insight, would later use to develop an account of what he calls "*signans* with a zero *signatum*"—the same passage that Viktor Shklovsky had already appropriated in 1916 for his programmatic essay on *Zaum* or trans-sense language.[32] The protagonist of Hamsun's novel reports the following:

> I imagined I had discovered a new word. I rise up in bed and say, "It is not in the language; I have discovered it. 'Kuboa.' It has letters as a word has. By the benign God, man, you have discovered a word! . . . 'Kuboa' . . . a word of profound import." . . . With the most singular jerks in my chain of ideas I seek to explain the meaning of my new word. There was no occasion for it to mean either God or the Tivoli; and who said that it was to signify cattle show? . . . No; on second thoughts, it was not absolutely necessary that it should mean padlock, or sunrise. It was not difficult to find a meaning for such a word as this. I would wait and see. . . . Some minutes pass over, and I wax nervous; this new word torments me unceasingly, returns again and again, takes up my thoughts, and makes me serious. I had fully formed an opinion as to what it should *not* signify, but had come to no conclusion as to what it should signify. . . . "No! It is just this, it is impossible to let it signify emigration or tobacco factory.[33]

Here is the "expressionless and creative word": something neither irrecoverably lost nor permanently postponed, nor simply diffused throughout language as a whole, but just a word, transmissible from past to future and enunciable in the present. The encounter with such a word—belonging to a given language but not included in its lexicon, allowing no particular meaning to attach to itself and (not least) afflicting anyone who discovers it with unceasing torment—is the encounter with language as such.

Modernist literature is of course full of such meaningless words. It is not only Hamsun and the *Zaum* poets who "discover" them, but also Lewis Carroll ("Jabberwocky"), Christian Morgenstern ("Das grosse Lalula"), Hugo Ball ("Karawane"), James Joyce (*Finnegans Wake*), and Virginia Woolf (*The Years*) among many others.[34] Indeed, what Gertrude Stein called "in between no sense" is to a great extent the very matter of modernist letters.[35] Just as painting does, literature seems to become preoccupied toward the end of the nineteenth century with its own materiality, abandoning the task of representation and giving rise to abstraction: in its case, linguistic abstraction, what Stéphane Mallarmé (and André Gide after him) calls *inanité sonore*.[36] Samuel Beckett's Molloy would speak for a whole era—the era of the death of God, of the splitting of the atom, of the "transitory, the fugitive, the contingent"[37]—when he declares: "Yes, the words I heard, and heard distinctly, having quite a sensitive ear, were heard a first time, then a second, and often even a third, as pure sounds, free of all meaning, and this is probably one of the reasons why conversation was unspeakably painful to me. And the words I uttered myself, and which must nearly always have gone with an effort of the intelligence, were often to me as the buzzing of an insect."[38]

The literary critics and philosophers of modernity, at least on the continent, also turn their attention to this question, that of what Mladen Dolar calls, in his monograph of the same title, "a voice and nothing more." Such a voice, whose importance within twentieth-century thought he demonstrates conclusively, Dolar defines as "what does not contribute to making sense," that is, "the material element recalcitrant to meaning," so that "if we speak in order to say something, then the voice is precisely what cannot be said . . . it is the non-linguistic, the extralinguistic element which enables speech phenomena."[39] So much would be at stake, for instance, when Roland Barthes defines literature as an "intentional cacography" and points to the "rustle of language" as a "utopic state" in which "language would be enlarged, I should even say *denatured* to the point of forming a vast auditory fabric in which the semantic apparatus would be made unreal; the phonic, metric, vocal signifier would be deployed in all its sumptuosity, without a sign ever becoming detached from it."[40] Or in Jacques Lacan's dictum that "*Lalangue* is the precondition of meaning"; or Julia Kristeva's identification of a "heterogeneousness to meaning and signification" within poetic language; or Giorgio Agamben's suggestion that "the search for the voice within language is thought itself."[41] It is unmistakable, in short, that linguistic nonsignification is a preoccupation of the modern era. The point goes practically without saying, in fact, though Friedrich Kittler, for one, has made it explicit: "our epoch," he writes, is "the epoch of nonsense."[42]

Which would seem to suggest that the epoch before this one was, quite simply, not. In this regard it is worth recalling a perhaps surprising fact. Scholars of the Middle Ages have been bringing to collective attention in the last decade that some of the most influential twentieth-century thinkers took a serious formative interest in the Middle Ages, and developed their most characteristic ideas on the basis of this interest.[43] As it happens, the thinkers in question are exactly those just mentioned. Benjamin undertook his dismantling of the "bourgeois conception of language" only a few months after he had composed the fragment "On the Middle Ages"; Lacan's most important discussion of *lalangue* is in Seminar XX, built around an account of courtly love; Barthes's *bruissement de la langue* is manifestly indebted to medieval models (and he even belonged to a group named after Rutebeuf's *Miracle de Theophile*, a play that includes lines of gibberish that I will discuss momentarily); Kristeva's close study of medieval texts, much in evidence in her later works, is already apparent in her earliest publications; Jakobson was an eminent medievalist; as is, of course, Agamben, whose whole theory of *vox* is indeed explicitly grounded in medieval *auctoritates*.[44]

As with the theorists, so with the poets and novelists. Hamsun's protagonist in *Hunger*, the discoverer of the word *kuboa*, will turn out to be working on a play about the Middle Ages; Mallarmé was fascinated with manuscript culture and with medieval English alliterative poetry; Morgenstern was reading Meister Eckhart during the period when he wrote "Das grosse Lalula"; Ball, that "alchemist of the word," took an interest in the *lingua ignota* of Hildegard of Bingen, recited Mechthild of Magdeburg at the fourth Dada soirée, and would go on to devote himself to the study of patristics (notably Pseudo-Dionysius); Woolf, whom we have already seen pointing to Chaucer as the "great originator," turned her attention to the Middle Ages in both novels and essays; Joyce was quite learned in medieval thought, as evidenced in *Finnegans Wake* in particular; Beckett was as well; and what is Carroll's "Jabberwocky" itself if not some "stanzas of Anglo-Saxon poetry"?[45] As for Stein, who referred often to Chaucer and copied lines from his "Merciles Beaute" into a notebook, she gives an account of that poet's work in the lecture "What Is English Literature" whose hermeneutic insight has never been surpassed:

> You do remember Chaucer, even if you have not read him you do remember not how it looks but how it sounds, how simply it sounds as it sounds. That is as I say because the words were there. They had not yet to be chosen, they had only as yet to be there just there. That makes a sound that gently sings that gently sounds but sounds as sounds. It sounds as sounds of course as words but it sounds as sounds. It sounds as sounds that is to say as birds as well as words. And that is because the words are there, they are not chosen as words, they are already there. That is the way Chaucer sounds.[46]

It is possible that chance alone suffices to explain the fact that the very writers, thanks to whom nonsignification came to seem a characteristically modern preoccupation, also happen to have spent careful time in the study of medieval texts. But if nonsignification was already a preoccupation of medieval writers, as it has been shown to be (and as Stein confirms) at very least in the particular case of Chaucer, another possibility comes into view: that modernist nonsense might in fact be the afterlife or recrudescence of a specifically medieval theory and practice of nonsignification. At least two things would follow if this turned out to be true: first, modernist nonsense would demand to be restored to its place in a history much longer than has been widely suspected; second—and more importantly for the purposes of this book—medieval literature would demand to be read according to the protocols of the modernist avant-garde.[47] For it is in the experiments of the latter-day alchemists of the word that the most perceptive, faithful, and thus exemplary readings of medieval letters would turn out to have been undertaken. But if this possibility is to be seriously entertained, it will first be necessary to determine whether nonsignification was, in fact, a matter of importance not just for Chaucer but for medieval writers more generally.

DREIT NIEN

Consider first the case of St. Anselm of Canterbury, sometimes called—and not without reason—the "first scholastic."[48] Anselm, writing in the second half of the eleventh century, did much to determine the course that would be taken by philosophy, theology, theory of language, and devotion in the centuries to follow; it is in no small part to his sensibility that both the characteristic rationality ("scholasticism") and the characteristic emotionalism ("affective piety") of the later Middle Ages can be traced. In the present day his fame rests chiefly, though not exclusively, on the basis of a treatise that he wrote toward the end of the 1070s and that came to be known as the *Proslogion*.

This treatise is remembered for two reasons. The first is the motto that provided the work with its original title: *fides quarens intellectum*, faith in search of understanding.[49] As Anselm writes, "I do not seek to understand so that I may believe; but I believe so that I may understand."[50] This precept might seem, to modern ears, to signal a subordination of reason to blind belief. But what will strike anyone who does not skip over the preface and first chapter of the *Proslogion*—that is, the sections in which the motto is introduced and explicated—is that *fides* refers not to unshakeable belief in the existence of God but to something altogether different. It names a willingness to be submitted to a certain ordeal: the ordeal that afflicts the mind when it withdraws into itself and discovers that it is entirely without ground.[51] *Fides*, as Anselm uses the term, is the name of a certain kind of imbecility that makes itself available, despite every instinct of self-preservation, for an experience of desolation, or atheism. For this questing faith arrives at the "understanding" that it has gone in search of only on one condition: that it declare, in its very heart, that there is no God. So much is clearly indicated in the treatise's first chapter, where mind is summoned to withdraw into itself, there to find nothing at all and be forced to conclude that there is no God. And it has been indicated already in its preface, where Anselm recounts that, tormented unceasingly by the absence of a proof for the existence of God, he came finally to grab hold of nothing else than that absence itself as the proof he had been seeking.[52] The discovery transmitted in the *Proslogion* is simply that to be deprived of the thought of God is already the proof of the nothing that that thought is.

But the true object of *fides* can be seen still more clearly in the formula of the *unum argumentum* that Anselm discovers in this fashion, which is of course the second thing still remembered about the *Proslogion*: the so-called ontological proof of the existence of God. The operation of Anselm's *argumentum* depends entirely on the fact that "the fool hath said in his heart, 'there is no God.'"[53] Recall the stages of Anselm's reasoning. To say "there is no God" is necessarily to have the idea of God in one's mind. But the idea of God is that of *quo nihil maius cogitari potest* ([something] than which nothing greater can be thought). And since it is greater to exist both in the mind and in reality than to exist merely in the mind, if the idea of *than which nothing greater can be thought* exists in the mind, it must also exist in reality—otherwise it would not be *than which nothing greater can be thought*. And thus, it seems, just to utter the word *god*—or, more to the point, to say, "there is no God"—is in itself sufficient to prove that God exists in reality.[54]

To put it mildly, this argument did not meet with universal assent. Indeed, as soon as it had begun to circulate it elicited a rebuttal from a certain Gaunilo of Marmoutiers. For Gaunilo, as for more than a few subsequent readers, the argument seemed absurd. A person can be familiar with the sound of the word *god*, he objected, without knowing what it means. Such a person would know that the utterance is not just a sound (*litterarum sonus vel syllabarum*) but a sound possessed of a certain meaning; but not having any idea of what that particular meaning might be, he could do no more than imagine (*effingere*) it to himself on the basis of the effect that the sound has upon his mind. As Gaunilo concludes: "it would be astonishing if he could ever attain to the truth of the thing" on such a basis—astonishing if by mere utterance of a word of unknown meaning a person could arrive at an understanding of the existence of God.[55]

In his reply to Gaunilo, Anselm strangely—even conspicuously—neglects to counter Gaunilo's central objection. But the reason for this neglect is not far to seek: as he explains, Anselm is not responding to a "fool" like himself, that is, to someone with *fides*, but to a Christian.[56] Because he has not attained to the state of foolishness, in Anselm's sense, Gaunilo does not realize that this "astonishment" of his—at the idea that the truth of the divine being would be made known in a word of no conceivable meaning—is the very experience of the proof itself. Gaunilo is exactly correct, in other words, only he has not gone far enough. As Daniel Heller-Roazen has shown, Anselm's formulation of the proof already anticipates Gaunilo's *cogitatio secundum vocem solam*: "one could define the entire philosophical *probatio* of the *Proslogion* as a single attempt to construct a metaphysics on the basis of a specific type of speaking without meaning; and the absolute novelty of the Anselmian 'demonstration' could be said to lie in the fundamental position it assigns to the limit point of language at which the mechanisms of reference and signification, faltering, give way to a speech that quite literally expresses nothing."[57] For it is precisely the fact that the word *deus* signifies nothing whatsoever that makes the proof operate. The God whose existence it proves is no more and no less than *quo nihil maius cogitari potest*, that is, not a subsistent entity but the mere trace of a relation: a *than which*. Moreover, what that *quo* is in relation to is itself not a something but rather *nihil maius*, a "nothing greater." The God in question here is neither a something nor a nothing, but a *than which nothing*—a relation to nothing. And the undergoing of such a relation, as Gaunilo saw without realizing what he was catching sight of, is just the mind's encounter with the *litterarum sonus vel syllabarum* of the word *deus*: the experience of getting caught in the mere sound-shape of a word of unknown meaning. The so-called ontological proof is the staging of an ordeal or *probatio* of incomprehension in the face of the "expressionless word," the excruciation of a *fides* or imbecility that does not know what it means when it says *non est deus*. In short, the key experience and doctrine of the "first scholastic" is, essentially, a thinking of nonsignification.

So, too, with literature. Consider the case of William the Ninth, Duke of Aquitaine, who wrote his songs within a few decades of the composition of the *Proslogion*. William, for his part, has long been known as the "first troubadour"—a designation to which we will return. His songs, the inauguration of the new practice of singing that would soon spread across Europe, are the seed of the late medieval literary tradition and indeed of all subsequent literature in the European vernaculars to the present day. With William the preoccupation with nonsignification could hardly be more evident. He famously begins a song with the declaration that he will "make a verse about absolutely nothing" (*farai un vers de dreit nien*). The poem that follows answers very neatly to this description:

> Farai un vers de dreit nien:
> non er de mi ni d'autra gen,
> non er d'amor ni de joven,
> ni de ren au,
> qu'enans fo trobatz en durmen
> sus un chivau.[58]
>
> [I'll make a verse about absolutely nothing:
> it won't be about me or about other people,
> it won't be about love or about youth,
> nor about anything else,
> because it was found while asleep
> on a horse.]

As Agamben has emphasized, William is alluding here to an "ancient exegetical tradition of the Gospel of St. John," in which *logos* is said to ride on the horse of *phone*, that is, thought is expressed by vocal utterance.[59] In this case, though, in which the poet is asleep on his horse, speech goes on while thought is suspended. The poem announces the arrival of a kind of vocalization that does not signify.

And just such a vocalization is spelled out at the heart of another of William's inventions. In the song that begins "Farai un vers, pos mi sonelh" (I will make a verse, because I am asleep), the poet declares that, meeting two women on the road, he responds to their greeting in the following manner:

> anc no li diz ni "bat" ni "but,"
> ni fer ni fust no ai mentagut
> mas sol aitan:
> "Babariol, babariol
> babarian."

> I said neither "baf" nor "buf,"
> I named neither metal nor wood,
> but only:
> "Babariol, babariol,
> babarian."[60]

The utterance of "babariol, babariol, babarian"—articulate, versifiable, and meaningless—makes up the crucial moment in the events narrated in the poem: the two women, thinking him incapable of telling tales, take the poet with them and have their way with him.[61] They also make up the crucial moment of its reflection on the being of language. What William provides here are materials for a taxonomy of ways of saying nothing at all: for it is not simply a matter of either signifying or not signifying. In the phrase "neither 'baf' nor 'buf'" what is established is that the utterance "baf" is irreducible to the utterance "buf"; in the following lines both of these are made distinguishable from utterances that would refer to things in the world (metal, wood); and finally all of these possible utterances are distinguished from what the poet says that he did, in fact, say aloud: namely, the sequence "babariol babariol / babarian." In this cobla various modes of saying *dreit nien* are distinguished and, at the same time, coordinated together. "Verse" is, for the first troubadour, a place in which speaking can be about nothing at all and yet be subject to linguistic differentiation, form the *materia* of literature, and bring about certain effects in the realm of love.

Nor did the poets who wrote in William's wake abandon his practice of versifying in what Paul Zumthor calls *jargon absolu*.[62] In the *Inferno*, written a decade into the fourteenth century, Dante describes an encounter with the giant Nimrod. The giant, suffering the punishment of Babel, says only "Raphèl maì amècche zabì almi."⁶³ This famous line, alongside that of Pluto ("Pape Satàn, pape Satàn aleppe"), has defied the efforts of interpreters to identify it as an instance of Arabic or Hebrew, Basque or Greek.⁶⁴ It is composed in no particular language, serving rather as an instance of barbarolexis, a form of speech that cannot be assimilated to any known idiom.⁶⁵ As Virgil explains to the pilgrim, the giant's speech is unintelligible to all who hear it, just as the giant himself can understand no one else's speech.⁶⁶ "Raphèl maì amècche zabì almi" thus announces a condition of absolute linguistic incomprehension, in which the experience of unintelligibility cannot be overcome by means of translation, explanation, or learning.

As Peter Dronke and others have indicated, Nimrod's "convincing line of spoken Babelese" participates in a wider medieval tradition of invented languages.⁶⁷ Nor is the hellish location of the giant's utterance incidental to its incomprehensibility: the demonic, necromantic, and heathen realms have been associated, immemorially, with meaningless incantations and illegible inscriptions.⁶⁸ The phenomenon is evident not least on the stage. A century before the composition of the *Inferno*, Jean Bodel included in his *Jeu de Saint Nicolas* a golden statue that comes to life long enough to say

> Palas aron ozinomas
> Baske bano tudan donas
> Geheamel cla orlaÿ
> Berec .he. pantaras taÿ⁶⁹

—which means nothing at all. The other play invariably cited in this connection is Rutebeuf's *Miracle de Theophile*, from about 1261, in which Salatin conjures the devil with the following invocation:

> bagahi laca bachahé
> lamac cahi achabahé
>   karrelyos
> lamac lamec bachalyos
> cabahagi sabalyos
>   baryolas
> lagozatha cabyolas
> samahac et famyolas
>   harrahya⁷⁰

Incomprehensible incantations of this sort exist also in Latin liturgical drama and appear widely in late medieval English plays.⁷¹ In the Towneley *Judicium*, for example, the demon Tutivillus announces himself in a macaronic speech that combines English, Latin, and sheer nonsense:

> Mi name is tutiuillus,
> my horne is blawen;

ffragmina verborum,
tutiuillus colligit horum
Belzabub algorum
belial belium doliorum.[72]

Likewise, in *Mankind*, the character Mischief reads aloud a writ copied out in an untidy hand:

Here ys blottybus in blottis,
Blottorum blottibus istis.[73]

And in the N-Town *Adoration of the Shepherds*, a shepherd, having heard the phrase *Gloria in excelsis Deo,* explains that he has understood it perfectly and memorized it exactly:

I have that songe ful wele inum.
In my wyt weyl it is wrought,
It was "Gle, glo, glas, glum."[74]

These lines of dog Latin constitute a kind of phonesthetic parody or *grammelot*, as Dario Fo will call his "method of producing the semblance of a given language without adopting real or identifiable words from that language."[75] They are made up of words that sound like they would belong to a certain language, without for that being lexically recognizable; words uttered in one language as though they belong to another; words represented as in a game of telephone.

Such a survey, preliminary as it is, makes plain that any history of medieval literary culture that does not include *jargon absolu* and other forms of nonsense will be incomplete and any account of modernist nonsense that assumes it to be a novelty misconceived.[76] For linguistic nonsignification was evidently a matter of basic importance both in the first philosophy and in the literature of the Middle Ages—and indeed in other fields as well.[77] If a medieval writer such as Chaucer devotes his attention not to the kernel of meaning but to the mere shell of the empty word, and to the poetic possibilities of nonsignification that might be found there, there is thus nothing anachronistic about his doing so. But simply to recognize that a poet comes by his *materia* honestly is still to know very little about that *materia* itself.

ELVISSHE CRAFT

The purpose of this book is to make discernible, in the shadow cast by the emblem of Chaucer's windmill under a walnut shell, the possibilities of thinking linguistic nonsignification that obtained in the world of letters when and where the poet recorded his vision. It marks out a constellation of texts, all of them either written or widely known in what used to be called the Age of Chaucer, that seem to have been constructed in such a manner as to transmit axioms, techniques, and aspirations by means of which the being of *reine Sprache* as the extinguishing of all sense might come into awareness. It is not a book about Chaucer himself, whose name indeed henceforth scarcely appears in it, but about the very possibility of his vision's having arisen in the first place. It consists of four commentaries on paradigmatic works or clusters of works. In chapter 1, I examine authoritative textbooks in the arts of language—by Priscian, Boethius, and Augustine—that the Middle Ages inherited from Mediterranean late antiquity; in chapter 2, an Aristotle commentary by Walter Burley; in chapter 3, the anonymous contemplative manual called the *Cloud of Unknowing*; and in chapter 4, the hagiographical poem *St. Erkenwald*.

It will be apparent to anyone familiar with these texts that they would not seem to fit comfortably under any single heading. The *auctoritates* studied in chapter 1 thoroughly determined the literary culture of fourteenth-century England, where all the other texts were written, but they were themselves composed a millennium before and in an altogether different part of the world. Moreover, chapters 1 and 2 focus on works written in Latin, whereas chapters 3 and 4 are readings of texts written in the Middle English vernacular. Chapter 4, on *Erkenwald*, is about an imaginative poem, whereas all the other chapters consider prose works that could be called works of literature only in a strained or outmoded sense of the word. However, the bringing together of these particular texts in this order is not by any means arbitrary. Their sequence recapitulates that of the fundamental linguistic model of the Middle Ages, the fourfold Aristotelian schema that Boethius calls *orandi ordo*. What occurs in an act of speech, according to this schema, is that four elements are brought together and coordinated in a sequence: the things outside the mind that are being referred to, the concepts that are formed of them in the mind of the speaker, the spoken words that communicate those concepts, and the written inscriptions that communicate in turn those spoken words. The four chapters of this book correspond, in order, to these fundamental linguistic elements: chapter 1, on the *auctoritates*, focuses on inherited definitions of *vox sola* (bare utterance) as a kind of "thing"; chapter 2, on Burley's logic, is about what kind of concept in the mind could be adequate to such a thing; chapter 3, on the *Cloud*, proceeds to consider what sort of spoken word could correspond to such a concept; and chapter 4, on *Erkenwald*, broaches the problem of such a word's being inscribed. Each reading, in other words, approaches the question of nonsignification from a different vantage point—that of its nature in itself, its relation to the mind, its relation to speech, and its relation to writing—and these four vantage points taken together constitute the basic medieval model of language. And if at times the chapters seem nonetheless to be joined only provisionally together, their doing so is also in keeping with that model; for, as will become plain in chapter 1, the *orandi ordo* was precisely understood as being constituted by its essential failure to cohere. This failure—the constitutive inoperativity of the structure by which meaningfulness is produced—is of course the very subject matter of my inquiry as a whole.

It will also be apparent to anyone familiar with medieval letters more generally that there exist many other texts that might have been studied in the present connection. There are other *auctoritates*, other works of Oxford logic, other contemplative treatises, other poems that concern themselves with non-signification than the ones that happen to appear here; moreover, those that do appear are in certain cases scarcely typical of the fields they are taken from. But what this book hopes to offer is neither the completeness of a historical survey nor the exemplificatory adequation of a representative sample but, instead, the generative possibility of a constellation of paradigms.[78] The texts examined here have been selected not as expressions, symptoms, exhibits, evidence, or artifacts of some posited phenomenon but, rather, insofar as they offer themselves as textual apparatuses that might still allow for thought, or indeed the suspension of thought, to arise in the moment of their being read.

To approach a text in this way is just to treat it—in good medieval fashion—as an *auctoritas*. For the authority of a text is simply its never ceasing to inspire contradictory interpretations: its retaining, in the face of sustained attention, the quality of not being able to be said to signify anything in particular. As the poet has it: "out of olde bokes, in good feyth, / Cometh al this newe science that men lere" (out of old books, in good faith / comes all this new knowledge that human beings learn).[79] The text as *auctoritas* is a transmission system for the preservation of incomprehensibility, an *engyn* constructed so as to shelter an obscure speech addressed to those still to come. Perhaps counterintuitively, the further removed the readers of a text find themselves from the circumstances of its composition, the better will they be able to receive the obscure speech that resounds in it. Or so teaches Marie de France, who has been the tutelary spirit of this inquiry, in what has rightly been called "as close to a vernacular *art poétique* as the High Middle Ages produced."[80] This is because those who imagine that they have understood what a text means are liable, to the point of inevitability, to pass over the core of obscurity that it transmits. Only those who really and truly fail to grasp what a text is about have a chance of discerning what always remains to be encountered in it: the mere letter out of which it is fashioned. This inscrutable letter is the real object of commentary, in which a gloss is produced not in order to retrieve the meaning the letter might once have carried but in order that, by virtue of its irreducible emptiness, it might again be made to resound. The task of the commentator, on this model, is to expose the seemingly inassimilable details of the textual object to sustained attention so as to activate whatever possibilities of contemplation the text itself, because of its nature as a linguistic construction, might still afford. Not to discover what its author actually thought—a tasteless presumption, not to mention an impossibility—nor to identify how such a thought does or does not fit in with some statistically significant trend, but to follow the logic of the text to its point of undecidability and thereby arrive at the real, contentless, and undiminished awareness of its maker.

All of which is to say that the purpose of the sequence of commentaries that makes up this book is not, finally, to make a claim about an extratextual reality—be it even literary historical—nor to bring the texts it examines under the jurisdiction of a given field of critical concern but rather to activate by making use of them a set of mind-engines that, both individually and in their mutual resonances within the fourfold structure of the *orandi ordo*, allow for awareness to encounter itself in the mirror of the past. "Not system but *commentary*," as Scholem says, "is the legitimate form through which truth is approached."[81] Nonetheless, and by way of bringing these prolegomena to a close, it is also possible to abstract from the individual commentaries three general implications.

First, as will be evident throughout, I have proceeded in the light of Rita Copeland and Ineke Sluiter's invaluable *Medieval Grammar and Rhetoric*; in the wake of the groundbreaking studies of medieval linguistic thought carried out by Irène Rosier-Catach; and following the lodestar of Giorgio Agamben's "unwritten work" on the voice.[82] More generally, there can be no doubt that in recent years the importance of theories and practices of sound, voice, and meaning to medieval culture (and to that of other periods) has been coming increasingly into view. The issue of *Speculum* devoted to the topic of "Sound Matters" and a recent edited volume on the topic of *Voice and Voicelessness in Medieval Europe*, for example, take up a line of inquiry that runs from the work of Paul Zumthor and Eugene Vance on poetics and sign theory to more recent studies such as Elizabeth Eva Leach's work on birdsong, Emma Dillon's on cacophony, Valerie Allen's on flatulence, and David Lawton's on the voice.[83] These exemplary studies have had a salutary effect on the study of medieval literary culture, and the present book is itself thoroughly in their debt.

Within the context of this broader inquiry, what this book underscores is first of all that medieval linguistic thought was not, despite everything, grounded in a hierarchical arrangement by which the rational articulations of human, nonforeign, learned, male discourse would be privileged over their alterities.[84] To the contrary: it was grounded in a theory of meaninglessness; it never ceased to concern itself with nonsignification; and its most creative inheritors did not fail to elaborate the materials they received into new modes of thinking and practicing nonsense. Furthermore, the incomprehensibility of these elaborations makes them not less but more readable, and indeed not less but more literary. In other words, if medievalists continue to turn their attention to noise, sound, and the bare voice, they should not assume them to be the site of some extra-linguistic meaning but should rather recognize in them what the medieval thinkers themselves did: the site of language itself, in its most essential extinguishing of meaning. It would be judicious, to put the point more polemically, to hesitate before diagnosing in medieval texts that include *jargon absolu* or *vaniloquium* or *barbarolexis*, much less in their composers, an "anxiety" in the face of sociological or species difference.[85] The pseudo-foreign babble, feminized chatter, and animal vocalizations that abound in medieval texts need not be approached either as evidence of a sorry view taken toward the subaltern nor as the latter's refusal to be silenced; they can, instead, be understood as participating in and developing a medieval theory of language far stranger and more capacious than has been understood. This is not, of course, to suggest that there were not hierarchies of various kinds that patterned the thought and behavior of the Middle Ages, nor that those hierarchies do not make themselves known in the texts they have left behind. It is to suggest, instead, that the very particular hierarchies that inhere in and are enforced by the "bourgeois conception of language" might not, in fact, organize the textual remains of a world that did not yet know the reign of the bourgeoisie; and that to proceed as if they do might be in effect to rule out, in advance, the possibility of experiencing the extent to which that conception, so crucial a foundation of contemporary ideology, might be merely adventitious.

Second, if I train my attention on the English fourteenth century it is because the latter has seemed to be the site of a particularly rich, but also peculiarly neglected, efflorescence of a millennial, transregional tradition of thinking and practicing linguistic nonsignification. Nor perhaps is it an accident if that time and place was also the site, with the emergence of what is now called Middle English as a written language, of crucial elements of the geopolitical and aesthetic orders that shape global affairs seven centuries on. It has been my working hypothesis that medieval linguistic thought will be better understood if these English contributions—both Latin and vernacular, scientific and imaginal—are taken into account; and that the political and aesthetic regimes that arose from this moment will be better understood if they are restored to their place within this medieval and ancient lineage of thinking signification and its outside.

To consider the objects of the following commentaries "English," in any fundamental sense, however, or even European, would be a grave misunderstanding. Because this misunderstanding is widespread, in a more sinister but no more mistaken fashion among its celebrants as among their critics, it is necessary to dispel it wherever possible. This can be accomplished without difficulty. Take, for instance, the writers treated in the preceding pages. Chaucer is a poet who receives, as he signals at every turn, much of both the matter and the form of his works—not least of all the *House of Fame*—from Asian and African sources.[86] As for Anselm, the monastic practices of *lectio divina* and the like out of which his thought emerges are a desert phenomenon, transplanted from Egypt.[87] William IX, for his part, gives every indication of having been the "first troubadour" only in the sense that he learned his new art of song from the enslaved Andalusian Muslim and Jewish women singers who populated the courts of Provence in their thousands during his formative years; or from any of the countless men and women of various estates who were crossing and recrossing the Pyrenees during his lifetime, if he did not cross them himself; or indeed on the eastern shores of the Mediterranean, where he went on crusade.[88] It bears recalling that the very epithet "troubadour" may itself derive from the Arabic word *taraba*, to sing.[89]

The case is no different with the writers to whom the remainder of this book will be devoted. Priscian and Augustine were Africans, working in scholarly modes that are recognizably African; Boethius, the other late antique writer considered here, had as his task the transmission to the Latin-speaking world of "Greek" textual lineages, where Greek means Alexandrian, that is, Indian and Ethiopian as well as Athenian.[90] The scholastic institutions in which Walter Burley's work took shape were part of a trans–Afro-Eurasian phenomenon that also comprises Buddhist shedras and Islamic madrassas; among Burley's foundational dicta, as will be seen, is one derived from Averroes.[91] The *Cloud of Unknowing* is an Englishing of meditative techniques and teachings on the nature of reality that come from Syria and Egypt, if not indeed from further East and South. Finally, *St. Erkenwald* is about nothing else than the survival in the foundations of an English church of Eastern Mediterranean, Islamic, Pagan relics; and the genre to which it more or less belongs, hagiography, also included exceedingly popular *legenda* derived from Buddhist *Jataka* tales: Christopher, Eustace, Hubert, and most prominently Barlaam and Josaphat.[92] Each of the texts here studied stands as a confirmation of the fact that, as has been rightly said, "Afroeurasia has been linked, at least at the information and luxury goods exchange levels, for two and a half millennia or more. Thus, events and processes in Europe cannot be explained solely by examining European processes."[93]

Toward the end of the Middle Ages, in a postcolonial backwater of the Afro-Eurasian world system called England, as has happened at various times in many another of its corners, certain practitioners of the linguistic arts undertook to transform the multiplicative, unfixed, mutually uninterpretable dialects they had at hand into a language fit for instruction, memorization, and translation.[94] They did so in order that ancestral teachings from all across the world system, as well as records of the states and contents of awareness newly arising in this particular quarter, might be made transmissible among those persons (not least women and the poor) who were unlearned in the *grammatica* of the Latins. The vernacular texts studied in this book are among the sites in which this "aureation of the mother tongue" was carried out. But the very useful abstractions by means of which scholars have characterized the first generations of texts to be written in this idiom—"vernacular theology" chief among them—should not be reified into the purported content of these texts, which is what occurs when the *Cloud*, for example, is taken to express a kind of homespun "English" anticlericalism, or when *Erkenwald* is pigeonholed as a "propagandistic" apologia for orthodoxy directed to the masses in their own tongue. For if there is a recurrent and explicit concern in these texts, it is not their having been written in the vernacular but, instead, the same thing that is at stake in the Latin works studied in this book's first half: transmissibility itself, the possibility or impossibility of communication that both precedes and contains anticipatorily the distinction between particular languages. Here the problem of mutual incomprehensibility—in modern but not in medieval terms the site of the distinction among languages—gives way to the problem of the incomprehensibility that a language, any language, harbors within itself. In the minor literature of *jargon absolu*, a particular language is made foreign even to its own speakers, or again the foreignness of language itself is made familiar to those who find themselves speaking it.[95] For just as the bits of dog Latin cited above—"Here ys blottybus in blottis / Blottorum blottibus istis"—both preserve and abolish the distinction between comprehensibility and incomprehensibility, they also both preserve and abolish the distinction between grammatical and vernacular speech.

In other words, the aureation of the mother tongue does not occur because some speakers have a particular meaning in mind that they wish to communicate—a meaning that it would then fall to their scholarly readers to retrieve—but when, and only when, the mother tongue encounters, in writing, its own capacity to say nothing in particular, to say the bare potential of meaning anything. The alchemical process by which this aureation occurs—for it is in such terms that perhaps the most incisive account of the phenomenon, Chaucer's "Canon's Yeoman's Tale," describes it—is not the kind that creates gold out of lead, an ennobling of vulgar chatter into something weightier and more meaningful.[96] To the contrary, it is instead a wastrel science of absolute unproductive expenditure, an "elvysshe craft" in which by gimmickry all accumulated value is transmuted into irrecoverable loss.[97] This elvish craft is called literature.

Third, this book, which begins with a reading of the *House of Fame* and concludes with a reading of *St. Erkenwald*, is perhaps best understood as an archeology of the literary. And this notwithstanding the fact that the better part of its attention is turned to apparently nonliterary works. The overall itinerary is as follows: having now established that the *materia* of Chaucer's poetics of tregetry is the empty word, and suggested by cursory survey both that this poetics is squarely medieval and that it has more in common than might be suspected with that of the modernist avant-garde, I consider a series of medieval linguistic, logical, and contemplative works in which the emptiness of the word is explicitly theorized, in order to turn finally to a poem by a contemporary of Chaucer's in which such thinking is elaborated into what becomes recognizable as an account of literariness itself. Literariness, on this account, does not inhere in any particular kind of statement, representation, symptomatization, entertainment, or ornamentation, but in a text's being engineered in such a manner as to arrest the faculty of interpretation and force it to focus on the nonsignificative event of language itself.[98] If *Erkenwald* is a work of literature, it is so just insofar as it constitutes a trap for interpretation. Approaching such an instrument as though it were the record of the polemics or societal tendencies proper to the time and place of its composition—or, by contrast, as though it were an object of merely aesthetic interest—is (for better or worse) to ignore its fundamental purpose. No less than any other *engyn*—a windmill, an astrolabe, a bain-marie—the literary work discloses its affordances only in being put to use. And what the trap of literature affords, when it is sprung, is an undergoing, in the reader, of an experience of a very particular kind of unknowing, one that happens to have been an object of study in the medieval sciences.

The following commentaries are studies of some of the linguistic, philosophical, theological, and mystical ideas that contributed to the formation of the category of literature as it emerged at the end of the Middle Ages and remains perhaps in effect today. The argument implicit in their fourfold sequence is that this category came into being not only, as has been well and convincingly explained, as an elaboration by medieval writers of notions to be found in scripture and in the science of its explication, in ancient imaginative writing and the conventions of its schoolroom transmission, and in the unwritten rules of popular song and storytelling, but also in the light of the traditions of thinking the being of language itself, of inquiring into the properties of the utterance, that are preserved in works on grammar, logic, contemplation, and sacramental theology. Just as an appreciation of the precisely literary stakes of Gertrude Stein's experiments, for example, requires familiarity not merely with the work of the poets and novelists who were her predecessors and contemporaries but also with that of her professor William James on the "varieties of religious experience"; just as an account of the experiments of Lewis Carroll that made no reference to his contributions to the field of mathematics would be needlessly impoverished; so, too, with the medieval poets: they did not carry out their experiments in a state of isolation from the other practitioners of the various *scientiae vocis* who were their contemporaries and whose aspirations, insights, statements of method, and technical vocabularies remain available for study in their works. What is gained by engaging in such study has perhaps never been better expressed than by Edgar Wind:

> The process of recapturing the substance of past conversations is necessarily more complicated than the conversations themselves. A historian tracing the echo of our own debates might justly infer from the common use of such words as microbe or molecule that scientific discovery had molded our imagination; but he would be much mistaken if he assumed that a proper

use of these words would always be attended by a complete technical mastery of the underlying theory. Yet, supposing the meaning of the words were lost, and a historian were trying to recover it, surely he would have to recognize that the key to the colloquial usage is in the scientific, and that his only chance of recapturing the first is to acquaint himself with the second.[99]

CHAPTER ONE

PRISCIAN, BOETHIUS, AND AUGUSTINE ON *VOX SOLA*

In the second decade of the sixth century, the Roman senator Anicius Manlius Severinus Boethius composed a commentary on Aristotle's *De interpretatione* whose influence was to be far reaching.[1] Transmitted to the Middle Ages along with his translation of the text itself, the commentary would do much to determine the linguistic reflection that took place in the Latin West over the next one thousand years. For this reason, it bears remarking that the commentary, for all the authority it was granted, begins with an assertion about Aristotle's treatise that will elicit skepticism in anyone who has actually read it.[2] According to Boethius, and indeed not only to him, *De interpretatione* is an *inexplicabilis caligo*, an impenetrable fog: the most difficult of all of the Philosopher's works.[3] But Boethius claims to know a path through the fog. "Prius igitur quid vox sit definiendum est," he begins. "Hoc enim perspicuo et manifesto omnis libri patefiet intentio" (It is first of all necessary to define what *vox* is. With this clear, what the whole book is about will become apparent).[4] (I am leaving the word *vox* untranslated because its definition is precisely what is at stake here, but it might be rendered in English as *utterance, vocalization, voice, word*, or even just *sound*, depending on context.) And the commentator does not fail to provide the definition whose necessity he has announced: "Vox est aeris per linguam percussio, quae per quasdam gutturis partes, quae arteriae vocantur, ab animali profertur" (*Vox* is a percussion of the air by the tongue, one that is emitted by an animate being by means of certain parts of the throat called the windpipe).[5] Boethius's wager is thus clear enough: when you have understood the nature of a certain physical and physiological phenomenon that he calls *vox*, you will understand the point of *De interpretatione*.

But in fact nothing could be more improbable. *De interpretatione* has never been mistaken for a treatise on physics or physiology; it has always been understood to concern itself with something quite different: logical propositions and the terms that make them up. Although Aristotle does, in the course of his extremely influential few lines of introduction to the treatise, mention *vox* (*phone*), he hastens to add that "these matters have been discussed in the *De anima* and do not belong to the present subject."[6] No clearer statement of the irrelevance of defining *vox* for the purposes of understanding the treatise could be wished for. Still more, when you follow Aristotle's reference to *De anima*, what you find there is a definition of *vox* that runs fundamentally counter to the one that Boethius himself gives. In fact, it is in some respects its opposite:

for Boethius, as will be shown below, *vox* need not be meaningful; for Aristotle, only what is meaningful can count as *vox*. So that what Boethius claims will reveal the whole point of *De interpretatione* is not only a definition of the one thing that Aristotle himself happens to have called incidental to its purposes, it is also, and still worse, a definition squarely at odds with Aristotle's own thinking on the matter. As Hans Arens has concluded, with an unconcealed disdain that he shares with many other readers of the commentary: "It is hard to believe that this is the beginning of a book on logic."[7]

But this is precisely what it is. For Boethius, as for his medieval inheritors, the science of logic or dialectic deals not so much with terms, propositions, or arguments as it does with *vox*.[8] Accordingly, as far as he is concerned, to understand Aristotle's fundamental textbook of logic it will be necessary to establish *quid vox sit*. This position may not square with current scholarly reading of *De interpretatione*, or indeed with Aristotle's own intentions insofar as they can be reconstructed, but the commentator does not adopt it because he has failed to understand Aristotle. He does so because an account of *vox* really is the indispensable starting point of his own logic, which is not strictly Aristotelian but rather a "harmonization" of the Philosopher's works with other theories of language and reasoning that had come together in his own training and sensibility, and notably with Stoic linguistics in particular.[9] Although Boethius does not invent the idea that understanding the nature of *vox* is the key to logic, he is its primary transmitter to the Middle Ages, and it is because of his influence that medieval Aristotelian logic will continue to ground itself, for most of the next millennium, on the profoundly un-Aristotelian principle that logic is in the first place a science of *vox*.[10]

Neither will logic, as a science of *vox*, be alone among the medieval sciences. Collectively, the three elementary branches of study in the medieval education system (grammar, logic, and rhetoric) were called *scientiae vocis*, modes of knowing that pertain to *vox*.[11] Each of the three arts of this so-called trivium had as its proper object the same thing, as examined in one of three different lights: grammar concerning itself with the correctness of *vox*, logic with the truth of *vox*, and rhetoric with the persuasiveness of *vox*. And given that the more advanced disciplines of number, the quadrivium—and indeed medicine, law, theology, and any other possible path of study—were themselves learned through verbal instruction, their apprehension, too, was said to depend ultimately on *vox*. As Remigius of Auxerre would write in the ninth century, commenting on the grammarian Donatus, "*vox* is the foundation of all the arts."[12]

But those practitioners of the medieval *artes* who wished to inquire into their foundation discovered, when they consulted the pertinent chapters of the textbooks that they had inherited from late antiquity, that it was by no means a simple matter to determine *quid vox sit*. For just as today there is in the West no science of the voice neither was there ever.[13] As Daniel Heller-Roazen has emphasized, the ancient linguistic sciences constituted themselves as sciences first by fracturing *vox* and then by taking as their object not *vox sola*, *vox* in and of itself, but one of the fragments into which it had been broken.[14] As an object of study, *vox* is shared among disciplines, proper to none of them just as none of them is proper to it, and the accounts of it given in the different disciplines are not always in agreement with one another. Moreover, the gesture by which *vox* is split up and distributed among various disciplines is reduplicated within the disciplines themselves when they content themselves with defining *vox* by differentiating it into its species. The transmitters of ancient linguistic knowledge thus passed on to their later readers the task of pursuing certain scattered leads if they wished to piece together a satisfying account of *vox* as it would subsist over and above its various possible specifications. They passed on in particular the problem of whether it would be possible not only to conceive of the undifferentiated stuff of language but also to recognize an example of it, that is, the problem of what, if anything, would actually count as an instance of *vox sola*. And most of all, they passed on the question of whether that *vox* would mean anything at all or whether it would be nonsensical.

In this chapter, I follow an itinerary that a medieval investigator of *vox sola* might have followed, reading through key works by Priscian of Caesarea, Boethius, and Augustine of Hippo. What emerges is that all three of these *auctoritates* contain passages that indicate that it is in fact possible to conceive of nonsignifying *voces*; that it is even possible to encounter them; and indeed that meaninglessness is an inalienable property of *vox* in its every instance. The theories that would be inherited by the Middle Ages work together to suggest that this basic stuff of language exists independently of its signifying this or that—and independently even of its having the capacity to signify at all. This characteristic feature of the late antique linguistic *auctoritates*, though it has often gone unremarked, did not go unnoticed in the Middle Ages. And indeed, the doctrines of nonsignification in question here are by no means arcane. In the case of Priscian and Boethius, they are elaborated on the very first pages of their works; in that of Augustine, in a series of definitions that the saint returns to repeatedly over the course of his career, definitions that are by no means eccentric to his main designs. Moreover, the discussions of *vox* in Priscian, Boethius, and Augustine are recapitulated in the other small handful of late antique works that would serve as textbooks in the Middle Ages and show up, in scarcely altered form, again and again in medieval works of various kinds. What is at issue here are exactly those lessons that would have been retained in the memory of even the most apathetic students in the most elementary classrooms of the medieval West.[15]

COAX, CRA

The opening chapter of the *Institutiones grammaticae*, written in Constantinople by Priscian of Caesarea around the year 520, is devoted to the question *de voce.*[16] The first order of business in what will become the most authoritative textbook in the field of grammar for the next thousand years is to give a definition of *vox*. But the definition Priscian transmits is of notorious opacity and questionable utility. It reads as follows: "Philosophi definiunt, vocem esse aerem tenuissimum ictum vel suum sensibile aurium, id est quod proprie auribus accidit" (according to the definition of the philosophers, *vox* is "very fine air when it is struck," or "that which it is the property of ears to perceive," i.e., the characteristic accident of ears.)[17]

It will come as no surprise that later grammarians were to disagree among themselves about what this definition was supposed to mean.[18] But it seems reasonably clear that, for Priscian as for Boethius, *vox* is something essentially physical. The grammarian is drawing on the work of Stoic linguists here, and his definition bears all the marks of their emphasis on *vox* as "corporeal."[19] A phenomenon explicable primarily by reference to the physics of air and the physiological properties of animal bodies, *vox* would seem to constitute one particular variety of sound: sound insofar as it is produced by vocal means. But this is already to read too much into the definition: oddly enough, there is nothing explicit here that would restrict *vox* to the voice. "Struck air" and "what is heard by the ears" might as easily be produced by nonvocal as by vocal means. So much is borne out by the later Priscianic tradition, in which the opening chapters of grammatical and grammatico-logical treatises, those corresponding precisely to Priscian's chapter *de voce*, are as often as not rechristened *de sono et voce*.[20] For Priscian's students in the centuries to follow, it precisely did not go without saying that what he is discussing here is a matter of the voice.

And in fact, it soon becomes obvious that neither did Priscian consider *vox* to be solely vocal. After giving the definition just cited, Priscian proceeds to differentiate *vox* into four species. The famous passage reads as follows:

> Vocis autem differentiae sunt quattor: articulata, inarticulata, literata, illiterata. Articulata est, quae coartata, hoc est copulata cum aliquo sensu mentis eius, qui loquitur, profertur. Inarticulata est contraria, quae a nullo affectu proficiscitur mentis. Literata est, quae scribi potest, illiterata, quae scribi non potest. Inveniuntur igitur quaedam voces articulatae, quae possunt scribi et intellegi, ut: "Arma virumque cano," quaedam, quae non possunt scribi, intelleguntur tamen, ut sibili hominum et gemitus: hae enim voces, quamvis sensum aliquem significent proferentis eas, scribi tamen non possunt. Aliae autem sunt, quae, quamvis scribantur, tamen inarticulatae dicuntur, cum nihil significent, ut "coax," "cra." Aliae vero sunt inarticulatae et illiteratae, quae nec scribi possunt nec intellegi, ut crepitus, mugitus et similia.[21]

> [There are four differentiae of *vox*: *articulate*, *inarticulate*, *literate*, and *illiterate*. *Articulate vox* is compressed, that is to say, it is expressed in combination with a mental meaning of the speaker. *Inarticulate* is the opposite, namely, *vox* that does not originate in any mental affection. *Literate vox* is that which

can be written, *illiterate* is that which cannot be written. Thus one may find certain articulate *voces* that can be both written and understood, e.g., *I sing of the weapons and the man*, some that cannot be written, but can be understood, e.g., the hisses and groans of humans: for although these *voces* indicate some intention of the person who pronounces them, they cannot be written. But there are others that are called inarticulate because they do not signify anything, although they can be written, e.g., *ribbit, caw*. Others are both inarticulate and illiterate: they can neither be written nor understood, e.g., creaking, lowing, and so on.]

This gesture, unlike the preceding, is comparatively straightforward. There are two taxonomical questions to ask of *vox*: Can it be spelled? Does it mean anything? On the basis of the answers to these questions four distinct varieties can be distinguished: meaningful and writable (*arma virumque cano*, the opening words of the *Aeneid*); meaningful but not writable (hisses and groans); not meaningful but still writable (*coax, cra* [ribbit, caw]); and neither meaningful nor writable (creaking and lowing). And yet the difficulties multiply from there. Two of these difficulties are of particular importance in the context of this inquiry. The first has to do with the status of Priscian's examples. Tucked in among the others, all of which appear to be vocalizations, is one that confirms that *vox* is despite its name not in and of itself a matter of voice: *crepitus*, creaking. *Crepitus* is the creaking of a hinge, the snapping of fingers, the chattering of teeth, the rustling of trees—or the breaking of wind.[22] But it is given alongside *mugitus*, that is, the (vocal) lowing of cattle, as if the two were equivalent: an equivalency underscored by the fact that Priscian, here as in none of the other three examples, goes on to say *et similia*: "creaking, lowing, and other such things." There is, in short, nothing in the major textbook of grammar that will allow you to differentiate vocal from nonvocal *voces*, nothing that restricts the sphere of *vox* to vocalization. Whatever difference might obtain between them is such as cannot be registered by the grammatical machinery of differentiation, which, in fact, is set up specifically so as to produce their "similarity."

The second peculiarity is terminological. The grammarian's choice of *literata* (lettered) as a technical term for writability is easy enough to understand, but his term for meaningfulness, "articulata" (jointed), is another story altogether. What does jointedness have to do with signification? The somewhat strained explanation Priscian offers is that a meaningful *vox* is one *coartata* (compressed) together with a mental meaning. What he does not say is more interesting, however. This is that *articulata* was already a technical term in grammar, one to be found prominently in the *Ars maior* of the Roman grammarian Donatus, written almost two centuries earlier. But for a Donatus, *articulata* means not meaningful but, of all things, writable. In other words, Priscian has chosen for the name of one of his two differentiating features the single word that will already be familiar as the name of the other.[23] It is impossible to do more than speculate as to why he might have chosen a term that could only provoke confusion. But whatever his reasoning, the result is unmistakable: in his misleading citation of earlier grammarians such as Donatus—who crucially *only* distinguishes between writable and nonwritable *voces*, leaving the question of their meaningfulness implicit—Priscian demands that the difference between writability and meaningfulness be thought through with utmost care. For as soon as you are not simply misled by the homonymy, you are forced to dwell on the idea that writability and meaningfulness are in principle absolutely distinct. That is, the apparently gratuitous confusion at the level of terms gives rise to a necessity of distinguishing not less but more precisely at the level of what those terms refer to. The terminological identity ends up being a means of producing conceptual differentiation.

And this distinction is of course what organizes the taxonomy as a whole. Priscian transmits to the Middle Ages the idea that *articulatio* or meaningfulness is something that can, but can also not, be joined to *vox*. It is even possible to have a fully writable *vox* that means nothing at all. In fact, Priscian gives as examples two such *voces*: *coax*, *cra*. Anyone who has read this textbook, in fact anyone who has gotten no further than its first page, has been given an authoritative disciplinary framework in which the existence of meaningless utterances of various kinds is demonstrated by example; a technical vocabulary is provided for naming them; and a conceptual schema is laid out by which to distinguish them from other sorts of words—as well as to draw connections among them.

For, although it might seem as though Priscian is constructing this schema in order to limit the scope of grammar to what is writable and meaningful, as indeed most of his modern readers have taken him to be doing, this is not in fact the case. Nowhere does he suggest that any hierarchy obtains among the four varieties of *vox*. He simply lists them, explains what they are, and passes on. And although his examples are no doubt suggestive, neither does he identify any of the four varieties as belonging exclusively to humans as opposed to other beings, or vice versa. In fact, what is most forcefully implied by this opening passage of the *Institutiones* is the strange idea that *vox literata articulata* is *vox* before it is anything else. Nothing would have stopped Priscian from just beginning his analysis with writable and meaningful *voces*, but he insists on the point—which is far from self-evident—that these are substantially the same thing as the sonic events produced by other animals, by humans yelping spontaneously in pain, and by things that creak.

He does so because, as a matter of fact, grammar will not confine its analysis to meaningful and writable *voces*. It is true that Priscian will not devote any more attention in the *Institutiones* to those *voces* that cannot be written. But it hardly seems remarkable, much less damning, that what is by definition unwritable should be largely unrepresented in what is, after all, a written text—and one that belongs to a discipline whose very name, *grammatica*, announces that it will pertain to the written. If anything is remarkable here, it is that the science of the writable turns its attention even in this minimal degree to what cannot be written—and thus ensures that its existence will be acknowledged and, in however elementary a fashion, theorized for the next thousand years.[24] But however that may be, the writable but meaningless utterance is another matter altogether. For it must be affirmed that *vox literata inarticulata*, here exemplified by *coax* (ribbit) and *cra* (caw), is by no means excluded from Priscianic grammar. So much is indicated first of all by the example *coax*, a conventional representation of frog noise familiar from, among other places, the *Frogs* of Aristophanes, in which an amphibian chorus sings *brekekekéx koáx koáx*.[25] When it appears in Priscian—no less than when it does, a millennium and a half later, in *Finnegans Wake*—the word *coax* can only constitute a citation: what is given here is not of course animal utterance itself, not even a representation of such utterance, but first of all a literary allusion.[26] And to this extent what is important about *coax* is actually what it has in common with the example that has just been given of writable meaningful speech. *Coax* no less than *arma virumque cano*, the one a fragment of verse as much as the other, will make itself available to grammatical analysis. If the opening lines of the *Aeneid* are a proper object of the science of grammar, so, too, is *vox literata inarticulata* in the form of a line from the *Frogs*. Far from excluding consideration of nonsignification, the study of poetic language demands it essentially. As Peter Comestor was to write in the twelfth century, the figments of poets are like the croaking of frogs.[27]

Such an analysis may seem to make too much of what is, after all, only an example. But this will not be the last time Priscian addresses himself to the question of *vox literata inarticulata*. He returns to it in connection with something that is so close to the heart of the discipline of grammar that it could be said without exaggeration to constitute its characteristic preoccupation. That thing is the syllable. After defining it as "sound expressed in letters, pronounced under one accent and in one breath," Priscian makes a further specification, one that will prove crucial. He declares that it is in the very nature of the syllable to mean nothing at all. As he writes, "numquam syllaba per se potest aliquid significare" (a syllable in itself can never signify anything).[28] (The syllable *-king* in the word *smoking*, unlike the word *king*, would be entirely devoid, on Priscian's account, of signification.) The syllable is, by definition, *vox literata inarticulata*: it is in its nature to be written, and it is in its nature to signify nothing. This is a point that will prove of the greatest interest, as will be seen in chapter 3, to the author of the *Cloud of Unknowing*. Let it be retained for the moment only that, to the extent that it is concerned with syllables as syllables rather than as parts of words, grammar will be by definition concerned with utterances that are writable but meaningless.

And this extent could not be greater. For grammar is nothing if it is not the discipline that treats of *vox* insofar as it exists syllabically. It is hardly necessary to point out that a grammatical reading of a given text, in the medieval sense and as the *Institutiones* attest, will necessarily involve prosodic analysis, that is, attention to patterns of syllabic number, length, stress, and so forth. Nor was grammar's interest confined to those syllables that make up already existing words, lines of verse, or sentences—meaningful or otherwise. In actual practice, a major part of what went on in the elementary classroom was the rote memorization, recitation, and inscription of isolated syllables. These syllables, emerging and persisting apart from any words into which their meaninglessness could be absorbed, are not an explicit concern of the *Institutiones*, but they were very much the concern of the discipline in which it served as the chief textbook. Historians of education have established that for almost three millennia, from at least the seventh century BCE until the nineteenth century of the current era, a fundamental aspect of grammatical instruction was something called the syllabary.[29] Students were asked to copy out, chant aloud, and memorize, combinatorially, all of the possible syllables: *ba, be, bi, bo, bu; ca, ce, ci, co, cu*; and so forth; and then *bab, beb, bib, bob, bub*, and on and on in like fashion. Raffaella Cribiore draws attention to a record of syllabic training that includes the sequence *bras-bres-bris-bros-brus*, pointing out that such an exercise would be of only the most questionable use in learning to read actual words.[30] But the grammarians, it seems, were fully committed to this practice of nonsense. As Quintilian put it, the syllables "must all be memorized thoroughly and there must be no putting off the most difficult of them."[31] Neither was the practice of the syllabary, so basic to grammatical instruction, restricted to the latter's initial stages; it served sometimes as a kind of daily warm-up even for advanced students. That syllables are meaningless, and that to think grammatically is to tarry with that meaninglessness, is nowhere more evident than in the chanting and writing out of *baba, beba, biba, boba, buba* that must have been the bane of students everywhere.[32]

Finally, grammar's preoccupation with *vox* as syllabic was not just a matter of actual practice. So essential did the connection between grammar and vocal nonsignification appear that it became proverbial. According to a commonplace, the grammarian is someone who is content to manipulate words and word fragments without ever bothering to ask himself whether what he is dealing with has any meaning. His would be precisely the realm into which the question of signification never enters. That this description is inaccurate is demonstrated by Priscian's division of *vox* into meaningful and meaningless; but that it is a misrepresentation does not make it any the less notable. Not least because the existence of the commonplace is in itself a demonstration that, for those who made use of it, grammar specifically did not appear to privilege *vox articulata* over mere nonsense. To the contrary, it could be referred to knowingly and in passing as the very science of babble. For examples of this commonplace it is not necessary to look any further than the works of the other two writers to be considered in this chapter, Boethius and Augustine.[33]

GARALUS

It was to remain axiomatic that, as Priscian teaches, there exist *voces* that do not signify. And this despite the fact that there would have been good authority on which to maintain exactly the opposite—the authority of the Philosopher himself. *De interpretatione* begins, as already noted, with a few remarks about *phone* (*vox*) that Aristotle almost immediately interrupts with the claim that such matters do not pertain to his present inquiry and that, in any event, he has treated of them elsewhere. Nonetheless, no other part of the treatise has ever generated more than a fraction of the interest that these remarks did, to the extent that they became (as is often repeated) the most influential passage in the history of linguistics. And this not least because of their inscrutability. Here is the passage in question: "Now spoken sounds are symbols of affections in the soul, and written marks symbols of spoken sounds. And just as written marks are not the same for all men, neither are spoken sounds. But what these are in the first place signs of—affections of the soul—are the same for all; and what these affections are likenesses of—actual things—are also the same."[34] What this appears to mean, first of all, is that any act of speech consists in the coordination of four separate elements: the things outside the mind that are being referred to, the concepts that are formed of them in the mind of the speaker, the spoken words that communicate those concepts, and the written inscriptions that communicate in turn those spoken words. So, in any event, does Boethius explain the passage, and it was in Boethius's translation and through the lens of his commentaries that Aristotle was to be known to the Middle Ages.[35] In the hands of the Roman senator, Aristotle's brief indications are elaborated into a whole theory of what will henceforth be called *orandi ordo*, the arrangement or sequence of speech:

> Tribus his totus orandi ordo perficitur: rebus, intellectibus, vocibus. Res enim ab intellectu concipitur, vox vero conceptiones animi intellectusque significat, ipsi vero intellectus et concipiunt subiectas res et significantur a vocibus. Cum igitur tria sint haec per quae omnis oratio conlocutioque perficitur . . . quartum quoque quiddam est, quo voces ipsae valeant designari, id autem sunt litterae. Scriptae namque litterae ipsas significant voces. Quare quattuor ista sunt, ut litterae quidem significent voces, voces vero intellectus, intellectus autem concipiant res, quae scilicet habent quandam non confusam neque fortuitam consequentiam, sed terminata naturae suae ordinatione constant. Res enim semper comitantur eum qui ab ipsis concipitur intellectum, ipsum vero intellectum vox sequitur, sed voces elementa id est litterae.[36]

> [The whole *orandi ordo* is achieved in these three things: things, concepts, utterances. For the thing is conceived by the concept, and the utterance

signifies the notions and concepts, and these same concepts both conceive the underlying things and are themselves signified by the utterances. Besides these three things through which all speech and conversation is achieved there is also a fourth thing, by which utterances themselves are signified, namely, letters. For written letters signify the utterances themselves. Thus, there are these four, so that the letters signify the utterances, and the utterances signify the concepts, and the concepts signify the things, and thus they have a certain sequence that is neither jumbled nor by chance but consists in a natural order. For things always accompany the concept that is formed of them, and the utterance follows the concept, and the elements, that is the letters, follow the utterance.]

According to the Boethian account of the *orandi ordo*, every single thing (*res*) that exists gives rise naturally and necessarily to a concept (*intellectus*) that corresponds to it; every concept, in turn, to an utterance (*vox*) that expresses it; and finally every utterance to an inscription (*littera*) that transcribes it.[37] For this reason, it should be possible, given an inscription, to utter it aloud, to form a concept on the basis of that utterance, and to pick out by means of that concept the thing of which it is the concept. In principle, there is no thing, concept, utterance, or inscription that would exist outside of this chain of signification.

What is strange, then, is that Boethius proceeds systematically to dismantle his own model. He takes pains to show that each link in the chain of signification is breakable, if not already broken.[38] For, as he explains, there is in fact a thing to which no concept corresponds: God. Given a concept, moreover, it is not possible to arrive at any specific utterance, since the same concept will be signified not by one word but by many: synonyms, new coinages, words in various languages. Likewise with utterances: since they can be transcribed in various alphabets (or by nonalphabetical conventions), they clearly do not give rise to any one inscription in particular. Still more, the *orandi ordo* also undoes itself at every point when it is traversed in the other direction. For there are inscriptions that cannot be vocalized: mysterious letterforms or unpronounceable sequences of letters. There are utterances that signify nothing whatsoever: sound-shapes to which no meaning has been assigned. And there are concepts to which no thing corresponds, those for example of imaginary beings such as the chimera.

This line of thought, in which the operation of language will prove to be inseparable from its own inoperativity, is just what Aristotle might have wished to forestall, and most of all where Boethius speaks of meaningless *voces*. For when the Philosopher refers his reader elsewhere for a discussion of these questions, the passage of *De anima* that he has in mind is doubtless the one in which he asserts that "not every sound made by a living creature is a voice (for one can make a sound even with the tongue, or as in coughing), but that which even causes the impact, must have a soul, and use some imagination; for the voice is a sound which means something, and is not merely indicative of air inhaled, as a cough is."³⁹ The point is made unmistakably: an animate being, such as a human, can cause a sound to emerge from its throat, can even shape that sound into a specific form, but if the sound does not mean anything it will not count as *phone* (*vox*). There is not and cannot be any such thing as a *vox* that does not signify. But the commentator asserts just the opposite view, and does so just as baldly: "Nec si voces sint, mox intellectus esse necesse est. Plures enim voces invenies quae nihil omnino significent" (Nor if there are utterances is it necessary for there to be thoughts. For you will come across many utterances which signify nothing at all).⁴⁰ Without drawing attention to the fact, in transmitting Aristotelian logic to the Latin West Boethius thus subjects it to a profound alteration.⁴¹

To understand the history of linguistic ideas in the Middle Ages it is necessary to understand what it is that Boethius swapped out Aristotle's conception of the subject matter of logic for: namely, his own doctrine of the fundamental meaninglessness of *vox*. As already noted, Boethius begins his second commentary on *De interpretatione* by defining *vox* as the lingual striking of air emitted through the throat.⁴² With the same gesture as Priscian, he now proceeds to differentiate it into species. Among *voces*, some are *articulatae*, "writable" (note that Boethius still uses this term in its traditional sense and not in Priscian's), and others are not. Leaving aside the unwritable *voces*, he divides up the writable *vox*, to which he assigns the technical term *locutio*, according to whether it does or does not signify. But rather than simply distinguishing meaningful from nonmeaningful, as a Priscian will do, Boethius identifies four distinct relations that a writable *vox* can have with signification:

> Sive autem aliquid quaecumque vox significet, ut est hic sermo homo, sive omnino nihil, sive positum alicui nomen significare possit, ut est blityri (haec enim vox per se cum nihil significet, posita tamen ut alicui nomen sit significabit), sive per se quidem nihil significet, cum aliis vero iuncta designet, ut sunt coniunctiones: haec omnia locutiones vocantur.⁴³

> [Whether an utterance signifies something, such as this word *man*; or signifies nothing at all; or can signify if it be assigned to something as its name, such as *blityri* (for while this utterance signifies nothing in itself, nevertheless when it is assigned to something as a name, then it will signify); or signifies nothing in itself, but does signify when it is joined with others, such as is the case with conjunctions—all these are called "words."]

The commentator's division seems fairly straightforward at first glance. Participating equally in the nature of *locutio* are four varieties of writable utterance. There are first of all words that mean something, such as the word *homo*; only this sort of word, he will soon specify, is at issue in *De interpretatione* and indeed in the discipline of logic as a whole. But there are three other sorts of words in addition to this one, and although they are not the concern of logic they can nonetheless be enumerated and characterized. These are as follows: words that mean absolutely nothing, words that mean something only when you combine them with other words (conjunctions), and words that do not mean anything for the time being but could at any moment become the name of something (the nonsense word *blityri*).

And yet the passage presents a serious difficulty. Boethius gives examples of the first, third, and fourth of the four varieties of *locutio*. Of the third and fourth he also provides short explanations, which he does not do in the case of the first, no doubt because such will be the task of the commentary as a whole. Of the second, however, he gives neither example nor explanation. In keeping conspicuously silent on this single point, Boethius transmits to his readers a problem, whether they are paying attention or not. It is by no means clear what the determining traits of *vox quae nihil omnino significat* (a *vox* that means absolutely nothing) might be, nor where an example of such an entity could be found. And this is, in fact, a real problem: how can there be a word that is totally refractory to signification, whose absolute nonsensicality neither coinage nor combination with other words will ever be able to reduce? In order to try to answer this question, we must determine whether Boethius, despite his seeming merely to leave the question open, provides any clues as to how he himself might answer it. The only indication given thus far is that *vox quae omnino nihil significat* is to be distinguished from words that are meaningful in themselves (*homo*), words that are meaningful in combination (conjunctions), and words that have not yet been assigned a meaning (*blityri*). This last point is the strangest and the most suggestive.

Blityri is by no means an invention of Boethius's. Apparently of Stoic origins, it is first attested in Diogenes Laertius.[44] Along with the word *skindapsos*, with which it is strictly equivalent, it was the stock example of what in Stoic linguistics was described as a *lexis* that is not also a *logos*: a word-shape that carries no sense.[45] As such, these words are actually quite unsatisfactory—and not only because, insofar as they have the status of stock examples, they end up "standing for" what they exemplify and thus not being entirely without meaning. Still worse, both of them originated as meaningful words in their own right. *Skindapsos*, originally the name of a kind of lute, had come to be the equivalent of English *thingamajig* or *whatchamacallit*; and *blityri*, for its part, appears to have been an onomatopoeic formation on the order of *zing* or *twang*—it signified "nonsignifying sound" and thus did not in fact constitute such a sound.[46] It is for these reasons, perhaps, that Boethius also offers his own more suitable example, unattested elsewhere: *hereceddy*.

This hapax, which really does appear to not yet mean anything, is introduced to illustrate the mechanics of what Boethius calls *impositio*, a theory about the origin of linguistic meaning that the Middle Ages would inherit from him. According to the theory of imposition, an empty sound-shape (*locutio*, rendering the Stoic *lexis*) is "imposed on" or assigned to a particular concept in order to signify it, thereby becoming a meaningful word (*interpretatio*, rendering *logos*). This theory ascribes the meaningfulness of words to an arbitrary exercise of will on the part of whoever has coined them. Boethius illustrates the theory of imposition by enacting it: he invents a new sound-shape, *hereceddy*, and then summarily imposes it:

> ... scindapsos vel hereceddy. Haec per se nihil quidem significant, sed si ad subiectae alicuius rei significationem ponantur, ut dicatur vel homo scindapsos vel lapis hereceddy, tunc hoc quod per se nihil significat positione et secundum ponentis quoddam placitum designabit.[47]

> [*Skindapsos* and *hereceddy* signify nothing in themselves, but if they are imposed so as to signify some underlying thing, so that man is called *skindapsos* or stone *hereceddy, then* this thing that signifies nothing in itself *will* signify by its imposition and according to the particular desire of the impositor.]

In short, meaningful words are produced by assigning an empty sound-shape to a given thing as its name. According to this doctrine of imposition, all words are originally meaningless, taking on signification only through a secondary operation of imposition: the meaningful word *stone* was once as meaningless as the newly invented *hereceddy*, and that did not prevent it from being a full-fledged word even then.[48] On the other hand, although they are in the first place meaningless, they are no less essentially susceptible of acquiring meaning. The only reason *hereceddy* is meaningless is that it has not yet been imposed. Since it will become meaningful as soon as anyone comes along and imposes it, there must be something in it that is liable to signify even if it happens never to have signified before.

What this means is that if an example of *vox quae nihil omnino significat*, which Boethius has conspicuously failed to give in his fourfold taxonomy of *vox*, is to be discovered, it will have to be somehow unimposable. It is in this light that the importance of the following, neglected passage of the commentary makes itself known:

> Vox enim quae nihil designat, ut est garalus, licet eam grammatici figuram vocis intuentes nomen esse contendant, tamen eam nomen philosophia non putabit, nisi sit posita ut designare animi aliquam conceptionem eoque modo rerum aliquid possit.[49]

> [A *vox* that signifies nothing, such as *garalus*, although the grammarians, paying attention to the shape of the utterance (*figura vocis*), claim that it is a noun, nevertheless philosophy will not consider a noun, unless it be imposed to signify some concept in the mind and in this way be able to designate an aspect of the things.]

Garalus is an invention of Boethius's; it is not a word known to speakers of Latin. In this, it resembles *hereceddy*. But the resemblance only goes so far. For *garalus* has a sound-shape (*figura vocis*) that allows it to be identified as belonging to a particular part of speech, since in Latin it is invariably the case that a word ending in *-lus* is a noun.[50] To the extent that it is possessed of what Taki Suto calls a "noun-like form," and even though it has no meaning, a grammarian, says Boethius, will not hesitate to submit *garalus* to grammatical analysis.[51] In the same manner, a "grammarian" of English would be able to identify *sladdiest* (to invent an example) as a superlative adjective, *to sladdify* as an infinitive, and so forth; such a grammarian could also assert with confidence that *kindly refrain from sladdifying* is an admissible formulation, whereas *sladdifying refrain from smoking* is not. Grammar is the name, here, of a realm in which the distinction between meaningful and nonmeaningful utterances does not obtain, in which words function no differently before they have been imposed as after. Grammarians are simply indifferent to the signification or nonsignification of the words they use; meaning is, to them, an irrelevance, or it would be if they bothered to give it any thought at all. Grammar is just the inoperativity of imposition.

Suto rightly notes that such a remark should not be read as a description of the actual activities of grammarians. What is at stake here is rather the constitution of the discipline of logic itself, or indeed of philosophy as a whole, which delimits its own realm by calling the sphere in which a meaningless word can circulate by the name of some other discipline. Logic, the science of the truth of *vox*, cannot and must not allow meaninglessness into its domain—even as it always fails, constitutively, to exclude it. For this apotropaic gesture has always been, for better or worse, ineffectual.[52] Despite continuing to publish Boethius's ban on nonsignifying utterances, the logicians of the Middle Ages found themselves face-to-face with them and did so squarely in the middle of their own domain (see chapter 2).

Nonetheless, it is also the case that Boethius's invented word does, by all rights, belong to the realm of grammar as it was actually practiced. For although it is true that *garalus* signifies nothing, it is also true that it resembles another word so closely as to be unmistakably an alteration of it. That word is *garrulus*, which—to add to the confusion—means "chattering, babbling, chirping." Some modern readers, indeed, have even taken *garalus* as nothing more than a scribal error for *garrulus*, but this is a misunderstanding.[53] What Boethius has done he has done with precision: he has submitted a word that already exists in the lexicon of a particular language to an operation of disfigurement. The technical term for a word produced in such a way is *barbarismus*, and the discipline to which the study of *barbarismus* belongs is of course grammar. It is—for example—the first of the *vitia* or faults discussed by Donatus, on the basis of whose *Ars maius* Boethius's medieval readers would have been able to recognize *garalus* as an instance of *barbarismus per detractionem et inmutationem litterarum* (barbarism through the omission and substitution of letters).[54]

A linguistic error of this sort belongs to grammar insofar as grammar would seek to eradicate it from the usage of the speakers and writers trained in its rules, but also insofar as it could constitute an instance of poetic license: Donatus refers to none other than Virgil and Lucretius for his examples of the sorts of barbarism that *garalus* represents.

It is because it belongs to grammar that *garalus* answers to the description of *vox quae nihil omnino significat*, and thus might be considered to represent the example missing from Boethius's classification of the types of utterances. Because it is not, in fact, a word (such as *garrulus*) that has already been imposed to signify something, *garalus* has no meaning; and yet, insofar as it is obviously no more than a fatuous form of *garrulus*, no one would mistake it for a truly unimposed word on the order of *hereceddy* and thus consider it available for coinage. *Garalus* is admitted to the realm of grammar on the strength of its morphology, since it is shaped like a noun; but having entered that realm it never leaves. As a barbarism, precisely, it remains the property of the grammarians: that is, it remains in that realm in which imposition is inoperative. Unlike *homo*, which means something already; unlike a conjunction, which means something in combination; unlike even the newly pronounced *hereceddy*, which will mean something just as soon as someone imposes it; *garalus* means absolutely nothing. If such a word could be translated into English—strange thought—it might come out as *chotering*, *bebling*, or *charrping*. Boethius's proposal, marginal as it remains within his work, is decisive: there exists a kind of nonsense that is absolute, and it can be encountered. The possibility of utter nonsignification arises within a given system of signification, and nowhere else. Only those speakers who are already familiar with the lexicon and morphological conventions of a language can make it permanently incomprehensible to itself. For each time an empty sound-shape is assigned a meaning, a new and irreducible form of nonsense springs into being. In a combinatorics of barbarization, around every imposed word will be arrayed the halo of all its possible deformations: not only *garalus* but *geralus* and *giralus* and *goralus* and so on, filling volumes in a Library of Babel.[55]

Because logic is the science of using language to determine truth and falsity, it must ward off the incursion of such words, for a proposition that contains even one of them will be impervious to any such determination. *Every garalus is mortal*, needless to say, is neither true nor false. And so Boethius relegates the *vox quae omnino nihil significat* to grammar. In so doing, he resumes a traditional gesture, one made, for instance, by Sextus Empiricus, who had maintained that truth "will not exist in that which has no significance, such as the words 'Blituri' and 'Skindapsos'; for how is it possible to accept as true a thing which is not significative?"[56] But he is not simply following convention. In an apparently off-hand remark he makes much later in the commentary—apropos of almost nothing, and only to let the matter immediately drop—he makes clear that he is familiar with another, more frightening reason to keep such words at bay. At issue is suddenly no longer logic but psychology: and thus the commentary reveals that it has never in fact left the realm of *De anima*, exactly where Aristotle had wanted to confine any discussion of *vox*, and where Boethius would not let it be confined. For it turns out that *vox quae omnino nihil significat* has a certain effect on the psyche:

> Si quis vero huiusmodi vocem ceperit, quae nihil omnino designet, animus eius nulla significatione neque intellegentia roboratus errat ac vertitur nec ullis designationis finibus conquiescit.[57]

> [If anyone hears a *vox* of the sort that signifies nothing at all, his mind—not strengthened by any signification or understanding—will wander and twist around on itself, and not come to rest at the limits that would be provided by a signification.]

These few lines represent Boethius's only other discussion of this entity. They are precise, despite their brevity, and far from incidental. The mental faculty, he suggests, is susceptible to the utterances it encounters, which impress themselves upon it without regard for its wishes. Utterances that signify—whether actually, in combination, or once they are coined—give the mind of a person who hears them something to work with. The mind can establish itself on their basis, drawing strength from their meaning and thereby taking up a position on solid ground. Discourse, as might be said, produces and consolidates subjectivity. But something quite different happens in the encounter with *vox quae nihil omnino designat*: mind has its ground taken out from under it, and it is cast into exile. Without any signification to rely on, the sense of self is deracinated, enucleated, and forced to undergo the issueless experience of its own unworking. As Michel de Certeau explains, in another context: "the nonsense of glossolalic discourse sets a trap for interpretation and drives it to delirium."[58]

For an utterance to be permanently and absolutely empty—unimposable—is thus not for it to simply hang in the air. The unrecognizable sound of a mere *figura vocis*, a *lexis* without a *logos*, far from simply passing you by, makes a claim on your attention. Without meaning anything, indeed insofar as it does not mean anything, it causes something to happen in the psyche. If you ever chance to hear it, your mind will become debilitated; deprived of an object, it will be forced to circle around itself. The word will go on harassing you, provoking you to cognize it but providing nothing that can be cognized, so that your mind is sent off in search of a signification that it will never discover. To encounter *garalus* is to undergo an experience of confusion with no conceivable end.

SARABARAE

Around the year 387, somewhat more than a century before the composition of the two works just examined, Augustine of Hippo began work on a treatise on logic whose Stoic influence is as marked as that of Priscian and Boethius. The unfinished *De dialectica*, known although relatively neglected during the Middle Ages, is chiefly remembered today for a single reason.[59] In chapter 5, the saint gives an account of four distinguishable linguistic elements coordinated together into a schema. This gesture will seem familiar from Priscian and Boethius. But just as the elements of Boethius's quaternity were not those of Priscian's, so are Augustine's again distinct:

> Haec ergo quattuor distincta teneantur; verbum, dicibile, dictio, res. Quod dixi verbum, et verbum est et verbum significat. Quod dixi dicibile, verbum est, nec tamen verbum, sed quod in verbo intellegitur et animo continetur, significat. Quod dixi dictionem, verbum est, sed quod iam illa duo simul id est et ipsum verbum et quod fit in animo per verbum significat. Quod dixi rem, verbum est, quod praeter illa tria quae dicta sunt quidquid restat significat.[60]
>
> [Therefore, these four are to be kept distinct: the *verbum*, the *dicibile*, the *dictio*, and the *res*. *Verbum* both is a word and signifies a word. *Dicibile* is a word; however, it does not signify a word but what is understood in the word and contained in the mind. *Dictio* is also a word, but it signifies both the first two, that is, the word itself and what is brought about in the mind by means of the word. *Res* is a word which signifies whatever remains beyond the three that have been mentioned.]

The first thing to notice about this rebarbative set of distinctions is that it differs from those in the works already examined not only in its elements but also in that what is being differentiated is not *vox*. In fact, though he makes much use of the word *vox* in the treatise, Augustine nowhere stops to define it. What then is being distinguished? It is impossible to say. For his part, Augustine just calls his elements *haec quattuor*, "these four," which is no help at all.[61] And in fact this whole passage, not to mention the chapter of which it is the core, is scandalously obscure. There has never been any agreement, among scholars who have written about *De dialectica*, as to how it should be construed; and when Tzvetan Todorov calls it a "terminological muddle" he does not overstate the case.[62] Nonetheless, the convincing indications of its modern editor, B. Darrell Jackson, allow for the following set of provisional glosses to be offered: the technical term *verbum* refers to a word insofar as it is mentioned rather than used (e.g., in the sentence *"weapons" is a noun*); *dicibile* refers to the concept intended by a person using, not mentioning, a word (e.g., the concept of weapons); *dictio*, perhaps the most obscurely described of the four, appears to refer to a word itself insofar as it is used rather than mentioned (e.g., in the sentence *Aeneas had weapons*); and finally *res* refers to the thing itself (e.g., the very weapons that can be held in the hand).[63]

But whatever Augustine may have meant to distinguish in his schema, and into whatever elements, one thing seems beyond dispute. Under none of these four headings would it be possible to classify Priscian's *coax, cra* or Boethius's *hereceddy* or *garalus*. The meaningless word has no place here. But this fact should arouse wonder. In a work in which Augustine is—as is often remarked—at his most explicitly Stoic, absent is the very thing that stands as the mark of a specifically Stoicizing tendency in Priscian and Boethius: a consideration of the word as *lexis* or empty sound-shape. At least, it would seem to be absent. But here is Jean Pépin on this very point, in his important book on Augustinian logic: "the Stoics, in order to designate the articulated utterance as opposed to the mere sound, used the word *lexis*, of which [Augustine's term] *dictio* constitutes an adequate and attested translation."[64] In other words, *dictio* (e.g., *weapons* in the sentence *Aeneas had weapons*) is the equivalent of *lexis* (e.g., *blityri*). The suggestion appears absurd. But Pépin is not alone in identifying Augustine's *dictio* as the equivalent of the Stoic *lexis*; his lead has been followed on this matter by a succession of eminent expositors.[65] How can this be?

An explanation is not far to seek. Marc Baratin has shown that Augustine's quaternity bears the traces of an "adaptation of the Stoic classification" by Alexandrian grammarians.[66] While maintaining the technical terms of their predecessors, the Alexandrians assigned them new definitions—and notably in the case of *lexis*. No longer referring to a sound-shape in isolation from any meaning it might or might not bear, for a Dionysius Thrax the word *lexis* will now designate the minimal unit of the proposition, that is, the logical term. The property of meaninglessness, formerly capable of being possessed by full-fledged words, is now relegated to the letters and syllables that make them up; and *lexis* goes from being the name of a unit of sound to being that of a unit of sense. According to the Alexandrian revision of Stoic logic, it is not that logic restricts its attention to that particular group of words that bear meaning, but that this group is coextensive with the category of word as such. In other words, there will be no such thing as a meaningless utterance: the sound-shape is subsumed in the term and can no longer exist on its own. And thus behind Augustine's treatise there stands a "reinterpretation" that in fact represents a banishment of nonsignification from the domain of logic even more forceful than the one that will be found in Boethius.

But if there is no place in Augustine's schema for utterances such as *blityri*—let alone *garalus*—this fact cannot be explained solely on the basis of the saint's familiarity with certain Alexandrian materials from which they also happen to be absent. For this absence is by no means peripheral to Augustine's thought as a whole. The question of whether it is possible for there to be a word without meaning is one that he addresses explicitly at the beginning of this chapter of *De dialectica*, one he has already addressed elsewhere, and one he will address again.[67] The answer is a firm *no*: by definition, for Augustine, "loqui est articulata voce signum dare" (to speak is to give a sign by means of the articulate *vox*).[68] Indeed, the principle that utterance is by nature meaningful has seemed to many modern readers to be characteristically Augustinian.[69] It is a commonplace of the history of linguistic ideas that Augustine is the first to have combined semantics with semiotics, that is, to have made the study of signs and the study of verbal signification a single discipline. Put more forcefully, what he accomplished was a subordination of semantics to semiotics: words become for him a species of signs, one of the many things that signify. Instead of considering (with Priscian and Boethius) the meaningful word as one of a number of species of *vox*, Augustine identifies it as one of a number of species of that which is meaningful.[70] As he will go on to write in *De doctrina christiana*, words are "signa quorum omnis usus in significando est.... Nemo enim utitur verbis nisi aliquid significandi gratia" (signs whose whole function consists in signifying.... Nobody uses words except in order to signify something).[71]

This is not just a terminological or taxonomic difference. What is at stake in Augustine's insistence on the meaningfulness of words becomes clear in his Sermon 288, where *vox* and *verbum* are made analogous to John the Baptist and the Christ, the former merely preparing the way for the latter, as the sensible aspects of a word are first received by a hearer and then give way to the concept that they signify.[72] The two elements are given wholly different values: "A word has full value, even without a voice; a voice is worthless without a word."[73] As Augustine develops this line of thought, the importance granted to *verbum* at the expense of *vox* is increased to such an extent that *verbum* sheds even its minimal attachment to the *vox* that precedes it, and the "voices fall away as the word grows."[74] In short, and as his modern readers have noted, Augustine gives a "lowly place" to mere words, insisting on the "powerlessness of external things"; it is the meaning in words that matters, and not what they are made of.[75] In such a theologically motivated theory of language, in which vocalization bows before intention, it should not be surprising if the meaningless word—an "external sign" so external that it would even be without an "inner meaning" with respect to which it could be external—should be neglected. It is easy enough to rehearse the diagnosis that this passage seems to call for: in order to shore up the reign of the master signifier, in a logocentric privileging of transcendental signification, Augustine forecloses the possibility of words that do not signify.

But what he is actually doing is more interesting. "Omne verbum sonat," he writes in chapter 5 of *De dialectica*: "every word sounds." The sonorous aspect of the word, moreover, can even be treated as an object of disciplinary knowledge: "De sono enim verbi agitur, cum quaeritur vel animadvertitur, qualiter vocalium vel dispositione leniatur vel concursione dehiscat, item consonantium vel interpositione nodetur vel congestione asperetur, et quot vel qualibus syllabis constet, ubi poeticus rhythmus accentusque" (We concern ourselves with the sound of words when we ask about or attend to the use of vowels to make speech lighter, or to the combination of vowels in a word, or again to the arrangement of consonants for articulation, or their concentration for asperity of speech, to the number and quality of syllables, or the matter of poetic rhythm and accent). But the discipline to which these concerns belong is not logic—"quod sonat nihil ad dialecticam" (sounds are not the concern of dialectic)—and they are therefore of no interest in this treatise *de dialectica*: they are rather the business of the grammarian.[76] Grammar functions here just as it does in Boethius: it stands for a realm in which words operate and are studied without reference to whether or not they signify, and its invocation allows Augustine to delimit the field of logic as over against it. Logic will be that realm in which the grammarian, as grammarian, cannot appear. Or so it would seem. For no sooner is the grammarian declared to have no business in the realm of logic than he reappears, this time in the guise of a mere example. Barely a page later, after Augustine has given his schema of *verbum, dicibile, dictum*, and *res*, he offers an illustration as a necessary clarification of what even he can see is a "terminological muddle." The example is that of a grammarian speaking to his class: "Let us take as an example a grammarian questioning a boy in this manner: 'What part of speech is "arma"?'" What was constitutively excluded from logic is smuggled back in, as an "example," in order to supplement the properly logical definitions that are evidently unable to stand on their own account.

The gesture is notable rhetorically insofar as it appears to take back with the left hand what has been offered with the right. But what is important about this example is that Augustine will repeat it later in the treatise, in the chapter on ambiguity and obscurity. There are in fact only two "examples" of this kind given in the whole treatise, and they are the same: a grammarian—and not, for instance, a logician—is speaking to his class. But in the second invocation of this scenario, in the chapter on obscurity, the grammarian is no longer discussing the opening line of the *Aeneid*. He does not say "arma" to his class, but something else:

> Constitue animo quempiam grammaticum convocatis discipulis factoque silentio suppressa voce dixisse "temetum."[77]

> [Imagine a teacher of grammar who, when he had called his class together and gotten silence, said in a low voice, "temetum."]

Augustine does not have much to say about the word *temetum* itself. An antiquated word for wine that appears in scripture, it appears to stand self-evidently for the class of arcane terms with which a schoolboy would be unfamiliar. The grammar school classroom is the site of an utterance to which no meaning attaches in the minds of those who hear it. But *temetum* is not just any antiquated word. It is one that he will make use of again a decade later, in *De trinitate*:

> Ita etiam signum si quis audiat incognitum, veluti verbi alicuius sonum, quo quid significetur ignorat, cupit scire quidnam sit, id est, sonus ille cui rei commemorandae institutus sit: veluti si audiat cum dicitur temetum, ignorans quid sit requirat.[78]

[Suppose someone hears an unknown sign, like the sound of some word which he does not know the meaning of; he wants to know what it is, that is, what thing that sound was fixed on to remind us of; he hears someone say *temetum*, for example, and not knowing what it is he asks.]

Giorgio Agamben, drawing attention to this passage on multiple occasions, has shown it to be crucial to Augustine's thought overall. As Agamben summarizes:

> In this passage, the experience of the dead word appears as the experience of a word uttered (a *vox*) insofar as it is no longer mere sound (*istas tres syllabas*), but not yet a signification—insofar as it is the experience, that is, of a sign as pure meaning and intention to signify before and beyond the arrival of every particular signification. For Augustine, this experience of an unknown word (*verbum ignotum*) in the no-man's-land between sound and signification is the experience of love as will to know.[79]

What Agamben goes on to underscore is the fact that the experience undergone by a person who happens to hear a *vocabulum emortuum* serves Augustine as the very model of contemplative devotion. The love of God, as the saint conceives of it here, has nothing to do with understanding what is meant by the word *God*, or by any other, but takes place in incomprehension. The highest capacity of the human psyche would be analogous with, if not simply identical to, the unknowing that is produced in the mind of a person who hears a word such as *temetum*. And yet, as Agamben shows, if for the Augustine of *De trinitate* what is revealed in *temetum* is not any signification in particular, nor is it a *vox inanis*, the mere syllabic sounding of the utterance. It is rather something apparently even more meaningful than a particular signification: the pure intention to signify. For Augustine claims that the person who hears *temetum* will know that the word has some meaning, whatever it might be, and so will apprehend this "whatever it might be" of meaning rather than some more limited particular signification. Even if you do not know what an utterance has been imposed to signify, in other words, you nonetheless know that it has been imposed to signify something. When you overhear a conversation held in a language that you do not speak, for example, you assume that its participants understand each other even if you yourself have no idea what they are talking about.

Still, it is by no means clear how this knowledge, minimal as it is, is meant to have been acquired. If you do not know what a word means, how can you be certain that it means anything at all? On what basis can you rest assured that what you are hearing is not just a newly invented *figura vocis*, a barbarism, the speech of someone putting on airs, a fool, an evil genius trying to delude you? The mere assertion that a person hearing *temetum* will know that it signifies something-or-other does nothing to reduce the possibility that something you hear without recognizing it might not be a dead word but a word that never lived at all, *vox inanis* and nothing more. And in fact Augustine is fully aware of this possibility. He keeps silent about it here, but he has already wrestled with it at great length in a dialogue written a bit more than a decade earlier. In *De magistro*, in the context of a spectacularly unconvincing demonstration of a doctrine that will by now be entirely familiar—namely, that if every word is a sign, there can be no word that does not signify—he introduces an obscure word from the book of Daniel, *sarabarae*, that "non enim mihi rem quam significat ostendit" (doesn't show me the thing it signifies).[80] The example is strictly equivalent to *temetum*. In the case of *sarabarae*, however, Augustine maintains that when confronted with such a word you cannot know "utrum vox ista sit tantummodo sonans, an aliquid etiam significans" (whether that utterance is a mere noise or also signifies something). He makes this point, which is in direct opposition to the one he will go on to make in *De trinitate*, repeatedly. And it pertains not just to *sarabarae* but to every word without exception. For here is how he sums up the argument, which he will famously return to in the *Confessions*, and which concerns both the abrogation and the persistence of the state of infancy: by hearing a given word used more than once in a particular connection, "reperi vocabulum esse rei quae mihi jam erat videndo notissima. Quod priusquam reperissem, tantum mihi sonus erat hoc verbum: signum vero esse didici, quando cujus rei signum esset inveni" (I discovered that it was the term for a thing already familiar to me by sight. Before I made this discovery, the word was a mere sound to me; but I learned that it was a sign when I found out of what thing it is the sign). Nor does he hesitate to emphasize what this means: "si ea quae signa non sunt, verba esse non possunt, quamvis jam auditum verbum, nescio tamen verbum esse, donec quid significet sciam" (if things that aren't signs can't be words, then although I have already heard a word, I don't know that it is a word until I know what it signifies).[81]

This last specification is astounding. Until now, it has seemed as though the Augustinian subordination of words to signs entailed that it is impossible to find a full-fledged word that does not signify. Even if you are ignorant of its meaning, you can assume that any given word means something. But here the doctrine is turned on its head: it is not that meaningless words do not exist, but that—as with Boethius—to encounter one is to undergo an experience of psychic debilitation. To hear such a word is to be without knowledge of whether what you are hearing is even a word at all. And this experience of ignorance is the originary experience of language, undergone by everyone in infancy and returning every time you happen to hear a word you do not yet know. Such an experience consists not in apprehending the pure signifyingness of language but, inversely, in a failure to recognize language as language, or nonlanguage as nonlanguage, in a word whose signifyingness is withheld. But if Augustine seems to be arguing in a different direction here than he does elsewhere, his doing so brings him remarkably close to Priscian. For the grammarian, as we have seen, *vox* is something not necessarily vocal, for it might just be a creaking; something that, even insofar as it is vocal, is produced by both human and nonhuman animals; and finally something that is not, in itself, either significative or nonsignificative. Augustine's very decision to define *vox* as necessarily significative leads him, despite everything, back to the realm of grammar: for what he suggests here is not that nonsignifying *voces* do not exist but rather that *vox* includes itself as non-*vox* and ceaselessly defies any attempt to tell the difference between the two.

Did Augustine change his mind when he changed his example from *sarabarae* to *temetum*? Perhaps. In the end, it probably makes no difference. The dead word, the unknown word, is the site of a hesitation in which it only indicates and does not yet symbolize, as Agamben puts it, or again in which it is not even identifiable as a word.[82] These are the two halves of a single broken coin. The experience of knowing the pure *intentio significandi* of the utterance matches up exactly with the experience of not knowing whether it is even a word. The desire to understand *temetum* or *sarabarae*, the very model of the love of God, is not only a desire to know what is being signified—or even, as Augustine will develop the idea, to know meaning in its totality—but also an inability to know for certain whether signification is taking place at all. Barely hidden by Augustine's emphasis on pure meaningfulness is thus something else: the originary experience of hearing a word in a language, every word in every language, and not recognizing it as a word.

Such is the conclusion to which a reader might be led by approaching chapter 5 of *De dialectica* with an eye for its lexical choices, the status of its examples, and the webs of allusion into which it enters. That is, by reading it rhetorically. Attention to the rhetorical dimension of Augustine's expositions of his theory of language shows that the saint's familiar emphasis on meaning—which would be so decisive for the Middle Ages, tiresome as it has become for some of his modern readers—is inseparable from a thinking of meaninglessness that is no less fundamental. And it should be said that if such a mode of reading is available now, and was available in the Middle Ages, it is of course in no small part due to Augustine's own efforts, notably in the massively influential "redeemed rhetoric" or Christian hermeneutics he lays out in *De doctrina christiana*. And reading, as it is both taught and practiced in that treatise, has no other purpose than to reveal the obscurities of its object—and not so as to clear them up, but in order that they might be released into their own permanent incomprehensibility.[83] The highest specifically rhetorical possibility of the word, that is, its ability to move its hearers to an experience of God, lies in its emptying itself of all content, to such an extent that it is no longer even clear whether it constitutes a word at all. The task of a redeemed rhetoric, of a properly "Christian" hermeneutics, is to turn scripture into so many mere syllables, to make its every word into *sarabarae*. The esoteric vocation of Augustinian rhetoric is in fact the mortification of holy writ: to bring about a kenosis of scripture itself.

But what is to be done with the *vocabulum emortuum* so produced? Augustine has given instruction on this matter, too, in a brief remark in *De doctrina*: "Nulla sane sunt magis mandanda memoriae quam illa verborum locutionumque genera quae ignoramus" (Nothing is better to commit to memory than those types of words and phrases of which we are ignorant).[84] No doubt he means that unfamiliar terms should be noted, so that you can inquire about their meaning at some later and more opportune moment. But, given everything that has been said so far, it is far easier to read this dictum to the effect that you should engrave in your heart the word insofar as you do not know whether it is a word or not.[85] There can be no doubt that Augustine transmits to the Middle Ages a whole metaphysics of the presence of the word. But he includes with it, inseparably, a counter-transmission in the form of this injunction to memorize the word as *coax cra*, to inscribe *garalus* indelibly on the psyche. And Boethius will have identified exactly what kind of an inscription this must be: the kind that puts the mind to flight, that leaves it exiled forever in a desert of sense.

ERRAT AC VERTITUR

Friedrich Kittler draws attention, in *Discourse Networks*, to the exemplary case of Hermann Ebbinghaus, a German psychologist who carried out a strange course of experiments on himself over the course of a handful of years beginning in 1879. "Reading aloud at a tempo dictated by the ticking of his pocket watch, the professor spent years reading line after line of meaningless syllables, until he could recite them from memory."[86] Memorizing series of syllables and taking every pain to avoid investing his material with meaning, Ebbinghaus made his way through the entire range of possible syllabic combinations. The experiments had as their object the quantification of memory; however, they also had a side effect on the man who was at once their subject and their administrator: "Dizzy, numbed by all the syllables, his mind became a tabula rasa.... With his head spinning, Ebbinghaus achieved an unthinkable distance where nothing, but nothing, means anything. He instituted the flight of ideas."[87]

As is clear from his manner of speaking, for Kittler these experiments are fundamentally novel, and indeed their pride of place in his schema is due to their illustrating the epochal fissure that he says bisects the nineteenth century, whose beginning and end are characterized by the transcendence of the signified and by the mechanization of the signifier, respectively. Kittler could hardly be more explicit about this point:

> Never before had such passion been devoted to syllables. Of course, Reformation primers did, to the dismay of the classical age, play through single vowel-consonant combinations of the second order. But their *ab eb ib ob ub / ba be bi bo bu* was only an example; the goal was not a mathematically guaranteed completeness of assembly. The discourse network of 1900 was the

first to establish a treasury of the signifier whose rules were entirely based on randomness and combinatorics. It is not that, with Ebbinghaus's numbered sounds and sound combinations or Mallarmé's twenty-four letters, an old-European discursive practice returns from its repression circa 1800. The fact that combinatory groups do not necessarily produce sense also applied to the letters and words of the miserable scribes of 1736. But not even Liscov's satire had the scribes systematically avoid "agreement among the letters" the way Ebbinghaus did.[88]

Kittler's description of the "dizziness" Ebbinghaus experiences in the "unthinkable distance" of "the flight of ideas" brought on by the encounter with the meaningless utterances is remarkably close to Boethius's description of what happens to someone who hears a *vox quae nihil omnino significat*: "his mind—not strengthened by any signification or understanding—will wander and twist around on itself, and not come to rest at the limits that would be provided by a signification." It would be absurd, of course, to suppose that Kittler is alluding here to a forgotten sentence from the middle of the second of the Roman senator's two commentaries on *De interpretatione*. Much more reasonable would it be to conclude that Ebbinghaus at the end of the nineteenth century and Boethius at the beginning of the sixth are familiar with the same experience, one that persists as a linguistic and psychic possibility independently of them both.

But if this is so, the novelty of Ebbinghaus's experiments in the decades leading up to the year 1900, and of the unthinkable knowledge of the "flight of ideas" that is their product, seems less sure. Kittler's misleading allusion to the ancient practice of the syllabary as if it were a matter of nothing more than "Reformation primers" only reinforces this suspicion; and not least because the "goal" of the practice of *ba be bi bo bu* was, in fact, exactly the thing that seems to Kittler characteristically modern: "a mathematically guaranteed completeness of assembly." For that is just what Quintilian insists, that the syllables "must all be memorized thoroughly and there must be no putting off the most difficult of them." It cannot in fact be maintained that Ebbinghausian nonsignification was unknown to earlier centuries and millennia. The apparently modern notion of the meaninglessness of the *res linguistica*, in short, would not only have been perfectly thinkable in the Middle Ages but was, in point of fact, a key element of the basic instruction that every literate person received. For the very *materia* of language, *vox sola*, was understood to be a matter of obscurity: neither vocal nor nonvocal, linguistic nor nonlinguistic. It could signify, but it need not, and it existed in varieties in which signification could never attach to it at all. These instances, it was held, belong by rights to the realm of grammar; but the realm of grammar, as it turns out, includes any place where *vox* is heard as such: in poetry, in infancy, in scripture, in the syllable, in the halo of disfigurement that surrounds every word.

CHAPTER TWO

WALTER BURLEY ON *SUPPOSITIO MATERIALIS*

In the middle of the thirteenth century, Roger Bacon drew attention to a point of contention in the field of logic, what he called a "quarrel, not small, among well-known men" (*non est modica contentio inter viros famosos*).[1] Some forty years later, John Duns Scotus could still refer to this quarrel as ongoing; for him, it had attained the status of a "great dispute" (*magna altercatio*).[2] The problem was this: the theorists of language could not agree on whether words are the names of things or of concepts. Does *vox*, the utterance, directly signify a thing in the world or does it instead signify the concept of the thing that exists in the mind of the person who speaks it? The debate turned on the status and operation of *vox*, the fundamental object of linguistic knowledge according to the models that had been transmitted to the Middle Ages from late antiquity. This inheritance, discussed in the previous chapter, was to be the site of a great deal of uncertainty and contestation, not least thanks to the fundamental inscrutability of the *auctoritates*. Already the earliest medieval readers of Priscian, Boethius, and Augustine struggled with their manifold obscurities, and it is these struggles that gave shape to the schools and doctrines that characterize medieval thought.[3]

Among those obscurities was the problem of what *vox* signifies: left ambiguous in the *auctoritates*, by the fourteenth century it had developed into a *magna altercatio*. The main authority in this matter was Aristotle's *De interpretatione*, read in Boethius's translation and according to his indications.[4] And Boethius seems to teach clearly that if a given *vox* is, in some sense, the name of a thing, it is so only through the mediation of the concept (*passio animae, intellectus*) that a person has of it: so that, in fact, the utterance signifies only the concept and not the thing at all. Indeed, he puts the matter in what are apparently the most unequivocal terms: "praeter intellectum namque vox penitus nihil designat" (other than a concept, an utterance signifies nothing at all).[5] Boethius's position was the dominant one among the schoolmen of the eleventh, twelfth, and thirteenth centuries.[6] Not everyone was convinced, however. Already in the twelfth century some authors suggested that words might refer directly to things, without conceptual mediation.[7] But this view comes into its own in the middle of the thirteenth century, with Roger Bacon. The Franciscan's objection is simple, and cogent. If, as Boethius also claims, the meaning of a word is given by the intention of its speaker, is it not the case that when you intend to name a thing, a thing is what will be named? And is it not also the case that when you utter a name you are usually intending to name the thing whose name it is? Therefore, concludes Bacon, there is no reason to maintain that words are the names of our concepts of things, for more often than not they are just the names of things directly. This new doctrine of "intentionalism," though Bacon claimed otherwise, represented a thoroughgoing rejection of the Boethian position.

Nonetheless, the prominence of the *magna altercatio* as to whether *vox* signifies a concept or a thing distracts attention, both for the partisans in the dispute and for their modern interpreters, from an even more fundamental question: that of whether it must necessarily signify at all. For any debate about what it signifies rests on a prior decision that it does in fact signify. And it by no means goes without saying that it does. As I have shown in the previous chapter, nonsignification is an essential possibility of *vox* as the late antique *auctoritates* define it. So much is even indexed in the very Boethian dictum, just cited, that underlay the whole *magna altercatio*: for while "praeter intellectum vox penitus nihil designat" (other than a concept, an utterance signifies nothing at all) indeed seems to mean that *vox* signifies a concept and only a concept, it can also be read as saying that—at a level beyond that of its signifying or not signifying any given concept—*vox* in any case signifies nothing at all. And it must be affirmed that such a construal would not be far-fetched but would much rather represent a straightforward way of interpreting Boethius's thinking of the ineradicable meaninglessness of the utterance.

In this chapter I turn to certain traces of what might be called a *parva altercatio* over the possibility of nonsignification that subsisted, more or less out of sight, underneath the *magna altercatio* over the signification of words. My main focus will be a commentary on *De interpretatione* composed by Walter Burley, at Oxford, in the first decade of the fourteenth century. The commentary is very much a school text, steeped in centuries of pedagogical tradition; still more, its author took an uncommon interest in the history of logic at Oxford in the centuries preceding him. What this means is that it is effectively illegible outside of that context, for at every moment Burley is either endorsing or taking issue with the teachings of the masters who have gone before him. The commentary might profitably be understood as a kind of collage of those earlier teachings, which is to say that its interest lies in what happens when Burley expropriates their elements and recombines them in a new form. Accordingly, in order to retrieve the specificity of Burley's thought it is necessary to reconstruct the twelfth- and thirteenth-century history of *vox non-significativa*, a history that has remained largely unwritten. First, I will show how *vox non-significativa* continues to function, as it had for Augustine and Boethius, as an excluded precondition in the constitution of the discipline of the new logic, laying out the problems as they were posed in Oxford logical works from the anonymous *Logica "Cum sit nostra"* to the *Introductiones in logicam* of William of Sherwood.[8] I then proceed to show, following the indications of the historian of linguistics Irène Rosier-Catach, how the logicians were forced, despite themselves, to reckon with *vox non-significativa*. What made them do so was the problem of what they called *suppositio materialis*, or autonymy: the use of a word to refer to itself, as in a proposition such as *human has two syllables*.

It becomes possible, in the light of the exclusion of *vox non-significativa* and its reappearance in connection with *suppositio materialis*, to read closely certain enigmatic passages of Burley's commentary. And the reason that, of all the works in the medieval logical tradition, I have picked out this commentary of Burley's for particular attention is that it takes up the question of nonsignification in a manner that is at once singularly faithful to that tradition and radically innovative. Burley was quite familiar with ways of overcoming the difficulty that nonsignification poses for the discipline of logic. In particular, he was a careful reader of the writings of Roger Bacon, whose solution to the problem of *vox non-significativa* in material supposition will thus be examined in detail. But he did not adopt Bacon's solution, or anyone else's. Instead, he did something altogether strange: he proceeded as though there was no problem to speak of. He transmitted all the incoherencies of the doctrine of vocal nonsignification inherited from late antiquity, despite their having been in some sense overcome by Bacon. By embracing these incoherencies and pushing them to an extreme, he transformed them into a new line of thought. The result is that, far from being forced to reckon against his will with the possibility that logic might have to deal, after all, with *voces non-significativae*, Burley indicates that such words belong in the most proper way possible to the science of propositions. He points finally toward the possibility, however unrealized, of a logic of nonsignification.

BU, BA, BUF

The most immediately noticeable innovation of the new logic of the Middle Ages with respect to the inherited curriculum is that its textbooks begin with a discussion that until then would have been properly postponed until the student had arrived at the third treatise of the *Organon*, *De interpretatione*. For, following what Jean Isaac has called a "nouveau plan," the authors of the *logica modernorum* considered it a necessary prolegomenon to the teaching of their science to discuss the question of the nature and status of *vox*.[9] This phenomenon can be seen clearly in William of Sherwood's *Introductiones in logicam*, an influential textbook from the mid-thirteenth century whose opening lines are typical of the genre. In order to undertake the study of the science of the truth and falsity of propositions, he affirms, it is necessary to know what propositions are made up of; and they seem to be made up of nouns and verbs.

> Prius autem agendum est de nomine quam de verbo, quia est principalior pars quam verbum. Ideo ab eo inchoandum est. Et quia omne nomen est vox et omnis vox est sonus, ideo a sono tamquam a primo inchoandum est. Est autem sonus proprium sesibile aurium. Et dividitur sic: Sonus alius vox, alius non vox. Sonus vox est vox, ut quod fit ab ore animalis. Sonus non vox,

ut strepitus pedum, fragor arborum et similia. Vox sic dividitur: Alia significativa, alia non significativa. Vox significativa est, quae aliquid significat; non significativa, quae nihil significat, ut: "buba blictrix."[10]

[The noun ought to be considered before the verb because it is a more important part than the verb, and so we must begin with it. And since every noun is an utterance and every utterance is a sound, we must begin with sound. Sound is the property to which the ears are sensitive; it is divided into vocal and nonvocal. Vocal sound is an utterance such as is made by an animal's mouth. Nonvocal sound is footsteps, the crashing of trees, and the like. Utterances are divided into significative and non-significative. A significative utterance is one that signifies something; a non-significative one signifies nothing; for example, "buba blictrix."]

The discussion establishes that the object of the science of logic is, at the most basic level, sound. But there are many varieties of sound, and logic does not concern itself with just any of them: only sounds that are made by the voice and that signify something can serve as the material of a proposition.

In the process of defining this proper object of their science, the logicians bring in examples of a kind of utterance from which it must be distinguished, which they call *vox non-significativa*, nonsignificative utterance. William, for his part, adduces "buba blictrix" in this connection, in which there survives, in garbled form, the ancient stock example *blityri*, accompanied here not by its sometime twin *skindapsos* but by a more characteristically medieval made-up word, *buba*.[11] The twelfth- and early thirteenth-century treatises in whose tradition William is working give variations on this theme: the *Ars emmerana* gives *blictrix* and *sindiarsis*; the *Ars burana* has *blictrix* alone. In the *Introductiones parisienses* the pertinent example is *buba*. The *Logica "Ut dicit"* gives *buba* and *plectrix*; the *Ars meliduna* mentions *biltrix* and *buba*; and various manuscripts of the *Logica "Cum sit nostra"* have *bon, bau,* and *beltrix*; *buba* and *bultrix*; *bon, bau,* and *bletrix*; *bou, bau,* and *beltrix*; and *bu, ba,* and *buf*.[12] There are a number of remarkable things about these words, which are by no means recondite, appearing as they do on the very first page of logical works written over the course of many centuries. They are lexically void, impervious to gloss, without definition. Never used but only mentioned—at least in theory—their existence seems to be that of an exemplar and nothing more. And they are invoked for a single purpose: that they might be cast out of the realm of logic altogether.

This exclusion is programmatic, as is made clear in the first lines of the *Logica "Cum sit nostra"*—a treatise of particular interest for my purposes, since Walter Burley will produce an adaptation of it:

> Cum sit nostra presens intentio ad artem dialeticam, primo oportet scire quid sit materia artis dialectice. Materia artis dialectice est vox significativa, quia de voce non significativa nullus intellectus ageneratur in animo alicuius.[13]

[Since our present concern is the discipline of logic, it is appropriate in the first place to know what is the material of the discipline of logic. The material of the discipline of logic is significative utterance, since no concept is produced in anyone's mind by nonsignificative utterance.]

The *materia* of the discipline of logic is *vox significativa*, and thus *buba* and *bufbaf* can have no place there. *Vox non-significativa* is what logic must by definition exclude, following the ancient protocol examined in the previous chapter, if it is to attain to the status of logic at all. For if it did not exclude them, it would amount instead to a kind of grammar.[14] And indeed the medieval examples on the order of *bu*, *ba*, and *buf* can only have been chosen in order to evoke the scene of grammatical instruction. Although their derivation seems never to have been investigated, they are evidently of a piece with the locution "to say neither *bu* nor *ba*"—meaning "to say nothing at all"—found in various forms across the languages of medieval Europe.[15] And for its part this locution has its origin in the grammatical practice of the syllabary, discussed in the previous chapter, in which students were made to copy out, pronounce, and even memorize meaningless sequences of syllables.[16] Such modes of treating *vox* without regard for whether or not it signifies are what logic must exclude if it is to be the science of the truth and falsity of *vox*, rather than the mere science of vocal form.

The crucial but ambiguous role of *vox non-significativa* in the articulation of the difference, for logic, between logic and grammar can be seen in a puzzling passage in the *Ars meliduna* where the word *biltrix* is subjected to grammatical manipulation:

> Amplius queritur utrum hec vox "biltrix" modo sit hec vox "biltricis." Quod necessario dicendum videtur. Nam hec vox "biltrix" instituetur cras ad significandum et tunc declinabitur: "biltrix, biltricis," nec alia vox erit "biltricis" quam "biltrix," sed eadem.[17]

> [Additionally, it is asked whether this utterance *biltrix* is the same as this utterance *biltricis* (i.e., whether the latter is just the former in the genitive case). Which it must be said to be. For this utterance *biltrix* will be imposed tomorrow to signify, and then it will be declined: *biltrix, biltricis*; and *biltricis* will not be a different utterance than *biltrix*, but the same one.]

The question of *biltrix* leads the logician to engage in a discussion that would seem to befit a grammarian instead: he sets up a paradigm for *biltrix*, listing and coordinating its declensions. The Melun master insists that such declension will happen "tomorrow," that is, only once the word has become meaningful, and thereby appears to observe the ban on working with *vox non-significativa*. And yet, needless to say, by writing "biltrix, biltricis" he does nothing else than demonstrate that it is already possible to produce such declension "today," while the word remains meaningless. The absurdity of his claiming to postpone the declension of *biltrix* until tomorrow while in fact carrying it out shows the importance, and no less the incoherence, of the role played by *vox non-significativa* in the marking out of logic as separate from grammar. For if logic can only secure the true object of its research by excluding *buba* and *bufbaf* from consideration, what this means is of course that this exclusion is constitutive. Logic requires *vox non-significativa* for its very being, and it requires that it remain outside of its domain, or at least intrude no further than these prefatory distinctions *de sono et voce*.

But the exclusion of *buba* and *bufbaf* from the field of logic could not be maintained. Despite all their indications to the contrary, the logicians found themselves forced to consider the question of *vox non-significativa*, which was to reappear at the very heart of their debates. It did so in connection with a phenomenon that the author of the *Fallacie parvipontane* endeavored to dismiss as a *transumptio grammaticorum*, a mere metaphor of the grammarians.[18] But the phenomenon proved more intractable than the Petit Pont master seems to have hoped. Indeed, it became a sticking point in the elaboration of supposition theory, the signature accomplishment of the logic of the medieval Latin West, its main contribution to the history of philosophy. The "mere metaphor of the grammarians" in question was something called *suppositio materialis*, or material supposition.

VOCUM CONGERIES

What is characteristic of the new, "terminist" logic of the Middle Ages is its formalization and elaboration of a distinction that was familiar to the logicians of earlier eras but had never before been formulated technically or treated at length. This is the distinction between *significatio* and *suppositio*. These two linguistic operations correspond more or less neatly to the *Sinn* and *Bedeutung*, or sense and reference, of Gottlob Frege.[19] It is one thing, the terminists teach, for a word to signify something: it signifies whatever it is "imposed on," that is, whatever it is assigned to as a name.[20] Thus the word *homo* signifies the mortal, rational animal. But when that word comes to be used in various propositions, even though its *significatio* does not change it nonetheless refers to (or "supposits for") a number of discrete things. So much can be seen in the following sentences, which are the classical examples. The word *homo* supposits here for three distinct things and in three distinct manners, while its signification is said to remain unaltered:

> *Homo currit.* [A man is running.]
> *Homo est species.* [Man is a species.]
> *Homo est nomen.* [*Man* is a noun.]

Setting aside for a moment the disagreements that these matters provoked among the schoolmen, the supposition of the subject terms in these three exemplary propositions can be identified provisionally as *personal*, *simple*, and *material*, respectively. In the first, the word *homo* stands for a particular individual; in the second, for a species or universal; in the third, for itself.

In short, whereas its *significatio* is what it means when it is considered in isolation, the *suppositio* of a term is the way that it stands for something in a particular proposition. As Peter of Spain writes,

> Differunt autem suppositio et significatio, quia significatio est per impositionem vocis ad rem significandam, suppositio vero est acceptio ipsius termini jam significantis rem pro aliquo.[21]
>
> [Supposition is distinct from signification, in that signification consists in the imposition of an utterance to signify a thing, whereas supposition consists in the reference of a term that already signifies a thing to something in particular.]

The theory of supposition tries to account for the fact that, while the signification of words seems to be relatively stable (words signify what they are imposed to signify), the same word will pick out different things in different contexts. Sometimes when you say "human" you mean humanity as such, other times a particular human, still other times the word itself—not to mention when you mean a picture of a human being or a fictional person in a literary work. The purpose of the theory is to classify these various instances and thereby control for the way that the truth of a proposition depends on the variable usage of words in contexts. The logicians' discussions of these matters were enormously influential outside of the field of logic narrowly conceived, and indeed outside of the university; they were crucial, notably, in determining the hermeneutic practices and assumptions of educated readers of literature in the later Middle Ages.[22]

Although supposition is distinct from signification, they are not entirely separable. It was regularly claimed that a word can signify without suppositing—for example if it is uttered by itself, outside of a proposition—but that it cannot supposit without first signifying. As this principle, common to all of the early treatises, is formulated in the *Cum sit nostra*, "terminus supponit quando ponitur in oratione; terminus significat sive ponitur in oratione sive extra oratione" (a term supposits when it is placed in a sentence; a term signifies whether it is placed in a sentence or [remains] outside).[23] Signification would be essentially prior to supposition, and supposition would be impossible without it: in order for an utterance to pick out a particular thing, it would first have to become a meaningful word. And yet there seems to be an exception to this rule: material supposition.[24] *Suppositio materialis* is what takes place in a sentence on the order of "man is a noun" or "man is a monosyllable," in which the proposition is true only insofar as the subject term *man* supposits for itself.[25] (Medieval Latin did not make use of quotation marks, by which a modern logician might indicate the mention as opposed to the use of a term, although the Old French article *ly* was sometimes imported into scholastic Latin in order to mark the occurrence of material supposition: for example, *ly homo est nomen*.) What the theory of material supposition tries to explain is what is sometimes called autonymy: the use of a term as the name of itself.[26] The strange thing about the autonymous use of a term is that in standing for itself the term appears to cease signifying. A term in material supposition does not supposit for what it signifies, inasmuch as the truth or falsity of the proposition *man is a monosyllable* has nothing to do with the nature of the rational mortal animal. Flying in the face of the principle that a word must first signify if it is going to supposit, the term in material supposition, in referring to itself, appears to break off its dependence on its signification and enter a realm in which it only supposits, and might as well be meaningless.

This nonsignificative quality of a word in material supposition was already identified in the middle of the twelfth century by the grammarian Peter Helias. As he explains, this variety of reference is known as *material* because what is picked out by its use is the material of the word itself. For, he says, the meaningful word can be distinguished from its material substrate. Considered in isolation, this substrate—possessed by every word—should be understood on the model of *blictrix*:

> Dicendum est quod vocabula quandoque se ipsa nominant, ut cum dicitur, "Homo est nomen." Hic enim non de homine loquimur sed potius de hoc nomine "homo." Et hoc appellabant antiqui "materiale impositum," quod quid sit ut intelligas, materiale impositum est vox representans seipsam, id est, posita ad loquendum de seipsa et dicitur materiale impositum quia nomen, si ita contingit, representat materiam suam, id est, vocem que quasi materia preiacet ut inde fiat nomen. Ex voce namque fit nomen per impositionem. Quod inde videri potest quia "blictrix" vox est tamen nondum nomen est, sed si alicui rei imponitur nomen erit.[27]

> [It should be said that words sometimes serve as the names of themselves, as when someone says "man is a name." For we do not say this about man but about this noun "man." And this the ancients (i.e., Priscian) called *imposed materially*, which you should understand as follows: material imposition consists in an utterance representing itself, that is, imposed to speak about itself. It is called *imposed materially* because the noun, taken in this instance, represents its own material, that is, the utterance which like a material precedes the noun, which is made out of it. For the noun is made out of the utterance by means of imposition. And this can be seen in the case of *blictrix*, which is an utterance although it is not yet a noun, but it will become a name if it is imposed on something.]

According to Peter, in the proposition *homo est nomen*, the word *homo* is used as though it did not yet have a signification. The use of a word in material supposition (called "imposition" here, reflecting the different context in which Peter is writing) picks out that aspect of a word that is no more than *blictrix*, that is, its *figura vocis* or sound-shape.

Homo, in this example, is a meaningful word being used in a way that brackets its significative function. But if the word *homo* in the proposition *homo est nomen* has been reduced to what it has in common with *blictrix*, the question arises as to why *blictrix* itself could not take its place in this proposition. The proposition *blictrix est nomen* would be false, since *blictrix* is just a sound-shape, not a noun; but to produce a true proposition it would only be necessary to introduce a negation: *blictrix non est nomen*—or indeed to make the very declaration that *blictrix est vox non-significativa*. If logic has no difficulty with a proposition containing a *vox significativa* in material supposition, it thus ceases to be at all clear on what grounds it would refuse to consider one in which a *vox non-significativa* functions in precisely the same manner. In their elaboration of the doctrine of material supposition, in short, thirteenth-century logicians found themselves unable to avoid the very words whose exclusion constituted the foundation of their discipline. Once supposition had been distinguished from signification, it became possible to conceive of the former in the absence of the latter: of propositions made up of nonsense words. Either the discipline of logic *can* admit *voces non-significativae*, and logic—its foundational gesture rendered inoperative—threatens to become indistinguishable from grammar, or meaningless utterances in material supposition will have to be shown to be meaningful after all. The logicians realized that they had no choice but to address the point directly.

The task of making a case for the meaningfulness of the utterance in *suppositio materialis* fell to Roger Bacon. In his late work, Bacon, who early in his career had written an important logical textbook that remained faithful to terminism, abandoned the terminist position and elaborated his own account of signification.[28] His new account represented a revision of Oxford logic on two notable fronts: he denied that any *vox* could fail to signify; and he denied that there was any difference between signification and supposition. And crucial in the elaboration of his theory was its treatment of material supposition. The Franciscan was a careful reader of a work otherwise little known in the Middle Ages, Augustine's *De dialectica*—where, as we have seen in the previous chapter, both of these matters are treated; he was also thoroughly familiar with the more widely known *De doctrina christiana*.[29] In the *Compendium studii theologiae*, composed at Oxford in 1292, Bacon follows the saint's lead: rather than treating meaningful utterances as a species of noise, he identifies them as a species of sign.[30] *Vox*, for him, is a sign in the same sense that damp earth is a sign of the falling of rain, or lactating breasts of motherhood: it points to something besides itself.[31] Before it is imposed to signify, in other words, *vox* already signifies by its very nature: and according to Bacon, what it signifies first of all is that the person who pronounces it has in his mind a certain model of the sound that is spoken.³² The example that Bacon uses to demonstrate this point is carefully chosen: *buba*. What he is arguing is that even a so-called *vox non-significativa* necessarily signifies, if only the presence of its own sound-shape in the mind of its speaker. The consequence of his new account of utterance as a natural sign is thus that, strictly speaking, there can be no such thing as *vox non-significativa*. Accordingly, the opening gesture of the terminist treatises—to bar meaningless utterance from consideration—becomes strictly unnecessary, for no such utterances exist in any case.³³

But Bacon is not of course interested solely in the natural signification of words. *Vox*, he says, can also signify conventionally. Here too his account departs from the terminist one. The centerpiece of Bacon's semiotics is his "intentionalism," the doctrine that a word means whatever its speaker intends it to mean. In Bacon's telling, this is true not only of a word's first being assigned a meaning, the moment of its original imposition, but of its every use thereafter. For Bacon, it is not that a word has a given meaning, and then comes to stand for various things depending on its usage; rather, with each new use of a word, its speaker newly intends to name a thing, or in other words reimposes the word he is using. If *homo* refers to something different in *homo currit* and *homo est species*, this is because in each case it is imposed anew: it is not that its signification remains the same while it is applied to a different sort of thing, but that its signification itself changes with each imposition.³⁴ In other words, there is no difference between signification and supposition. Accordingly, by the end of his career Bacon has stopped using the word *suppositio* altogether, speaking only of *significatio*.

All of this emerges in a discussion of what other thinkers called material supposition but which Bacon, having abandoned the concept of supposition altogether, no longer does. Here is what he says about the proposition *buba est vox*—exactly the sort of sentence that would seem to furnish proof that a *vox non-significativa* can, after all, appear in a proposition: "Quod enim possint tales orationes esse verae et significativae, non potest fieri, nisi post impositionem huius vocis 'buba' sibi ipsi" (such propositions could not become true and significative except after the utterance *buba* had already been imposed on itself).³⁵ Recurring as is his custom to the will of the speaker, Bacon argues that in *buba est vox* the speaker intends *buba* to name its own utterance. When we use *buba* in such a proposition, what we are doing is imposing the utterance on a thing: namely, the very vocal material out of which it is formed. In short, as soon as an unimposed word appears in a proposition, it becomes imposed: so that in *buba est vox*, the word *buba* has ceased to be an example of what it is meant to exemplify. According to Bacon's theory, speakers are continually imposing and reimposing words whenever they use them, and so what occurs in *buba est vox* is not the supposition of a meaningless word but the use of a word to signify itself. The phenomenon that terminists call material supposition would thus not be distinct in any nontrivial way from any other use of a word, since it involves just like every other act of speaking the use of an utterance to name a thing: in this case, itself.

Nonetheless, Bacon also imagines a case in which *buba* appears in a proposition without its having been imposed to signify itself. But even then, he claims, nothing would be demonstrated, for insofar as it contains unimposed utterances a series of words cannot in fact attain to the status of a meaningful proposition. Of the proposition *buba est vox* he maintains that:

> Dicendum quod haec vocum congeries non facit orationem significativam et nihil significat, quia prima pars huius sermonis, scilicet, "buba," est vox non significativa ante impositionem; ergo tota oratio est non significativa ab una parte non significativa. Sicut si scribantur hae duae dictiones "est" et "vox," et praeponatur eis lapis vel lignum vel pomum in eodem pergameno in quo illa duo vocabula sequuntur, tota congeries posita in pergameno nihil significaret.[36]

> [It must be said that this conglomeration of utterances (*vocum congeries*) does not make up a significative proposition and signifies nothing, because the first part of this expression, namely, *buba*, is a nonsignificative utterance before its imposition; therefore the entire expression is nonsignificative because one of its parts is nonsignificative. It is as if these two words *is* and *utterance* were written down, and a rock or a chunk of wood or a piece of fruit were placed in front of them on the same parchment where those words would follow it: in that case, the whole conglomeration placed on the parchment would signify nothing.]

Insofar as *buba* remains a *vox non-significativa*, it is no more than a *vocum congeries*, an amassment of vocal sounds, a mere thing, and is thus of a different order of reality than are the terms of a proposition. Unless *buba* has been imposed on itself, *buba est vox* does not constitute a proposition but subsists rather as an amalgam of physical objects. The physical object *buba* fails to attain to the status of a subject in relation with a predicate, and neither can the words *est vox* serve as a predicate in the absence of a subject, so that there remains no proposition to speak of.

In short, Bacon maintains that every *vox* signifies by its very nature, and that when it enters a proposition it takes on a conventional signification as well.[37] The whole terminist doctrine of *vox non-significativa* is rendered obsolete, as is the account of material supposition for which it poses such difficulties. In discarding the distinction between signification and supposition and denying that any word can be used in a sentence without imposition, Bacon thus provides what Rosier-Catach has called an "elegant solution" to the problem of material supposition. And yet this problem would continue to dog fourteenth-century thinkers, for they did not follow the Franciscan's lead.[38] Indeed, some fifteen years after the composition of the *Compendium*, one of Roger Bacon's closest readers remained unconvinced.

BUBA EST DISYLLABUM

The logical writings of Walter Burley represent the first major contribution to terminism since Bacon's own early, abandoned efforts in the field.[39] At the beginning of the fourteenth century, Burley—who was deeply familiar with the early Oxford logical textbooks, and made use of them in his teaching—began to compose new works in the style that Bacon had rejected.[40] Remembered mostly by specialists today, Burley was a major thinker of the fourteenth century, especially in the field of logic. His works were important for subsequent generations of scholars at Oxford's Merton College, where he wrote the commentary in question—the same Mertonians whose influence on Chaucer and on the author of the *Cloud of Unknowing* has been established.[41] He is chiefly remembered today for having engaged in a long-standing debate with William Ockham, a debate that shaped the latter's ideas to a great extent and in which Burley defended a position that has sometimes been called, more or less derisively, an "extreme realism."[42] Burley's logical writings reward attention in their own right, however, not least in connection with the question of the status of *vox non-significativa* and the nature of *suppositio materialis*. Late in his career, in the important longer version of *De puritate artis logicae* written in about 1326, Burley would develop an unusually complex taxonomy of material supposition, and indeed he paid close attention to the phenomenon in many of his works, discussing it already at notable length in the early *De suppositionibus* from 1302.[43] His most interesting thinking on the matter, however, can be found not in these more considered treatments of the varieties of supposition but in a series of remarks he makes at the beginning of a commentary on *De interpretatione*.

The *Commentarius in librum aristotelis Perihermeneias* or *Middle Commentary*—written in the first decade of the fourteenth century, while Burley was at Merton College or shortly thereafter—is the third of four commentaries he devoted to Aristotle's treatise.[44] The work is a close and thorough explication; the commentator proceeds line by line and devotes considerable attention to various points of difficulty. The very first such point arises almost immediately, in connection with the famous first sentence of the treatise. The difficulty concerns the nature of the logical term. A term, Burley writes, is a *vox*, as the tradition had always maintained. But this hardly seems possible:

> Sed tunc est dubium: Cum eadem vox non possit bis proferri, si vox prolata esset pars nominis, videtur quod idem nomen non possit bis proferri, et sic nulla propositio prolata posset converti, et sic in syllogismo secundum eius esse in prolatione essent sex termini.[45]
>
> [But a doubt arises: since the same utterance cannot be pronounced twice, if the pronounced utterance is part of the noun, it would seem that the same noun cannot be pronounced twice, and thus that no pronounced proposition

can be converted, and thus that insofar as the syllogism exists in pronunciation it would contain six terms.]

Burley's reasoning runs as follows: a *vox* is a unique occurrence, a particular sound that comes out of someone's mouth at a particular time and place, never again to be encountered. If a logical term is a *vox*, then it, too, would seem to be unrepeatable. But this would present a grave problem for syllogistic reasoning, which rests on the repetition of the same term now as a subject, now as a predicate ("conversion"). Without this iterability, nothing at all would be demonstrated by a syllogism such as

> Man is an animal;
> But this is a man;
> Therefore, this is an animal.

That is, since this utterance "man" is not this other utterance "man," nor this "animal" that "animal," nor this "this" that "this," the apparatus of the syllogism cannot get any hold on them. Burley's point is that logic depends for its operation on the capacity of a term to appear multiple times without ceasing to be itself. Since he has already identified the term as a *vox*, what he must establish is that *vox* can be repeated and remain identical to itself. And this is what he goes on to do.

His reply to the point of doubt is that the *vox* of which a term is composed is not simply *vox*. The gesture does not at first appear unusual, as it seems to resume the millennial restriction of the *materia* of logic to certain kinds of *vox*. And indeed, it is in exactly this connection that the terminist logicians introduced *buba* and *blictrix*: in order to specify that logic deals not with *vox* as such but only with *vox* possessed of the differentia *significativa*. But this appearance is misleading. In point of fact, Burley is making a point of an entirely different kind. His claim is that what makes up a term is not *vox* itself but a resemblance obtaining among various *voces*:

> Ad istud potest dici, salvando trinitatem terminorum in syllogismo, quod ista vox prolata quae est pars nominis non est aliqua vox una numero sed est unum commune ad istam vocem prolatam et ad quamlibet vocem consimilem. Circa quod est intelligendum quod ista vox "homo" prolata a te et illa vox "homo" prolata a me magis conveniunt quam ista vox "homo" et ista vox "animal."[46]

> [To this objection it can be replied, preserving the trinity of terms in the syllogism, that this pronounced utterance which is part of the noun is not some singular utterance, but is rather a single thing common to that pronounced utterance and to any other utterance similar to it. On account of which it should be understood that this utterance *homo* pronounced by you and that utterance *homo* pronounced by me accord with one another more than do this utterance *homo* and this utterance *animal*.]

Vox as such, as "itself," has no part in the term. The term is formed out of a *communitas* or *conveniencia* or *consimilitudo* among multiple utterances. This *communitas* alone, and not the *voces* among which it obtains, is the *materia* of the term. Nothing except what is fully iterable in the utterance will matter in the constitution of the elements of a proposition. Everything else about it, all the unrepeatable characteristics of a particular vocal sound, Burley separates out from the *vox communis* that is the *materia nominis et verbis*. But it should be said that even as he excludes the *vox singularis* from consideration, he draws attention to the variability of utterances produced by different speakers at different times and in different places. That is, insofar as it would have been entirely possible to avoid making this distinction, in making it Burley draws attention to the sound of the voice. What does not participate in the constitution of the term, in being separated out, also becomes thinkable in itself. So much would scarcely be worth observing, however, were it not the case that Burley will return to this excluded *vox singularis* within a few lines.

The drawing of a distinction between *vox singularis* and *vox communis* is the inaugural gesture of Burley's whole theory of terms. Burley stands apart from the earlier terminists insofar as he defines the *vox* that is pertinent to logic—that is, the kind of *vox* that can be used as a term—not as utterance that is joined with signification but as a *consimilitudo* among multiple utterances. He is entirely aware of the distance he is taking from the earlier mode of proceeding. In fact, he specifically distinguishes his isolation of the *commune ens* in the utterance from any question of meaningfulness, maintaining that significative and nonsignificative utterances alike are able to accord with one another in this resemblance. Immediately after declaring, in the passage just cited, that the utterance *homo* "goes together" with another utterance *homo* more than it does with the utterance *animal*, Burley extends the scope of his observation in order to include meaningless utterances in it:

> Similiter, haec vox "bu" prolata a me et haec vox "bu" prolata ab alio magis convenient quam haec vox "bu" et haec vox "ba." Habent igitur aliquod commune ens quod non est commune istis, scilicet "bu" et "ba."[47]

> [Likewise, this utterance *bu* spoken by me and this utterance *bu* spoken by someone else accord with one another more than do this utterance *bu* and this utterance *ba*. Therefore they have a certain common being which is not common to those others, namely, *bu* and *ba*.]

In citing *bu* and *ba*, familiar terminist examples of *vox non-significativa*, Burley signals unmistakably that he is interested in the utterance not insofar as it is meaningful but insofar as it conforms to other utterances. The *commune ens* is indifferent to sense or nonsense, even as it isolates something in *vox* that is distinguishable from the mere separated noise of different vocalizations issuing at different times and in different ways.

In short, although in citing *bu* and *ba* in the first pages of his commentary Burley appears to be following the conventions of the Oxford terminist tradition in which he is steeped, in fact he uses these examples not to distinguish *vox significativa* from *vox non-significativa* but in order to reveal the dimension in which they cannot be told apart. The gesture is perverse: in defining the term Burley uses as his example nothing else than the classical examples of what is not and cannot be a term. For *bu* and *ba* not only provide him with instances of the material out of which a term might be made, they themselves also already attain for him to the status of full-fledged terms. Without acknowledging that they exist for no other reason than to exemplify what cannot be used in a proposition, Burley begins using *bu* and *ba* in the commentary in just that way.

This fact, easily overlooked, is in fact decisive: the first four examples of propositions adduced here all contain either *bu* or *buba*. Having identified the material of the term as the *commune ens* obtaining among various *voces*, Burley specifies that this *commune ens* can already take part in a proposition even before it has been assigned as the name of something. A *vox non-significativa* no less than a *vox significativa* can supposit:

> Nec est solum reperire unum tale commune in vocibus significativis sed etiam in vocibus non-significativis. Unde aliquid est commune huic voci "bu" quae profertur a me et huic voci "bu" quae profertur a te, et pro tali communi verificatur ista "Bu est bu."[48]
>
> [Nor is such a common being only to be found in significative utterances, but also in nonsignificative utterances. Thus there is something common to this utterance *bu* which is pronounced by me and this utterance *bu* which is pronounced by you, and on account of this common thing the truth of the proposition *bu is bu* can be demonstrated.]

The proposition *bu est bu* is admissible and moreover true, on Burley's account, because both the first *bu* and the second *bu* naturally supposit for what is common to both of them. This resemblance is not, as he tells it, a form of signification. While Burley seems to subscribe to Bacon's intentionalist account of imposition, he maintains here that supposition occurs apart from the will of any speaker: there is already supposition before anyone utters a proposition, insofar as singular utterances in the world resemble one another and thus can stand for what is common to all of them. As he goes on to say, *voces singulares universaliter supponunt pro communibus*: singular utterances stand for what is common to them and their likes, whenever they are pronounced. The stronger resemblance between this *bu* and that *bu* than between this *bu* and that *ba* is not a matter of meaning or reference but of *conveniens*, a pattern to which disparate utterances are reducible. In the proposition *bu est bu* it is not, Burley thinks, that a speaker intends both *bu* and *bu* to name something like the form of the utterance *bu* itself, so that at stake in it would be the imposition of the word, as Bacon would have argued. Rather, such a proposition merely draws out the self-identity of the term insofar as it is a term, that is, something made out of what is common to both utterances. Thus, in *bu est bu* each singular utterance supposits for a *vox communis* that is itself singular in number, without the intervention of any will to signify; and the proposition is true, notwithstanding the presence of nonsense words in it. Though he makes the point without fanfare, it is a radical one. For Burley proceeds as though no difficulty whatsoever is presented by *vox non-significativa*.

The commentator brings his remarks on the *commune ens* and on the possibility of supposition without signification to a conclusion by drawing attention to a distinction that he thinks might otherwise escape notice. He declares that in the proposition *buba est buba* the subject term *buba* has personal supposition. In other words, even though *buba* is standing here for its own material as a term—what is common to this *buba* and that *buba*—it does not have material supposition. The point is necessary to make, insofar as material supposition would seem to be exactly, and definitionally, the phenomenon of a term's standing for its own materiality. But given Burley's definition of the term, that would be a misunderstanding. He proceeds to make this point explicit:

> Unde dico quod aliam suppositionem habet subiectum in ista "Buba est dissylabum" et aliam in ista "Buba est buba," quia in prima habet suppositionem materialem secundum quod est vera et in secunda suppositionem personalem.[49]

> [I maintain that the subject term has a different supposition in the proposition *buba is disyllabic* than it does in the proposition *buba is buba*, because in the first it has material supposition insofar as it is true and in the second it has personal supposition insofar as it is true.]

Although in both cases it appears to be the term *buba* itself that is referred to, the subject terms in *buba est buba* and in *buba est disyllabum* do not have the same supposition. It is here that Burley's unusual definition of the vocal materiality of the term becomes consequential for his theory of supposition. For it turns out that there are two ways in which a term can refer to the *vox* out of which it is made, because that *vox* itself has two aspects: *vox communis* and *vox singularis*. That is, to predicate something of *buba* can be either to predicate it of the sound-shape that remains identifiable across various pronunciations at different times and places—the material of the term, properly speaking—or, by contrast, to predicate it of the unrepeatable, unrepresentable, idiosyncratic noises that make up a singular utterance, which do not form any part whatsoever of the term. Material supposition can only be said to occur, Burley insists, when a term in a proposition stands for itself as *vox singularis*.

Burley uses the proposition *buba est dissylabum* as his example of material supposition, no doubt because it is the conventional one. But because the distinction he is making is not itself a conventional one, the example has to be examined carefully. For the *commune ens* that obtains among this *buba* and that *buba*, and that allows each to attain to the status of a term, itself also seems to have two syllables, but what Burley is saying is that if the proposition *buba est disyllabum* were a predication of disyllabism to that *comune ens*, the subject term would be in personal, not material, supposition. And his point is exactly the contrary: that it has material, not personal, supposition. His claim is thus that, in this instance, if it is true to say that buba has two syllables, it is not because *buba*, *buba*, and *buba* can all be seen to have two syllables, but just because this one *buba* does. Had he wished, he might have said that material supposition is what takes place in *buba is said loudly, buba is said with a regional accent, buba is stuttered*, or the like.[50] Insofar as *buba est disyllabum* is true when *buba* supposits materially, the subject term refers only to this one unrepeatable utterance *buba*, which is not an instance of the term but a mere *vox singularis*. What this means is surprising but follows necessarily from Burley's distinctions: the term *buba* in the proposition *buba est disyllabum* does not, after all, stand for itself. For it supposits for nothing else than what distinguishes this *buba* from that *buba*, for *buba* to the extent (and only to the extent) that it is not *buba*. Material supposition emerges here in an unfamiliar guise: it is not the autonomous use of a term after all, for it is not the use of a term as the name of itself. It is rather the use of a term to stand for its difference from itself. It is what takes place when a term stands for itself insofar as it is not a term and can never be a term.

In a proposition that is true when its subject term is taken in material supposition, in other words, something is said about the unrepeatable noise produced by a singular human voice. Although this noise is excluded from the term, it is not excluded from the proposition. Nor, by extension, is it excluded from the science of propositions. Logic, it seems, can accommodate not only empty terms but the very noises that attend their individual pronunciations. Not only can the mere *figura vocis* or *commune ens* appear in a proposition, but so can the irreproducible variability that desists from figuration. Burley points toward the possibility of a propositional knowledge of the variabilities of pitch, volume, timbre, tempo, and so forth that do not go into the term itself. This affirmation runs directly counter to Bacon's remarks on the possibility of *buba*'s appearing in a proposition. For the Franciscan, as we have seen, such a proposition would be on the order of a rock or piece of fruit sitting on a paper next to the words *est disyllabum*. Burley seems to think that Bacon is correct on this count, but that he has not gone far enough. In the proposition *buba est buba*, as Burley conceives of it, it is as though two unfamiliar but similarly shaped objects (two instances of a kind of fruit never before encountered, for instance) were set down on either side of the word *est*, and the resemblance among their shapes could be apprehended. But in the case of *buba est disyllabum*, he maintains, the subject term is like whatever there might be about a piece of fruit that would make it incomparably different from any other piece of fruit, and even from the piece that it itself is. In material supposition, the term is encountered not as an instance of an iterable but empty configuration, but as *vocum congeries* itself. But Burley does not see this as a problem. The truth of such a proposition, he insists, can be known.

IGNOTUM INTELLECTUI

Thus far I have emphasized three implications of Burley's unusual account of *vox* and *terminus*. In the first place, he maintains that there can be supposition without signification—indeed, whole propositions whose subject and predicate terms both mean nothing at all, such as *buba est buba*. Neither are such propositions to be thought of as exceptional cases. To the contrary, they are exemplary: for Burley, it is *homo est homo* that is to be understood on the model of *buba est buba*, rather than the inverse. *Vox non-significativa* is an essential element of Burleyan logic, which will thus be a kind of algebra, or gibberish—or grammar. In the second place, the terms of this logic will be made out of a *commune ens* or vocal iterability, in order that its syllogistic operation not fall apart under the pressure of the unrepeatable accidents of pronunciation or inscription that make up the *vox singularis*. And yet, in the third place, there is a variety of proposition in which even the unrepeatable can appear: material supposition, where the term stands for itself insofar as it is not a term—that is, insofar as it is not itself. The theory of *suppositio materialis* that would follow from this description would amount to a study of noise. Taken together, these three implications mark Burley's commentary as a radical return to the question of nonsignification—one that resuscitates the problems of the earlier, moribund theory of terms and repurposes them as its very foundations.

Let it not be imagined that the implications of this gesture were lost on him. As the commentary proceeds, Burley remains true to the vision of a logic of nonsense that animates its opening sections. This fidelity is especially marked in his explication of the famous Aristotelian passage about things, concepts, utterances, and inscriptions, which Boethius had elaborated into an account of *orandi ordo*. Although he does not draw attention to what he is doing, Burley points in the course of his remarks on this passage toward an account of cognition—and its failures—that merits close attention. For when logic dispenses, as it does in Burley's hands, with the ancient rite that marks out its difference from grammar, it is not possible to know in advance what will occur.

In these opening sections of the commentary, Burley aligns himself with Bacon in the *magna altercatio* as to whether words signify concepts or things. That is, he rejects the traditional account according to which words refer to concepts rather than things. He does so quite pointedly, arriving at the Franciscan's conclusion and following his argumentation to get there.[51] A word signifies a thing in the world rather than a concept in the mind, he writes; and it does so because the impositor wishes to name a thing, not a concept, and the will of the impositor is what determines the signification of a word. Nevertheless, to hear a word spoken is to be able to gather certain things in addition to what it has been imposed to signify:

> Potest enim vox esse nota alicuius cui vox non imponitur ad significandum. Nomen enim vel verbum prolatum est nota vel signum per quod proferens habet similitudinem in suo intellectu istius rei quae significatur per nomen vel per verbum vel quod ipse aliqua passione afficitur erga eum ad quem loquitur, videlicet amore vel odio. Unde vox est signum passionis animae non quia imponitur ad significandum passionem animae sed sic est signum passionis animae sicut est signum quod iste qui loquitur est homo.[52]
>
> [For an utterance can be a sign of something on which it is not imposed to signify. For a noun or a verb, when it is pronounced, is a sign by which it is made known that the utterer has a similitude in his understanding of that thing which is signified by the noun or verb, or that he is affected by some feeling toward the person to whom he is speaking, for instance love or hatred. Thus utterance is a sign of a concept in the mind (i.e., as Aristole says in the root text) not because it is imposed to signify a concept in the mind, but because it is a sign of a concept in the mind, in the same way that it is a sign that the one who is speaking is a human.]

Burley's point is that, in Peircean terms, a noun or a verb is not only a symbol but also an index. Even if someone uses a word whose meaning you do not know, you can be certain that she means something by it, that she harbors feelings of one sort or another toward you, and moreover that she is a human being. The use of a word to name something is an index of the rationality, and thus humanity, of the speaker; it is also an index of the presence of the particular concept of the named thing in the speaker's mind. If you happen to know the meaning of a word, you will know what concept its speaker has in mind; but whether you do or do not, the word in any case indicates the mere presence of the concept without disclosing which concept it might be. All of this seems to follow strictly the Augustinian-Baconian line of argument—that is, to reject the Boethian doctrine that the capacity to signify nothing is a constitutive and characteristic aspect of *vox*.

And yet this appearance is misleading. As Burley well knew, the Baconian argument that he is rehearsing is that every *vox*, without exception, is a sign. But in the passage just cited, Burley makes a slight but decisive alteration to that argument. He begins by discussing *vox* as such, but immediately proceeds to restrict his remarks to certain types of *vox*: "an *utterance* can be a sign of something on which it is not imposed to signify. For *a noun or a verb* . . ." He takes pains, in other words, to specify that his remarks about natural or indexical signification pertain not to *vox* itself but to the *nomen* and *verbum* alone. So that, whereas Bacon's argument is that words to which no meaning has been assigned already signify, in Burley's retelling the argument is rather that words that have already been assigned a meaning also signify naturally. And what must be emphasized is that, because of this revision, nothing at all is said here about words to which no meaning has been assigned. Given his marked concern with *vox non-significativa*, both in the passages just examined and further on in the commentary, there can be no doubt that when Burley restricts the Baconian analysis to nouns and verbs, as Bacon does not do, he is specifically signaling that the analysis does not apply to *vox non-significativa*. By confining the scope of this characterization to *voces significativae* alone, Burley effectively declares, by conspicuous omission, that nonsense words do not, for their part, allow their hearer to gather anything about the mind of their speaker.

Although Burley does not spell it out, what this means can be inferred. Because *buba* has not been imposed as the name of anything, its being spoken is not the effect of a knowledge of something named; and therefore it does not entail, and thus signal as effect to cause, the presence of such knowledge. It does not allow you to gather whether its speaker feels a particular way toward you. Hearing *buba* spoken does not even allow you to ascertain whether it has emerged from the mouth of a human being. In his exclusion of *vox non-significativa* from the discussion of what is signaled by *vox* apart from its imposition, Burley thus remains faithful, despite appearances, to the Boethian position that there exist utterances from which nothing at all can be gathered, not even that their speaker is present, speaking, human, cognizant, and so forth.

What is more, for Burley—as for Aristotle and Boethius—the implications of the existence of, and still more of the encounter with, linguistic nonsignification are not merely logical but psychical. His revision of Baconian semiotics opens onto the question of what happens in the mind of a person who hears a meaningless word: if the psychical event that takes place in the wake of the encounter with *vox significativa* does not take place in the case of *vox non-significativa*, what in fact does? A glimpse of an answer to this question can be found, in negative form, in the manner in which Burley sets up his argument in favor of Baconian intentionalism. Since the meaning of a word is freely assigned by a person's will, Burley declares, there is no reason why it should not signify a thing directly if that is the will of the impositor. He proves this point by means of the following reasoning:

> Intellectus prius intelligit rem extra quam intelligit aliquid exsistens in eo, quia intellectus non intelligit aliquid exsistens in eo nisi per reflexionem; nunc intellectio directa praecedit intellectionem reflexivam; igitur in illo priori in quo intellectus intelligit rem extra potest imponere nomen ad significandum rem extra. Et illud nomen sic impositum non significabit aliquid exsistens in anima, quia quodlibet exsistens in anima est adhuc ignotum intellectui et

nomen non imponitur nisi noto; igitur vox potest significare immediate rem extra et non oportet quod primo significet passionem animae.[53]

[The understanding understands an exterior thing before it understands anything that exists within itself, because the understanding does not understand anything existing within itself except by reflection; but direct understanding precedes reflexive understanding; and therefore, in order to signify the exterior thing, it can impose a name on that prior thing in which the understanding understands the exterior thing. And this name, imposed in this way, will not signify anything existing in the mind, because anything existing in the mind is still unknown to the understanding and a name is imposed only on what is known; therefore, the utterance can signify an exterior thing immediately, and it does not have to first signify an impression in the mind.]

A number of things are happening in this condensed passage. Whereas Burley has just demonstrated, on strictly Baconian lines, the possibility that an utterance signifies a thing directly by invoking the freedom of the will of the impositor, he now does exactly the contrary: placing a constriction on that will, he demonstrates the necessity that an utterance signifies a thing rather than a concept. This is to turn the Baconian argument on its head, as quickly becomes apparent: for it emerges that it is not even possible for a name to be assigned directly to a concept. Burley's argument rests on a dictum that he ascribes to Boethius, although the latter had never said anything of the sort: "vox non imponitur nisi noto" (a name is not given to something unless that something is already known).[54] The argument runs as follows. A concept (*passio animae*) is not that which is itself known but that by which something else is known.[55] Since the mind (*intellectus*) can only know its own operations in a secondary, reflexive moment, the thing known in the moment of imposition has to be something outside of itself (*res extra*). For the mind is necessarily unaware of its cognitions while they are occurring. While it is certainly possible for the mind to think and even to name one of its own cognitions, it can only do so by the mediation of another cognition which will remain for its part unthought for as long as it is in operation. The only way for *intellectus* to know itself is through an infinite speculative regression of thinking but unthought cognitions. If the impositor wishes to name a concept in his own mind, he can do so only by forming another concept of it by which to know it, which is to say by treating it as a thing. In short, although the impositor appears to be free to name anything, which is to say either concepts or things, he must know something in order to name it; and because he cannot in the first instance know a concept, in fact if he names anything it will be a thing. In short: the prior knowledge of the named thing on which every imposition depends is immediately the failure of that knowledge itself to be known.

This failure is itself communicated to others, in a certain sense, in speech.

For it so happens that in Burley's account of what occurs when you hear a noun or a verb, examined above, the knowledge of the presence of an *intellectus* that is at once an ignorance of its identity resumes a peculiarity of the circumstances of the original imposition of the word. For what else is it than this perpetual postponement of knowledge on the part of the speaker of a meaningful word that is signaled to its hearer when the utterance of that word entails the presence of a concept without disclosing the concept itself? In other words, not only the concept but the ignorance that it depends on is transmitted in the utterance of meaningful words. But the crucial point is that, if this is the case with a meaningful utterance, it is not the case with a meaningless one. The utterance that means nothing at all—that does not even allow you to conclude that its speaker is a human—operates exactly inversely to the model just described. Rather than being the effect of a prior knowledge, the pronunciation of a *vox non-significativa* will be the cause of a subsequent failure of knowledge. Such an utterance is the production of an inability on the part of the mind to cognize any object. This is of course exactly what Boethius had long before maintained:

> Si quis vero huiusmodi vocem ceperit, quae nihil omnino designet, animus eius nulla significatione neque intellegentia roboratus errat ac vertitur nec ullis designationis finibus conquiescit.[56]
>
> [If someone hears an utterance of this sort, which signifies absolutely nothing, his mind—bolstered neither by signification nor understanding—wanders around, turning upon itself, and does not come to rest at any such limit as would be provided by a signification.]

But Burley does not think that this effect is a reason to exclude *vox quae nihil omnino designat* from the field of logic.[57] To the contrary: his conspicuous inclusion of propositions containing *voces non-significativae* emerges instead as an insistence that this predicament of mental breakdown can itself be known. In *buba est disyllabum*, the unimposed word standing for itself (as other than itself) in its unimposability produces a failure of knowledge. The propositional knowledge of *vox singularis* in material supposition is thus not, after all, just an apprehension of the physical characteristics of a vocal entity; it cannot at all be said to consist either in quantitative or in qualitative study of accent, tone, and the like. It is, instead, the experience of the failure of knowledge that occurs when the mind is deprived of any object. As sheer differentiation, the *vox singularis* cannot be known. But the truth of the proposition in which it appears is a demonstrable and knowable truth.

In other words, the occurrence of *vox non-significativa* in material supposition should be understood, on Burley's model, as the inverse of the original event of imposition. If to assign an utterance as the name of something is to presuppose (and thus signal) a knowledge that is itself unknown, to use an utterance non-onomastically to stand for its singularity is to produce an absence of knowledge that is itself known. Rather than the unknowability of the mind to itself, what is produced in material supposition is a knowledge of the unknowable voice object. While the mind cannot ever hope to know its own operations without mediation, Burley implies that it is possible for it to know its failure to cognize the utterance as such. It does so in the minimal delay that interposes itself between *intellectus* as cognizing and *intellectus* as cognized. The irreducible lag that prevents the mind from ever being entirely present to itself, forcing it to know itself only across a duration, be it ever so slight, is the time of an unknowing at the basis of every operation of naming. In the de-naming or unimposition that occurs in material supposition, the mind is forced to while away in this duration, in the temporal noncoincidence that is a failure of self-understanding. The failure of knowledge amounts to a knowledge of that failure, and both the knowledge and the failure are produced in the reduction of a word to its status as a bare utterance. This reduction is the highest calling, and founding movement, of the discipline of logic as it constitutes itself in Burley's commentary.

Burley does not himself draw out these implications, let alone defend them. They emerge as if by the way in the course of his explications of Aristotle rather than as part of a systematic treatment of supposition. In later works, Burley would go on to produce such a treatment. The taxonomy he constructs in the *De puritate artis logicae*, for instance, distinguishes among five varieties of *suppositio materialis*: in all of them the utterance stands for "itself" (*pro se*), but without reference to any distinction between *vox singularis* and *vox communis*.[58] But if his position in the *Middle Commentary* is not reflected explicitly in this later taxonomy, it is not incompatible with it, and neither does it conflict with the definition of material supposition in his early treatise *De suppositionibus* as *suppositio pro voce sola*.[59] That is, while Burley does not pursue the line of thought of the *Middle Commentary* elsewhere, neither does he contradict or repudiate it. Indeed, throughout his career Burley maintained that material supposition occurs apart from signification, and he was by no means alone in that position. His slightly younger contemporary Ockham famously identifies both material and simple supposition as nonsignificative.[60] In fact, at the beginning of the fourteenth century it had become a commonplace that material supposition, if not other forms of supposition as well, is a kind of reference without signification. As D. Vance Smith has observed, "supposition theory in England in the fourteenth century . . . above all taught that one did not need to know what the primary imposition of a word or a thing was, when it happened, or who did it, in order to say something about the potential senses and shades of meaning of an animated body of signs."[61]

But this consensus was short-lived. Even as logic in the new styles of Burley and Ockham was incorporated into the arts curriculum at Oxford, it was the older notion of the dependence of supposition on signification that prevailed.[62] Elizabeth Karger has shown that, by the end of the century, logicians again denied that it was possible for there to be supposition without signification. Drawing on and extending Karger's findings, Stephen Read has argued that the notion of material supposition as nonsignificative is and always was fundamentally absurd, and that the fourteenth-century logicians caught on to this absurdity and corrected the mistaken notions of their predecessors.[63] Concomitantly, by the end of the century the use of *voces non-significativae* among Oxford logicians dropped off as well: in John Wyclif's important *Tractatus de logica*, for example, and even though much of it is drawn from Burley's works on supposition, there is no trace of *buba* or *bufbaf*; the same is true of the *Logica parva* of Paul of Venice, a widely circulated text that can be considered a kind of introductory summation of the logical doctrines ascendant at Oxford at the end of the fourteenth century.[64] *Vox non-significativa* is no longer even mentioned in the course of its being excluded: it is simply nowhere to be found. In short, the apprehension of *vox sola* adumbrated in Burley's *Middle Commentary* had no future in the field of logic. Burley did not pursue it in his mature works on supposition, his contemporaries did not take up his suggestion, and his successors developed theories about the material basis and properties of terms that do not invite such speculation.

All of which is to say that the meaningless utterance had been an irritant in the field of logic since its inception, the grain of sand around which it opalesced. Hidden in plain sight, it served as the unthinkable foundation for the discipline as a whole. Over the course of the Middle Ages, attempts were made to expel this irritant; some of them—notably *grammatica speculativa*—were more successful than others. But *buba* and *blictrix* persisted at Oxford, despite Bacon's assault on them, into the fourteenth century, where they found in Burley a devotee. Nonetheless, once the doctrine of vocal inanity was elaborated explicitly in the form of the Burleyan account of the apprehension of mental failure, it disappeared with startling speed. By the late fourteenth century, logicians at Oxford barely remembered that their predecessors had once paused over the existence of such words. But the millennial thinking of *vox non-significativa* did not disappear completely. For just when it was finally expelled from logic it reappeared in an unlikely place—not in logic, nor in any other university discipline, nor even in a text written in Latin. The place where Burley's line of thinking was pursued more faithfully, perhaps, than any other is the vernacular contemplative treatise called the *Cloud of Unknowing*. For the *Cloud* is about nothing else than the de-imposition of words, about the opening of a minimal duration, in the time it takes the bare utterance to sound, of a mental failure that attains to truth.

CHAPTER THREE

THE *CLOUD OF UNKNOWING* ON THE *LITIL WORDE OF O SILABLE*

This chapter is an extended gloss of the "litil worde of o silable" (little word of one syllable) that is mentioned several times in the *Cloud of Unknowing*, an anonymous mystical treatise written in Middle English in or around the 1380s.[1] Despite the fact that its utterance makes up a prayer whose practice is the work of unknowing itself, the *litil worde* has been given surprisingly little attention.[2] My aim in this chapter is to describe as accurately as possible the procedure of prayer taught in the *Cloud* and to suggest that this procedure can best be understood in the terms provided by the medieval linguistic sciences. For the prayer, as I will show, consists in the production of an utterance that is both a syllable and a word—and thus neither. It occurs in the mantric repetition of this utterance, and the "unknowing" that it brings about is nothing else than the experience of confusion that momentarily afflicts the mind of a person repeating a word to the point of nonsense.[3] Nevertheless, the *Cloud*-author has never been thought to take an interest in the *scientiae vocis*, and so a few words about the presuppositions of this reading are in order here.

What must be kept in mind is that the treatise is not all of a piece. The practical instructions in the prayer procedure that is the focus of this chapter take up only a small portion of the text.[4] The majority of the treatise is devoted to something else: explaining, situating, elaborating, and otherwise accounting for the prayer procedure in the terms of a particular discourse, what scholars would now call "late medieval affective apophaticism."[5] But the fact that the *Cloud*-author situates the prayer procedure within a particular discourse does not mean that the procedure belongs to that discourse. To the contrary: the effort he expends to assimilate the one to the other demonstrates precisely the necessity of such a labor. Neither does the prayer have anything essential in common with the models and corollaries that have been proposed for it, for example the aspirative prayer of a Hugh of Balma or the meditations on the name *Jhesu* of a Walter Hilton or a Richard Rolle.[6] Insofar as the procedure is inassimilable to the affective tradition, it can and must be read on its own terms.

The question is what those terms might be. Most of the attention paid to the treatise in recent decades that does not focus on its theological doctrines focuses instead on the fact that it is written in a particular idiom, Middle English, and in a particular ("homely" and "literary") style. But the pertinence of these observations does not go without saying. The *Cloud*-author, for his part, appears entirely uninterested in the fact that he writes in English; in any event, he never mentions it. I will discuss the question of the treatise's "vernacularity" at greater length below. As for the stylistic features of the treatise, three observations can be made. First, its tendency to recur to a homely register is entirely in keeping with pseudo-Dionysian indications as to the fitness of unlike figures and thus does not amount to an especially literary gesture.[7] Second, as J. A. Burrow cautioned thirty years ago, its rhetorical strategies are by no means uncommon in Middle English prose and are "better left unmarked by any special comment" unless they can be shown to be particularly significant as "part of the author's whole effort to realize a story or explore an idea."[8] Third, it has been suggested with frequency that these devices are, in fact, crucial to the *Cloud*-author's "whole effort to explore an idea," because his purpose is to produce in the reader an aesthetic experience that would amount to unknowing itself. In other words, just to read the treatise would already be to do the work it counsels.[9] This may well be. But there is nonetheless something unsatisfying about the idea, for not only does the *Cloud*-author never say anything of the sort, he does not fail to declare exactly what the work of unknowing consists in: and it is not the reading of literature, in a vague sense, but a very particular practice of prayer whose procedure is that of the *litil worde*. What, if anything, the *Cloud* has to do with literature can only be determined in the light of the specificity of that procedure.

Neither vernacular-theological nor aesthetic, the terms of the procedure are *sermocinal*: they bear on the nature of *vox* as it was theorized by the linguistic disciplines of the trivium: grammar, logic, and rhetoric. Confining itself largely (and for reasons that will soon become clear) to the first and most basic of these three, my reading suggests that the prayer is an elaboration of possibilities announced notably in Priscian's *Institutiones grammaticae*. It is not necessary to establish any particular evidence that the *Cloud*-author knew this work. The passages referred to here are those in which the most basic distinctions of the most basic medieval discipline are laid out, distinctions that were rehearsed in all the medieval grammatical textbooks and would have been intimately familiar to any literate person in the Middle Ages.[10] My argument does not rest on the notion that the *Cloud*-author took any particular interest in grammar; he did not. But he could by no means have been unaware of the foundational concepts of the "cradle of the sciences," *grammatica*, what Rita Copeland has called a "master discourse, providing the means of access to all other knowledge in the insistently textual culture of the Middle Ages."[11]

The *Cloud* consists, at its heart, of instructions in the peculiar devotional practice that its author refers to as "þis werk" (this work).[12] The first task of any reading of the treatise is thus to come to some understanding of the nature and status of that practice, which are not perhaps self-evident. A clue as to what is at stake can be found in chapter 34, which offers in the guise of a casual remark a formula that is in fact of the greatest importance. The formula bears on the possibility of the work of unknowing, and on its essence. "Þe abilnes to þis werk," it reads, "is onyd to þe selue werk, wiþ-outyn departyng" (the ability to do this work is united inextricably with the work itself).¹³ In its context, this sentence appears to do little more than extend a set of remarks counseling against taking pride in the work of devotion. The first half of the chapter in which it appears has established that whatever success you might have with the prayer is due not to any aptitude or effort on your part, but to God's prompting alone; and that God grants or withholds this prompting without regard for your merit. In one sense, the sentence in question merely reinforces this line of argumentation, by locating the ability to do the work of prayer outside of the the person praying. But its implications extend beyond the limits of a simple warning against pride. The formula establishes with precision the metaphysical status of the prayer: it is such that its possibility is inseparable from its existence. It is a prayer that can only exist when it is already underway; and, conversely, when it is not happening it is impossible that it should ever begin. The *werk* in question would thus seem to be an activity that, strictly speaking, would never occur, for how can something ever take place at all, if it only becomes possible once it already exists? The *Cloud*-author appears to be endorsing, in the case of the *werk* of prayer, a doctrine of existence and potentiality most famously refuted in Book IX of the *Metaphysics*, where Aristotle takes the Megarians to task for maintaining so absurd a principle as that a thing is only capable when it is acting.¹⁴

Nonetheless, although he is not unaware of the difficulties of his position, the *Cloud*-author does not modify it; instead, he puts the point only more forcefully. "Þe condicioun of þis werk is soche," he writes, "þat þe presence þerof abliþ a soule for to haue it and for to fele it. And þat abilnes may no soule haue wiþ-outyn it" (The condition of this work is such that its presence enables a soul to have it and to feel it. And no soul may have that ability without it).¹⁵ And yet he gives every indication that he is describing a prayer that he himself practices and that he believes others can practice as well. The question is thus practical as well as metaphysical: when can a work that is only possible when it is already underway ever come into being?

As it happens, this is a question that the *Cloud*-author does not neglect to address directly. Among the very first characteristics of the *werk* of unknowing that he sees fit to explain is its duration. As he writes in chapter 4:

> Þis werk askeþ no longe tyme er it be ones treulich done, as sum men wenen; for it is þe schortest werke of alle þat man may ymagyn. It is neiþer lenger ne schorter þen is an athomus; þe whiche athomus, by þe diffinicion of trewe philisophres in þe sciens of astronomye, is þe leest partie of tyme.¹⁶

> [This work does not require a long amount of time in order to be truly done, as some people believe; for it is the shortest work of all that may be imagined. It is neither longer nor shorter than is an atom—the atom being, according to the definition of the true philosophers in the science of astronomy, the smallest part of time.]

The time that the *werk* takes to occur is strictly equivalent to that of a temporal *athomus*, the minimal unit of duration.[17] It does not last for less time than an instant, that is, it does take place in measurable time; but it does not last any longer, either, so that it takes as little time as it is possible for anything to take. As Eleanor Johnson has remarked, the *Cloud*-author's reference to the discipline of astronomy aligns his interest in the elemental form of duration with the work of the so-called "Oxford calculators," the mid-century scholars associated with Merton College, where Walter Burley produced the commentary discussed in chapter 2. But, as Johnson shows, that atomism has much more to do with the disciplines of speech than it does with those of number: and, indeed, with the way that Burley himself conceived of *vox*. For the *Cloud*-author quickly makes clear that the "leest partie of tyme" in question is nothing else than the duration of a single syllable, or—to be precise—of what he will call a *litil worde of o silable*.[18] It is in such a word, and nowhere else, that a time opens up in which there might take place the impossible occurrence of a work whose possibility is one with its actuality.

SILABLE

The first invocation of the *litil worde* comes in chapter 7:

> what tyme þat þou purposest þee to þis werk, & felest bi grace þat þou arte clepid of God, lift þan up þin herte vnto God wiþ a meek steryng of loue. & mene God þat maad þee, & bouȝt þee, & þat graciousli haþ clepid þee to þis werk: & resseiue none oþer þouȝt of God. & ȝit not alle þeese, bot þee list; for it suffiseþ inouȝ a naked entent directe vnto God, wiþ-outen any oþer cause þen him-self. & ȝif þee list haue þis entent lappid & foulden in o worde, for þou schuldest haue betir holde þer-apon, take þee bot a litil worde of o silable; for so it is betir þen of two, for euer þe schorter it is, þe betir it acordeþ wiþ þe werk of þe spirite. & soche a worde is þis worde GOD or þis worde LOUE. Cheese þee wheþer þou wilt, or anoþer as þe list: whiche þat þee likeþ best of o silable. & fasten þis worde to þin herte, so þat it neuer go þens for þing þat bifalleþ.[19]

[When you apply yourself to this work, and feel by grace that you are called by God, lift up your heart to God with a humble stirring of love. And mean God who created you, and redeemed you, and who has graciously called you to this work: and admit no other thought of God. And yet not all of these, but only as it pleases you; for a bare intent directed to God is sufficient, without any other object besides himself. And if it pleases you to have this intent wrapped up and folded in a word, so that you might have a better hold on it, take just a little word of one syllable; for such a word is better than one of two syllables, for the shorter it is, the more fitting it is to the work of the spirit. And such a word is this word *god* or this word *love*. Choose whichever of these two you wish, or another as it pleases you: whichever word you like best that is of one syllable. And fasten this word to your heart, so that it is never separated from it, no matter what happens.]

In this passage the *Cloud*-author describes the work of unknowing as a prayer that does not praise or petition but rather attempts to mean God himself. As he explains elsewhere in the treatise, this "meaning" is in fact the attempt to remove all particular concepts from the mind, in order to bring about an encounter with what he calls the nought but God. This attempt appears to be a matter of the will alone, the directing of a bare intent toward God, so that the point would be to dispense not only with particular thoughts but also with any of the linguistic props in which prayer might be thought to take place. But immediately, and without marking any disjunction, the *Cloud*-author now recommends that the will be wrapped up in a *litil worde*. Many commentators have indicated that this practice would be optional and, what is more, better avoided by those more adept at the work of unknowing. Such a reading might seem to be borne out by the *Cloud*-author's reference here to the desire of the contemplative, "ȝif þee list" (if it pleases you, as you like). But in the context of the *Cloud*, in which what is essential is your being stirred to do the work of unknowing, a reference to the desire of the contemplative can only serve to emphasize the importance of the practice. For the desire to carry out the work of unknowing is coextensive with the work itself: "as moche as þou wylnest it & desirest it, so mochel hast þou of it, & no more ne no lesse" (as much as you will it and desire it, so much do you have of it, and no more nor less).[20]

Having recommended the practice of the *litil worde*, the *Cloud*-author now gives two examples of words fitting for the purpose: "And soche a worde is þis worde GOD or þis worde LOUE" (and such a word is this word *god* or this word *love*). These words are fitting because they fulfill the single requirement governing the choice of word: that it be "of o silable" (of one syllable). All that matters about the word is its syllable count, which must be one. That the littleness of the word is specifically a matter of syllabic quantity has not always been kept in mind, and its implications have never been remarked. The word *syllable* is a technical term in a particular discipline, and that discipline is grammar. Grammar is the science that takes as its object of study the utterance insofar as it admits of syllabification.[21] Conversely, syllable count does not pertain to words except insofar as their susceptibility to grammatical analysis is presupposed. The repeated and consistent terminological choice on the part of the *Cloud*-author to refer to the prayer word as "of o silable" places the *litil worde* within the field of grammar, and it suggests that the status of its littleness should be understood on the basis of the explanations of the syllable provided by grammarians.

What do the grammatical textbooks say about the syllable? The definition repeated throughout the Middle Ages is Priscian's:

Possumus tamen et sic definire syllabam: syllaba est vox literalis, quae sub uno accentu et uno spiritu indistanter profertur.[22]

[We can define the syllable as follows: the syllable is a writable utterance (*vox literalis*) that is emitted uninterruptedly under a single accentuation and a single breath.]

At the most basic level, the syllable is a variety of vocal utterance. It is a collecting, in a single unit, of the *elementa vocis*. It is a matter of accent and breath, something pronounced and emerging from the mouth. The first consequence of the *Cloud*-author's specification of the *litil worde* as syllabic is thus that it consists in something said aloud, something emitted by the voice.[23] It is not a form of silent meditation but an utterance. Nonetheless, there are indications to the contrary, the most serious of which is that the prayer is "goostly," uttered only in spirit, and that "it is best whan it is in pure spirit, wiþ-outyn specyal þou3t or any pronounsyng of worde" (it is best when it is in pure spirit, without particular thought or any utterance of words).[24] It is this idea of the prayer as silent that has been picked up by modern scholars.[25] For example, Jocelyn Wogan-Browne and her colleagues refer, in an influential recent anthology, to the practice as "a form of silent prayer" without further qualification, and Cheryl Taylor appears to consider the technique to be one of "mental prayer" consisting finally in "word-free, imageless contemplation."[26]

For his part, the *Cloud*-author allows that the prayer, though it is best when it is silent, might sometimes break into speech: the passage just cited continues "bot 3if it be any seeldom tyme, when for habundaunce of spiryt it brestiþ up into worde" (except for occasionally, when because of an abundance of spirit it bursts out in the form of words).[27] In his explanations of the procedure, in other words, he admits utterance as an exception. But insofar as it makes exclusive and invariable use of a word "of o silable," the procedure has its own itinerary. Utterance is inherent to the syllable, and a prayer consisting in a syllable is thus an inherently vocal one. The contradiction between what the *Cloud*-author says the prayer procedure actually is and what he says about it cannot be neatly resolved. Accordingly, the task of the interpreter is first of all to register the contradiction itself, and then to reconstruct each of the two itineraries on its own terms. Because the second of these itineraries has been much followed, I will pursue here exclusively that of the procedure itself. As a syllable, then, the prayer happens aloud. It consists not just in any sort of vocalization, however, but specifically in the utterance of a "worde." That is, it does not take place in moaning, whistling, or hollering, nor in the use of a made-up word such as *buba* or an animal noise on the order of *coax* or *cra*, but only in the pronunciation of a *dictio* or *vox literata articulata*, to use Priscian's terms: a writable word with a determinate *sensus*. Moreover, it is confined to the utterance of a single word. The *litil worde* is by definition not a collection of words that together make up a phrase, a sentence, *oratio*, but just a word by itself.

This last specification accords with a principle of vocal brevity announced repeatedly in the treatise. If a single word is to be used, it appears to be because utterance should be kept to a minimum: "for euer þe schorter it is, þe betir it acordeþ wiþ þe werk of þe spirite" (for the shorter it is, the more fitting it is to the work of the spirit).[28] That is, the shortness of the shortest possible word is most fitting to the work of unknowing because shortness in itself assists in prayer. But this principle of *breviloquia*, as it is found both within his treatise and elsewhere, does not account for the *Cloud*-author's insistence on the use of a *litil worde of o silable*.[29] As a rule, it is better to speak directly and succinctly than otherwise. But the prayer is distinct from utterance in general: it is not simply that its sounds should be kept to a minimum, but that this minimal utterance should take the form of a syllable. Needless to say, a word of one syllable could easily take longer to pronounce or contain more letters than a multisyllabic one, but the *Cloud*-author gives no indication that he is concerned with the length of the syllable that makes up the *litil worde*.[30] All that matters is that it be exactly as short as a syllable: "Cheese þee wheþer þou wilt [i.e., from the words *god* or *loue*], or anoþer as þee list: whiche þat þee likeþ best of o silable" (choose whichever of these two words you wish, or another as it pleases you: whichever word you like best that is of one syllable).[31] Although even the closest readers of the *Cloud* have regularly referred to the *litil worde* as "preferably" or "ideally" monosyllabic, in fact the *Cloud*-author admits no compromise on this point.[32] He has only one stipulation: you can choose whatever word you like, as long as it be monosyllabic. To use a multisyllabic word is not to perform the work of unknowing in a less than ideal manner; it is not to perform it at all.

In this injunction to choose whatever word you wish lies what is perhaps the most notable characteristic of the *litil worde*. This is its complete lexical indifference. If all that matters is that it be of one syllable, the *litil worde* could certainly be *god* or *love*, but it could also be *cloud* or *is* or any other monosyllabic word. The *Cloud*-author could hardly be more explicit on this fairly shocking point, which has nonetheless been overlooked by many modern scholars, who take the examples he gives to be the best and only words for the purpose. But if the words *god* and *love* are well suited to the task of praying, this in no way lessens the fact that they are only examples. This can easily be seen in the fact that the second discussion of monosyllabic prayer relies on two examples not quite the same:

> I maad no force, þof þou haddest now-on-dayes none oþer meditacions of þin owne wrechidnes, ne of þe goodnes of God . . . bot soche as þou mayst haue in þis worde SYNNE & in þis worde GOD, or in soche oþer, whiche as þe list.[33]

> [I would not mind at all if, at this point, you had no other meditations on your own wretchedness or on the goodness of God than such as you may

have in this word *sin* or in this word *god*, or in another such word, whichever you like.]

In the final clause, the *Cloud*-author makes the point explicitly: these are only examples. Moreover, the repetition of the phrase "as þe list" (as you like) from his earlier remarks calls attention to the fact that he is resuming a discussion begun earlier. What comes most to the fore, when the two passages are read together, is that the earlier examples have been partially replaced: *god* and *loue* have become *synne* and *god*. This discrepancy, and the substitutability of examples that it presupposes, is soon underscored still further. After describing a situation of emergency in which you shout "fiir!" (Fire!) or "oute!" (Alas!, or Help!), the *Cloud*-author returns his attention to the prayer that the emergency is supposed to be merely analogous to. But now, with the analogy ostensibly left behind, one of the words that appeared in it, *oute*, has become part of the prayer itself: "And crye þan goostly euer upon one: 'Synne, synne, synne; oute, oute, oute!'" (and then continually cry out, in your spirit, this one thing: "Sin, sin, sin; help, help, help!").[34] First *god* and *loue*, then *synne* and *god*, and finally *synne* and *oute*: as the *Cloud*-author proceeds, his first examples come to be entirely displaced.

The shifting instances of the prayer word are not the only evidence that its choice is arbitrary. For the *Cloud*-author does not fail to address the question of which word is to be used. In chapter 39, after repeating that one should pray in a "lityl worde of o silable," he poses the question explicitly: "& what schal þis worde be? Sekyrlyche soche a worde as is best acordyng vnto þe propirte of preier. & what worde is þat?" (And what shall this word be? Surely such a word as is most fitting to the nature of prayer. And what word is that?).[35] He explains that the words *god* and *synne* are very appropriate to the task, given that the meaning of these two words comprehends everything one would want to mean in a prayer. But the explanation does not suffice, as he knows, for he has made clear already that it is the number of syllables in a word that makes it appropriate rather than its meaning this or that. For this reason, he goes on to specify that the words *god* and *synne* are not necessarily better than any others. If God had taught him to make use of some others, he would have done it:

> ȝif I had be lernyd of God to take any oþer wordes ouþer, I wolde þan haue taken hem and lefte þees; and so I rede þat thou do.[36]
>
> [If I had been taught by God to take any other words instead, I would have taken them and left these; and I advise you to do the same.]

These are the words he himself has been moved to use, so that they should not lightly be set aside; and yet what is important is not what word is chosen but the fact that you are moved to choose some word, whatever it be. What determines the choice of the word is nothing else than this stirring:

> & þerfore take þou none oþer wordes to preie in—al-þof I sette þees here—bot soche as þou arte sterid of God for to take.³⁷
>
> [And therefore—even though I propose these ones—use no other words in your prayer than those you are stirred by God to use.]

If you are stirred to use the words *god* and *synne*, there is no reason to choose some other word instead; but these words make themselves available to the stirring for a single reason. They are "fully brief"—that is, they are of one syllable:

> ȝif God stire þee to take þees, I rede not þat þou leue hem—I mene ȝif þou schalt preie in wordes, & elles not; for whi þei ben ful schorte wordes.³⁸
>
> [If God stirs you to use these, I am not advising you to avoid them (that is, if you are praying with words, and not otherwise), since these words are fully brief.]

The point is made without ambiguity: it does not matter what word you use. And yet the examples given are not entirely without interest, in that they allow a final notable characteristic of the *litil worde* to become clear. What is pertinent about the examples *god*, *loue*, *synne*, and *oute* is that they are words known to any speaker of the language in which the treatise is written. But this has nothing to do with Middle English as a particular language—nor with its so-called vernacularity. It simply means that the *litil worde* is not a *nomen barbarum*: not an esoteric, foreign, or unfamiliar term but just any old word already known to you.³⁹

It might seem strange to affirm that the *werk* of unknowing is not a matter of vernacularity, for in the past few decades the *Cloud* has attained to the status of an example, if not the very paradigm, of what is called vernacular theology. And there is no denying that the treatise was composed right in the midst of what Nicholas Watson calls "an intense, approximately sixty-year cultural argument over the whole role of the vernacular in religious culture: an argument that took in larger questions about the intellectual capacities of the laity, the role of the clergy in ministering to them, and the suitability of vernacular theological writing as a vehicle for religious truth."⁴⁰ That the treatise as a whole, and the examples of the *litil worde* that it contains, is in Middle English clearly makes a difference in the context of that cultural argument. But does this fact make any difference to the argument or arguments that the *Cloud*-author is himself interested in making, that is, to the treatise's immanent concerns?⁴¹ The most crucial fact in this connection is that the *Cloud*-author—who concerns himself explicitly and at length both with matters of a broadly linguistic nature and with restricting the circulation of his treatise to particular communities of readers—never once draws attention to the fact that he writes in the vernacular. Nor is there in the content of the treatise any instruction or speculation on which the fact of the multiplicity of languages or that of the relations among them has any bearing to speak of.

In the absence of any such connection, what is pertinent about the examples provided for the *litil worde* is that they are drawn from the same lexicon as are all the rest of the words that make up the treatise, not that that lexicon belongs to the particular language that is now called Middle English. It stands to reason that readers of the *Cloud* in untranslated form, whatever else might or might not be said about them, will be competent enough in the language of its composition to be familiar with those examples.[42] Of course, the situation would be different with readers of the treatise in translation; and it is indeed instructive to consider the renderings of the examples of the *litil worde* in the two Latin versions of the *Cloud* prepared in the century after its composition. Both translators sometimes use Latin equivalents of the examples (*deus, amor, peccatum*— though neither ever translates the "interieccio" *oute*), sometimes leave them in the original, and sometimes include (with or without adverting to the fact) both the original and a translation: for example, "clamemus aut verbo aut desiderio nichil aliud, nec plura verba, nisi hoc vnum: 'God' Anglice, Latine: 'Deus'" (let us cry out, either aloud or only in desire, nothing else, nor in more words, than this one word: *god*, in English, *deus*, in Latin).[43] They adopt these various strategies because their Latin texts would be incoherent without the presence of the English words. Indeed, in the translation prepared by Richard Methley in 1491, the passage in which the *litil worde* is first mentioned is given without Middle English gloss and is thus effectively incomprehensible until later passages can be compared with it: "Assume proinde tibi vnicum verbum vnius sillabe.... Et tale verbum, vt est: 'Deus,' sive illud: 'Dileccio'" (thus, take for yourself a single word of one syllable. And such a word is *deus* or *dileccio*).[44]

The effort to avoid the absurdity of calling *dileccio* a word of one syllable suffices on its own to explain the translators' inclusion of the vernacular words. It is neither necessary nor warranted to suppose that they wished thereby to signal that a vernacular lexicon is more suitable for the purposes of the prayer.[45] In particular, there is no reason to believe—as has been suggested more than once—that English lends itself quasi-uniquely to the *werk* of unknowing because of its numerous monosyllabic words, whereas Latin's polysyllables would leave it constitutionally unsuitable for the purpose. For although it is evidently true that *deus* and *amor*—not to mention *dileccio*—do not fit the bill, it would in fact be a simple matter to find a "litil worde of o silable" in the language of *hic haec hoc*. All that is necessary is that the word answer to the description given by the *Cloud*-author.

HOELNES

To summarize, the description is as follows: it is a vocal utterance, a word, a single word, whichever word you are incited to choose from among your already existing vocabulary, as long as it be monosyllabic. Put negatively, the *litil worde* is not silent, not a sigh or a wail, not a phrase or series of phrases, not any particular word, not one belonging to an unknown or invented language, and not a word of two or more syllables. That such a thing would lend itself to the purposes of prayer does not go without saying. The utterance of the *litil worde* is immediately and evidently distinct from more familiar practices: praising or petitioning, for example, wordlessly, extemporaneously, or as structured by rosary, psalter, or book of hours. But the point is that this prayer takes a form that allows for as precise a description as does the *Pater Noster*. The question is why anyone might wish to pray in such a manner. The *Cloud*-author explains that if he insists on the use of the *litil worde* it is because such an utterance lends itself most fittingly to the purpose to which it will be put. This fitness inheres in a characteristic of this word that he calls its *hoelnes*: the way that it can be kept whole.

Recall that the purpose of the *Cloud*'s technique is to do away with all the thoughts in your mind in order that the intellect may encounter the very absence of thought, the so-called cloud of unknowing. This encounter will be accomplished by means of the *litil worde*, which, according to an improbable figure, you use simultaneously to bludgeon your thoughts and to pound against the cloud. The double operation of unknowing consists in this blow—to which the *Cloud*-author gives the name "loue put" (love-thrust)—which takes place when you turn the word into an accouterment of battle, at once a sword you bash against the cloud of unknowing and a shield to keep your thoughts at bay. In being wielded in this manner, the word produces "þis lityl blynde loue put, when it is betyng upon þis derke cloude of vnknowyng, alle oþer þinges put doun & forȝeten" (this little blind love-thrust, when it is beating upon this dark cloud of unknowing, all other things having been put down and forgotten).[46]

If the word of one syllable lends itself to this operation, it is because it can be kept whole. The *Cloud*-author explains that your importunate thoughts will constantly attempt to get you to explain the word, analyze it, break it up into its parts, but this is what you must not do.

> ȝif any þouȝt prees apon þee to aske þee what þou woldest haue, answere him wiþ no mo wordes bot wiþ þis o worde. & ȝif he profre þee of his grete clergie to expoune þee þat worde & to telle þee þe condicions of þat worde, sey him þat þou wilt haue it al hole, & not broken ne vndon.[47]
>
> [If any thought presses upon you to ask you what you are seeking, answer him with no more words than this one word. And if he offers to explicate that word for you, using his impressive learning, and to tell you about its various aspects, tell him that you want to have it entirely whole, and not broken or undone.]

To keep the word whole is to withdraw it from the grammatical and logical procedures that would break it up by distinguishing in it genus from species, root from ending, literal sense from figurative sense—or syllable from syllable.

This refusal of exposition by means of sheer repetition appears to seize upon the brevity and unity of the monosyllable, insofar as a longer word might be more readily articulated into parts. It would seem easier to keep whole a word made up of one syllable alone.

This appearance is deceptive. In fact, syllable count and word count are entirely unrelated, and it is the peculiarity of the coincidence of part and whole in the monosyllabic word that matters here. If the *Cloud*-author recommends the use of a word of one syllable, it is not because the syllable, as has been suggested, is "the shortest unit of audible language that carries meaning."[48] On the contrary, the syllable, as it is theorized in both the grammatical and the logical traditions, is, if anything, the largest part of a word that is not in itself meaningful. In Priscian's terms, *syllaba* differs from *dictio* first of all inasmuch as the one is a part of the other, but no less because it is in the nature of *dictio* to bear a complete meaning, whereas *syllaba* in itself does not necessarily signify at all.[49] Moreover, the grammarian demonstrates the meaningfulness of the word (its having *sensus*) exactly by opposing it to its parts. For it is self-evident that the syllable *-king* in the word *smoking* makes no reference to the monarchy; or, to use Priscian's example, that the meaning of a word like *vires* (men) is altogether distinct from that which might be imagined by someone breaking it up into *vi* (by force) and *res* (things).[50] The meaning of *vires* has nothing to do with that of the words *vi* and *res*, and more importantly the syllables *vi-* and *-res* have nothing to do with the words they resemble. Insofar as they remain syllables, they are subordinated to the word of which they are a part and do not themselves signify.

The meaninglessness of isolated syllables is a dictum of the logical as well as the grammatical authorities. Aristotle makes the point twice in the opening pages of *De interpretatione*. His explanation of why he has included, in his definition of the noun, the specification that "no part of [a noun] is significant separately" is that the syllable, its part, has no meaning in itself. Commenting on Aristotle's treatise, Boethius underscores this point: "although every noun is made up of them, syllables themselves do not yet mean anything at all."[51] So that when the commentator explains what Aristotle means in defining the noun as a kind of *vox significativa* (meaningful utterance), his contrasting example of a *vox quae nihil designat* (utterance that refers to nothing) is the syllable. The grammatical and logical authorities are in agreement on this point: the syllable has no semantic value, is as it were suspended in meaninglessness, until the word of which it is part has been uttered in its entirety.[52]

And yet there is one sort of word whose whole signification would seem to arrive in the understanding at the same moment that a single syllable is pronounced, and that is of course the monosyllabic word. The fact that the nonsignificative part and the significative whole of a word can and in fact not infrequently do coincide is not ignored by the *auctoritates*. To the contrary, it comes in for special treatment as the limit case that reveals the distinction between *dictio* and *syllaba* the more completely. Having already declared that the syllable does not always signify anything, Priscian explains that while it is true that a monosyllabic word can be called simply a syllable, this is the case only in an imperfect sense: for the syllable, he goes on, can in fact never signify anything by itself, since signifying is proper only to words.[53] It is nothing else than the existence of monosyllabic words that forces the grammarian to specify that the syllable is not just potentially but by nature totally and always nonsignifying. In other words, the entity that would seem to undo the distinction between word and syllable is rather the basis on which their total irreconcilability makes itself known. Until a syllable has been placed within a word, it has none of the characteristics of a word and will not admit of any of the modes of apprehension proper to a word.[54] Conversely, once a word can be considered as a word, it ceases to be apprehensible on the basis of the syllable or syllables that make it up. In Priscian, it is thanks to the monosyllabic word that the following principle can be formulated: insofar as it is considered as a syllable, a word does not signify; and insofar as it is considered as significative, a word is no longer a syllable.

The *Cloud*'s precept that the *litil worde* should be kept whole should be understood in the light of this double exclusion. On the one hand, it is a matter of insisting on the lexical indifference of the monosyllabic utterance by confounding the efforts of your thoughts to tell you what the word means. On the other, the utterance is not a syllable but a "worde" of one syllable, and the task is to keep it precisely "whole," that is, a word and not a syllable. The work consists, then, in producing an utterance that in being both syllable and word is emphatically neither. This *litil worde of o silable* is not, after all, just a "monosyllabic word" but something that might be better called a "syllable-word." Wholly and only a word, it is nonetheless retained at the level of the syllable: and this means that to utter it is to produce a word that is totally nonsignifying.

Both the end and the means of its own production, the syllable-word emerges only in repetition. This crucial point is one that the *Cloud*-author makes almost glancingly, though he declares in so doing that, while he barely addresses it, it is no less important than the one characteristic of the *litil worde* he has underscored so heavily. The word is to be repeated incessantly:

> al-þof þe schortnes of preier be greetly comendid here, neuerþeles þe oftnes of preier is neuer þe raþer refreynid . . . it schuld neuer sees tyl þe tyme were þat it had fully getyn þat þat it longid after.[55]

> [Although the shortness of prayer is much recommended here, this does not mean that the frequency of prayer is to be restrained . . . it should never cease until it has fully gotten what it longed after.]

And thus when the *Cloud*-author gives an example not just of the word used in the prayer but of the "crie" in which it sounds, he sets the word down repeatedly: "And crye þan euer upon one: 'Synne, synne, synne; oute, oute, oute!'" (and then continually cry out this one thing: "Sin, sin, sin; help, help, help!").[56] Now, this frequency of the utterance corresponds to its use as a *loue put*—a beating against the cloud of unknowing. The word is fixed to the heart so as to be always working: "fasten þis worde to þin herte, so þat it neuer go þens for þing þat bifalleþ" (fasten this word to your heart, so that it is never separated from it, no matter what happens).[57] But there is more to be said about it. The repetition of the single word prevents its entry into "ordered speech," it isolates it as a word outside of a grouping of words. To repeat the same word over and over again is to never produce a sentence into which it could be fit but to produce instead what Johnson has called a "recursive and asyntactic" prayer, or in Vincent Gillespie's phrase an utterance "syntactically uninhibited."[58] But this insistence on the single word is very far from an insistence on its signification, from a hammering home of whatever it might mean. This, too, is explicit in the Priscianic definition of the word as distinct from the syllable: for if a word has a *sensus*, the grammarian hastens to add that this status is exclusively granted by its placement within a sentence. The *sensus* of the whole and single word can only be gathered by reference to its participation in a sentence, an *oratio*, the ordered combination of words that taken together show a complete *sententia*.[59] That is, although the word has meaning in itself, this meaning is not granted by the word's being definable in itself but only insofar as it can be picked out from the succession of words. For instance, you cannot know if the word *smells* is a noun or a verb, if it is a verb whether transitive or intransitive, and (in speech if not in writing) if it is a noun whether nominative or genitive, without a sentence in which the word would appear: and its *sensus* would be different in each case. The repetition of a single word outside of a phrase or sentence as taught in the *Cloud* is a refusal of the kind of ordered speech that would complete itself and thereby allow its various parts to show the sense of their combination and therefore the sense of each part.

Repetition thus deprives the *litil worde* of its meaning from two directions: both by retaining it at the level of the syllable and by preventing it from forming part of a sentence. But perhaps it is not necessary to refer to the authority of a Priscian here. As the *Cloud*-author says, this word is "betyr lernid of God by þe proef þen of any man by worde" (better learned from God by experience than from any man by speech).[60] And you already know very well what happens when you say "cloud cloud cloud cloud cloud cloud cloud cloud." It is the same with the word *love*, or any other: repeating it ad infinitum does not reinforce its meaning but cancels it out. In a process familiar to everyone, sometimes called "semantic satiation," the more you repeat an utterance the less it seems to have to do with any concept or thing. A duration can be produced by the repetition of an utterance in which whatever signification might have attached to it before, and in all likelihood will do so again, just cannot possibly have anything to do with it for the time being. During this duration, not only does the semantic value of a word become uncoupled from its sound-shape or *figura vocis* but the sound-shape itself appears to change, though mysteriously, so that it would belong to a distinct and unknown other word. The method of prayer of the *Cloud of Unknowing* is nothing else than the child's game of repeating a word until it sounds like absolutely nothing you have ever heard before and cannot possibly be considered to mean anything, even while it is indistinguishable from a word with which you remain altogether familiar.

The procedure is thus a means of turning *god*, *loue*, *synne*, or *oute* into a nonsense word. It is a collection of ruses to be employed in the confounding of the concepts that will attempt to join themselves to an utterance. These are as follows, each reduplicating the effect of the others. The word should be maintained in a state in which it cannot be told apart from a mere syllable. It should be pronounced without regard for its lexical specificity. It should be repeated incessantly, so that it takes on the bizarre proportions of a sound estranged from its usual familiarity and sense. It should be kept in a state of nonexposition and wielded against all impulses to explain it or use it to explain anything else. Each of these stipulations conduces to the same end: the production of an utterance that enjoys an existence independent of reference and signification.

As I have established in the preceding two chapters, medieval scientists of language were not unfamiliar with such utterances, from the *coax* and *cra* of Priscian to the *buba* and *bufbaf* of the late medieval theorists of terms. But the *Cloud*-author does something unattempted in grammar or logic, not to mention in theology or devotional literature: he provides a method for the production of the meaningless word. His strange proposal is that you turn an ordinary word into a meaningless one, *vox significativa* into *vox non-significativa*. This operation is neither grammatical nor logical. A grammarian will accept a nonsense word blithely, whereas a logician will reject it—this being the proverbial difference between their two disciplines. But the work of unknowing consists neither in accepting such a word nor in rejecting it but rather in producing it. The prayer procedure takes place in a possibility inherent in *vox* that opens between grammar and logic, in which you make your own voice available as an instrument for the carrying out of a task. The innovation of the *Cloud*-author should be located here, in his pressing into service a sort of utterance widely recognized though widely ignored in the medieval sciences of language. He does this because he believes the syllable-word to be possessed of a particular efficacy: it causes something to happen; it works.[61]

HIDOUS NOISE

What does the repetition of the word to the point of meaninglessness bring about? Here, too, the syllabic nature of the *litil worde* is of central importance. For the efficacy of the utterance is a monosyllabic efficacy, as the *Cloud*-author explains by means of a comparison between the person carrying out the prayer and someone caught in a fire and crying for help. How, the *Cloud*-author asks, will such a person shout? "ʒe, how? Sekirly not in many woordes, ne ʒit in o woorde of two silabes" (Yes, how? Surely not in many words, nor in a single word of two syllables).[62] When praying, you should shout like a person in an emergency, who will not stop to think about what he wants to shout but will rather naturally emit a monosyllabic cry like "Fire!" This is because brevity befits the direness of your situation, that is, the wretchedness of sin. But the syllable-word is not only appropriate to the state of its speaker but also useful, and what makes it useful is that it strikes the ears of whoever hears it in a particular way:

> & riʒt as þis lityl worde FIIR steriþ raþer and peerseþ more hastely þe eren of þe herers, so doþ a lityl worde of o syllable. . . . & raþer it peersiþ þe eres of Almyʒty God þan doþ any longe sauter vnmyndfuly mumlyd in þe teeþ.[63]
>
> And just as this little word *fire* stirs more and pierces more quickly the ears of the hearers, so does a little word of one syllable. And it pierces the ears of Almighty God more than does any long psalter distractedly mumbled in the teeth.

Such a word more effectively brings succor than other forms of speech: whoever is within hearing distance will more readily come to your aid if you shout "Help!" than if you remark that you might benefit from their assistance should they be willing to consider offering it. And this is so even, the *Cloud*-author goes on, in the case of mortal enemies. He claims that you will jump out of bed—"ʒe! þof it be aboute midwintirs niʒt" (indeed, even on a midwinter night)—to help your "deedly enmye" (deadly enemy) without giving any particular thought to the chill or to the fact that he is your enemy, if only he cry out "Fire!"[64]

Despite its homely appearance, the figure of someone in a fire shouting for help was a commonplace in thirteenth-century grammatical discussions of what are now called "performative speech acts," where it was used to illustrate the doctrine that sentences need not be grammatically complete in order to be understandable and effective.[65] The *Cloud*-author employs this figure in the context of prayer: if the syllable-word forces even enemies to help one another, he suggests, how much more useful will it be when it is addressed to God. The *litil worde* all but forces the one hearing it to respond against her will, it puts out of commission whatever unwillingness to help might be present, and makes your enemy merciful toward you, or you merciful toward your enemy, "not aʒenstonding his enmite" (despite his enmity).[66] The *Cloud*-author does not go so far as to say that you will compel God to do anything unwillingly, but he comes remarkably close. This is how he explains it: if—through grace—the worst sinner, who is to God as it were an enemy, is able to "crye soche a lityl silable" (cry such a little syllable), notwithstanding this enmity "he scholde for þe hidous noise of þis crye be alweis herde and holpen of God" (he will, on account of the terrifying noise of this cry, be always heard and helped by God).[67]

What matters in the syllable-word is thus its *hidous noise*. This phrase (which is also to be found in Chaucer) should be taken as a technical term.[68] The efficacy of the little word is lodged in the *noise* of its *crye*, and it is for the sake of this noise that it is pressed into service in the prayer procedure. If God does not hear the particular word uttered, he does hear and respond to its noise, which is *hidous* (terrifying, horrifying). This is because, as the *Cloud*-author explains, you make something plain to God altogether differently than you do to another person. It would be exactly wrong to think that you should try to tell God anything, about yourself or himself or something else again, about a wish or a fear or a state of affairs. But this does not mean that if God hears and helps you when you emit a syllable-word it is because the clamor of its noise communicates to him the mere fact that you need help. Operating under this misconception might lead you to make

> a bodily schewyng vnto hym, ouþer in contenaunce, or in voyce, or in worde, or in som oþer rude bodely streynyng, as it is when þou schalt schewe a þing þat is hid in þin hert to a bodily man; & in as moche þi werk schuld haue ben inpure. For on o maner schal a þing be schewid to man, & on an-oþer maner vnto God.[69]

> [a physical display to him, either with your expression, or your voice, or your words, or in some other rude physical exertion, as you do when you want to display something hidden in your heart to a physical person; and insofar as you do this your work will be impure. For in one manner shall a thing be showed to man and in another manner to God.]

In speaking to God it is not a question of making known what is within you, as it is when you speak to another person. But what the *Cloud*-author's emphasis not just on the word but also on the voice, face, and gesture indicates is that the utterance will "not make known" not only insofar as its *sensus* is to be placed under suspension but because its force as a natural sign is too.

The hideous noise of the syllable-word is not, in other words, the sound of a yell or scream, it is not the recuperation in the voice of an originary cry. The *litil worde* does not cease to be a word, a *dictio* or *locutio*, an utterance fundamentally writable. But this is not because an inarticulate utterance would necessarily be outside the circuit of meaningful utterances. On the contrary, the problem with inarticulate utterances is that they say too much: that they, too, make something known. For (as seen in the last chapter) there are two ways in which the voice is understood to signify in the Aristotelian tradition: as encoding, arbitrarily, some idea to which a particular utterance would be assigned (or "imposed on"), and also as symptomatizing by its very presence the fact that some mental state is occurring, the same way that smoke indicates fire. In other words, when someone speaks you can gather from the noise produced not only some particular signified content but also the bare fact that a person is there, meaning something-or-other, whatever it might turn out to be.[70] Vocal sound may or may not communicate an arbitrarily imposed meaning, but it will always announce the presence of a will to signify. This is why sighs, yells of pain, and the like, are not without signification, even though they are unwritable and have not been imposed on any particular concept. And this is why if a person speaks a language you do not know, you are still able to gather that the person has something in his mind that he is attempting to make known by means of his voice. It is to this dimension of signification that the *Cloud*-author alludes in his celebrated prose castigating people who want to display their own imagined holiness in their bizarre modes of comporting themselves, and especially with their voices, expressions, and gestures. These wretches, gripped by their ill-advised wish to know things and to display what knowledge they have already, screw up their eyes like sheep knocked over the head, or tilt their heads to one side as though they had a worm in their ear; others "pipyn when þei schuld speke, as þer were no spirit in þeire bodies" (chirp when they should speak, as if there were no spirit in their bodies) or "crien and whinen in þeire þrote, so ben þei gredy & hasty to sey þat þei þink" (cry and whine in their throats, so greedy and hasty are they to say what they think).[71] In trying to show something with their voices and countenances, such squeakers and lispers fracture the voice into parts, rather than keeping it whole in the effort to display nothing with it.

In short, the *hidous noise* that makes God hear the syllable-word is not a clamor that makes it known that something is happening. What is frightful about the *litil worde* is that it does not even do that: it makes nothing at all known. Its hideousness is that of a word repeated to the uncanny point of perfect nonsense. It is for the sake of this particular hideousness that the *Cloud*-author insists that you should go so far as to conceal the meaning of your prayer from God, that you should hide your desire in as dark an obscurity as possible. Thus you should perform the prayer as if "þou on no wyse woldest lat hym wite hou fayne þou woldest see hym and haue hym or fele hym" (you would in no way let him know how much you would like to see him and have him or feel him).[72] And this because it is in concealment that your desire will make itself known to him most easily and fully: "it schuld more cleerly com to his knowyng, to þi profite & in fulfyllyng of þi desire, by soche an hiding, þan it scholde by any oþer maner of schewyng" (it will come to his knowledge more clearly, to your benefit and in fulfillment of your desire, by such a concealment, than it would by any other manner of showing).[73] If the point of the prayer procedure is to put the meaning of the *litil worde* under suspension, it is because the word will more effectively come to the hearing of God if its meaning is hidden as deep as possible: as it were concealed both from him and from yourself.

But what does it mean to be *holpen of God*? What is the success of a prayer that asks for nothing? It is a state of the intellect made possible by the *hidous noise*. The purpose of the word that makes nothing known is exactly to produce a failure of knowledge in which nothing is known. This is because such a failure of knowledge is itself the knowing of God. As the *Cloud*-author puts it, while a person can "neuer bi þe werk of his vnderstondyng com to þe knowyng of an vnmaad goostly þing, þe whiche is nouȝt bot God" (never come, by the work of his understanding, to the knowledge of an uncreated spiritual thing, which is nothing but God), this does not mean that knowledge of God is impossible. For he continues: "Bot by þe failyng it may; for whi þat þing þat it failiþ in is noþing elles bot only God" (But by means of the failure itself such knowledge may occur, since the thing that it fails in is nothing else than God himself).[74] While the work of the understanding will never allow a person to know God, in this very failure such knowledge may occur. It is the purpose of the prayer procedure to bring about this failure, by producing a thinking that does not extend itself toward any particular object. In the *Cloud*-author's most favored phrase, it is a thought "wiþ-outen special beholdyng," that is, free of particular regard. It intends nothing and is without object. The technique of the *Cloud* thus works as follows: the repetition of the syllable-word produces a null-word, in whose terrifying noise the intellect becomes suspended as a null-thought which is the knowledge of God.

GLOS

The experience of the cloud of unknowing is this remittance of the intellect to what Gaunilo of Marmoutiers had called, three hundred years earlier, *cogitatio secundum vocem solam*—to what Boethius had described, most of a millennium before, as the mind's ceaseless wandering, twisted and turned upon itself. The *Cloud*-author invents his own technique of "thought according to the utterance alone" on the basis of the familiar experience of what takes place when a word is repeated over and over again and on the basis of the properties of the utterance as they were theorized in the grammatical and logical traditions. In this the thinker closest to him is Burley, who points toward the possibility that the mind can come to a knowledge, faced with a *vox non-significativa* in material supposition, of its own failure to cognize the utterance as such. Burley was familiar with an irreducible lag preventing the mind from ever being entirely present to itself, forcing it to know itself only across a duration, be it ever so slight: the time of an unknowing at the basis of every operation of naming. In the de-naming or un-imposition that occurs in Burleyan material supposition, the mind is forced to while away in this duration. The *Cloud*'s werk of unknowing is meant to produce the same sort of truth that Burley considers to inhere in a proposition containing a subject term in material supposition. In the reduction, by repetition, of a word to its status as a bare utterance there takes place a failure of knowledge that is immediately a knowledge of that failure. It, too, takes place in a minimal duration: what the *Cloud*-author calls, using the language of Burley's descendants, an *athomus* of time—or a syllable. For the lag that opens up, sometimes, in all its brevity into the frozen time of a word repeated to the point of senselessness is the temporal noncoincidence that is the same failure of self-understanding that reveals itself in material supposition, the apprehension of *vox non-significativa* as such.

It is perhaps because *voces non-significativae* can produce such a mental effect, removed from all possibility of the apprehension of truth or falsity, that in the decades after Burley's death they were made to disappear from the discipline of logic as it was taught at Oxford. But it is for the very same reason that the *Cloud*-author develops, just when they would have seemed to be in danger of being forgotten in the university, a method for producing them himself. For the vertiginous state of mind that Boethius had long before identified is exactly what the *Cloud*'s technique is meant to bring about:

> For I telle þee trewly þat I had leuer be so nowhere bodely, wrastlyng wiþ þat blynde nought, þan to be so grete a lorde þat I miȝt when I wolde be euerywhere bodely. . . . Lat be þis eueriwhere & þis ouȝt, in comparison of þis noȝwhere and þis nouȝt.⁷⁵

> [For I tell you truly that I would rather be nowhere physically, wrestling with that blind nothing, than be so great a lord that, whenever I wanted, I could physically be anywhere at all. . . . Leave aside this everywhere and this anything, in favor of this nowhere and this nothing.]

The prayer-work of the *Cloud* follows a procedure whose single aim is to produce *vox non-significativa*, in order that the mind of the person uttering it might be forced to roam, without an object, in no place at all. This mental failure occurs only when you become caught up in the *hidous noise* of a word repeated to the point of senselessness. What the *Cloud*-author discovers is that, if the no-man's-land between grammar and logic belongs to psychology, it belongs with all the more reason to theology—and to prayer, or meditation. For the *Cloud*-author, the unknowing of God is an encounter with the limits of language in the form of a nonsense word produced by your own voice. Far from an escape from language, this encounter with the syllable-word is rather what Giorgio Agamben has called, in another context, "an experience which is undergone only within language, an *experimentum linguae* in the true meaning of the words, in which what is experienced is language itself."⁷⁶

But one characteristic of the *litil worde* remains unaccounted for: its familiarity. If the prayer procedure consists in stripping a word like *loue* of its *sensus* by means of repetition, why not simply start with a word to which no *sensus* is attached? If the particular word to be used is really a matter of indifference, as has been argued here, why not use a made-up or foreign word? Why does the

Cloud-author restrict himself to the examples *god*, *loue*, *synne*, and *oute*? There seem to be two possible answers to this question. The first is that something different happens when you hear a familiar word made meaningless by repetition than when you hear an unknown word. When a familiar word is stripped in this way of its meaning, it does not become a simply unknown word. Rather, it remains a known word even as your knowledge of it is withdrawn. What emerges is a ludicrousness, the overwhelming improbability that this utterance could be the same one you are familiar with, even as you have every reason to believe that it is. This ludicrousness occurs in the state of knowing that you know but not knowing. The "unknowing" of the *Cloud* is just this experience of language that occurs in the withdrawal of sense in repetition. In other words, the already known word would be possessed of a force which an unknown word is not: its familiarity gives rise to an incomprehension that is not merely a fact but a problem. Instead of sliding past the ears, the word sticks. Undeniably familiar, and yet wrenched from its recognizability by repetition, such a word cannot be a matter of indifference. It presses itself upon you, compelling the mind to take notice of its own inability to conceive.

I should probably allow to pass unmentioned the second reason that these particular examples might have been chosen, for as a reading it is strictly fanciful. This is that they might constitute a cipher, so that their choice would be neither purely arbitrary nor purely motivated but both at once. For it can be observed that, read as an acronym, anagrammatically, the words *god*, *loue*, *synne*, and *oute* resolve themselves into the word *glos*. And what else has the *Cloud*-author been saying all along than that the point of the *werk* is not at all to talk yourself into an "affective state" appropriate to contemplation of an exalted being outside you (god, love) or to your own lowly condition before such a being (sin, help), but is rather a matter of praying, as St. Paul says, "in gloss."[77] What he teaches is a technique, consisting in a very particular kind of glossolalia, designed to reveal to the mind its groundlessness, objectlessness, and finally nonexistence.[78]

And even if such a thing is not mere fancy, even if the *Cloud*-author really did wish to transmit the word *glos* in code, as a *mot sous les mots*, would not tact demand that the decipherers of such a message refrain from publicizing it? But just to have written about the *Cloud* at all, and especially in a scholarly context, is already to have defied the explicit instruction that is the very first thing its author sets down: to refrain from sharing its contents with anyone except the most devoted and accomplished contemplatives, among whose number there is no reason to think that the present book's readers—let alone its author—should be included. It is also, insofar as it proceeds by citation and paraphrase, to violate his second instruction, that the treatise be read only "al ouer," in its entirety: for, like the *litil worde* itself, he says that the treatise is to be kept whole. On the other hand, it could be that publicity and fragmentation amount to just another means by which the purposes of the *Cloud*'s occluded wholeness can be accomplished. The reason that its author cites for enjoining his readers to spend the time necessary to "rede it, speke it, write it, or here it, al ouer" (read it, speak it, write it, or hear it in its entirety) is that

> parauenture þer is som mater þer-in, in þe beginnyng or in þe middel, þe whiche is hanging & not fully declared þer it stondeþ; and ʒif it be not þere, it is sone after, or elles in þe ende. Wherefore, ʒif a man saw o mater & not anoþer, parauenture he miʒt liʒtly be led into errour.⁷⁹

> [perhaps there is some matter in it, in the beginning or in the middle, that is suspended and not fully declared in the place where it stands; and if it is not there, it is soon after, or else in the end. Wherefore, if a man saw one matter and not another, perhaps he might lightly be led into error.]

For what is this invocation of an ostensible danger if not a precise description of the very *werk* of unknowing itself, in which a certain linguistic "matter"—"suspended," "not fully declared where it stands"—causes you to be "lightly led into error"? In other words, what the *Cloud*-author seems to warn against is in fact nothing else than the work of unknowing itself.

This *mater* that leads you into the desert of sense, where you can do the *werk* of wrestling with the "nowhere and the nothing," is the *materia* of *vox*, the syllabic form that makes up every word and that, in being indistinguishable from it, also destroys it. This empty shell, which Augustine called *vocabulum emortuum*—the dead word, the word in its kenotic form, the *glos*—does not disappear when it is decrypted. Decryption is only a means by which it pursues its own kenosis. For the matter of the *Cloud* is self-secret; it is self-secrecy itself. That is why, finally, it makes no difference whether it is revealed here—or whether there is anything in fact to reveal. The *glos* is interminable. It is in this sense, and this sense alone, that the *Cloud of Unknowing* should be considered literature; it is in this sense alone that reading it would already constitute the *werk* in which it gives instruction. And what this sense might be is nowhere made clearer, perhaps, than in *St. Erkenwald*.

CHAPTER FOUR

ST. ERKENWALD ON THE *CARACTER*

There are texts that set traps for their readers. They include within themselves, allegorically, their every possible reading, so that just when you think you have found an exterior vantage point from which to apprehend them, you find yourself right back where you started: caught within their grasp. The most maddening thing about them is that the harder you struggle—the more readerly force you apply to them—the tighter they grip you. No such work is more exemplary of its kind, of course, than "The Turn of the Screw." As Henry James said of his little ghost story, it is not simply "a trap for the unwary" but, still more, "a piece of ingenuity . . . an *amusette* to catch those not easily caught . . . the jaded, the disillusioned, the fastidious."[1] Submitting its readers to a hermeneutic ordeal, to the inescapable allegories of its own interpretation, a work of this kind leaves no room for anything but a literal reading. For all that remains apprehensible in it is the mere letters that make it up. We call such a text a work of literature.

Suppose that *St. Erkenwald*—an anonymous, late fourteenth-century Middle English poem of 352 lines—is such a work, that it answers to the description of literature. The point would seem to be self-evident: it is an imaginative and indeed fanciful tale about the discovery of a corpse that has been mysteriously preserved for countless centuries; it consists of sophisticated alliterative verse, disposed according to an intricate formal system; it circulates, in the present day, alongside works to which no one would think of denying the name of literature. Still, it is likely that to set out to distinguish literature from other sorts of text is a fool's errand at best. An example of the difficulties involved is near to hand: the *Cloud of Unknowing*, a contemplative treatise and manual of prayer, is now regularly treated as though it called for analysis on literary lines, and on no others. This seems to be a misunderstanding, as I tried to establish in the preceding chapter. With *Erkenwald* the situation is exactly the inverse. Despite its apparently uncontroversial status as a work of literature, it is all but invariably treated by literary critics as though it were a work of historiography or pseudo-historiography; or as a bit of evidence for their own work of historiography; or again as a theological treatise or political pamphlet in the guise of a poem. It may well be all of these things. But if the poem proves to have backed its readers into the corner of treating it as such—if it can be shown to have anticipated its various scholarly interpretations allegorically—a suspicion might arise that its aims are less transparent than has sometimes been maintained. In that case, its propounding of what critics have not hesitated to call a "propagandist message" might after all show itself to be only a single move in a rather more complicated game. And if *Erkenwald* is in fact an *amusette* of this type, there might also be good reason to suspect that it will end, in Jamesian fashion, by pointing its readers back to the level of the letter itself.

The events narrated in the poem can be summarized without difficulty. While excavating St. Paul's cathedral, workmen come across a crypt covered in indecipherable inscriptions. Scholars are called in, but even they cannot make heads or tails of what is written there. The crypt is opened, and within it is found a body in a miraculous state of preservation. Scholarship proves of no more help now than it did before. Experts and archives are consulted, but nothing can be discovered about the dead man: not his name, not the meaning of the inscriptions on his tomb, and not how long he has been lying there. A great clamor arises among the populace. The bishop, Erkenwald, is summoned. Seeing that erudition will be fruitless, Erkenwald resorts to prayer and invocation, which seem to finally clear things up: the Holy Spirit intervenes, speaking through the corpse to explain the circumstances of the dead man's death and preservation. The voice reveals that, in life, the ventriloquized corpse belonged to a judge. This judge lived a spotless life, but he did so before the time of Christ, and thus his soul is now stuck in hell merely because he happens never to have been baptized. Erkenwald is moved to a tearful pity by this story. He expresses the wish that it might be possible to baptize the man, and in the process of expressing this wish he cites the baptismal formula that he would say if he were to conduct the rite. One of his tears, meanwhile, chances to fall on the corpse. Between this accidental sprinkling with water and the conditional expression of the formula, a baptism actually occurs. The dead man's soul is sucked up to heaven and the corpse instantaneously decomposes. The populace erupts in another clamor, and the poem ends with a celebratory ringing of bells.

As should be clear from this summary, everything that occurs in the poem does so because of an initial encounter with a set of unintelligible inscriptions. The work as a whole is about this encounter and its aftereffects, about what is generated by the inability to read. Neither is this inability ever overcome. The poem's celebratory ending is a kind of ostentatious diversionary tactic, a fanfare drawing attention away from the fact that it has avoided answering the very questions it raised. For although the spirit voice says many things about the circumstances of the life and death of the corpse through which it is speaking, it never resolves the mysteries that first prompted the wonder of the people: when exactly the man it belonged to was alive remains a cipher, as does his name; and so, most crucially of all, does the meaning of the inscriptions.[2] This point has been regularly, and inexplicably, overlooked.[3] It is, however, the fundamental gesture of the poem: to put forward certain ciphers as the engine of its plot, and to preserve these ciphers in a state of permanent indecipherability.

The failures of reading that provide the material of the poem can be divided into four types: illiterate, textual, historicist, and ventriloquistic. The crowd cannot understand the inscriptions at all; the clerks bring their linguistic knowledge to bear on them without success; consultation with the archive proves fruitless; even the miraculous intervention of a spirit voice fails to clear anything up. What is curious about scholarly readers of the poem is that they have not seen, in these failures, so many mirrors of their own attempts to make sense of the poem. Consider the four varieties of misreading described in the poem in the light of the poem's own reception. Most people of course simply do not read *Erkenwald* at all, or make no public interpretation of it if they do. Like the populace before the inscriptions, they make nothing of it whatsoever (though, unlike the crowd in the poem, thus far no hue and cry seems ever to have gone up from them). So much for the illiterate reading. Somewhat more can be said about the second type of failure to read, the one that proceeds by textual analysis. An early generation of scholarly readers tried to determine, on philological grounds, exactly the same things about the author of the poem that those in the poem want to know about the dead man—his name, floruit, and identity—and they did so precisely by attempting to decipher certain supposed anagrams and quasi-illegible ornamental inscriptions. Nothing much ever came of these inquiries.[4] The ornamental inscriptions are no longer mentioned in polite company. The author of the poem is still nameless; there has never been a consensus about when exactly he wrote it; and it remains a matter of controversy whether he also wrote the better known poems of MS Cotton Nero A.x. (*Sir Gawain and the Green Knight, Pearl,* and so forth).[5]

By far the majority of published accounts of the poem fall under the third variety of failed readings that it itself allegorizes, the historicist.[6] Just as the clerks in the poem consult the archive in order to try to clear up the mystery of the corpse, so modern readers try to explain it by reference to the debates and historical events with which it was contemporary. There has even been some discussion of whether the events it recounts actually happened.[7] And for a number of decades now scholars have been preoccupied chiefly with the "orthodoxy" of a writer about whom nothing at all is known. Some of the poem's most prominent interpreters have argued that the baptismal theology to which he subscribes is in accordance with the official position of the church and stands as a rebuke to the heterodox tendencies of his time.[8] Their work has shed much light on the poem's relations to the time and place of its composition. But it has done so by turning away from what is, it would have seemed, the central concern of the poem. For if *Erkenwald* is about anything, it is about the unaccountable presence, in the present moment, of something long expired but still unnervingly fresh, belonging neither to this time nor to any other that can be identified. And this noncontemporaneity is that of an extrahistorical doxa. The "just pagan judge" persisting as an uncorrupted corpse: what is this but a figure of the law insofar as it is neither orthodox nor heterodox but outmoded, incommensurable, inoperative, even as it remains, immaculately preserved, within the very foundations of the church itself—and indeed, by the "wonder" of the man's salvation, proves itself not entirely exterior to the present law. To proceed as though a poem organized around such a figure can be explicated by means of reference to the law in effect at its own historical moment is thus to ignore, in some measure, the poem's own indications about how it should be read. Or rather, to the extent that it proceeds in a manner that leads directly away from the central figure of the poem, such a reading exactly rehearses the efforts of those scholars depicted in the poem itself, poring over archival records to no avail.

But the real problem with the discussion of the supposed historico-theological commitments of the *Erkenwald*-poet is that it has remained both insufficiently historical and insufficiently theological. For it is not the case that what was at stake in medieval baptismal theology was only the tension between the official teaching of the church and dissent from that teaching. To the contrary, there were matters of doctrine that remained basically unthinkable to the theologians who took them up. There were gaps and ciphers in strictly orthodox baptismal theology, inconceivabilities that were transmitted in the form not of articles of faith but of thought experiments. And it is exactly these perplexities that *Erkenwald* takes up. This, in any case, is what I suggest in this chapter: not that *Erkenwald* sides with one faction as over against another in a controversy raging in the time of its composition, but rather that it forms itself around the abyss of an unknowing that was never reduced over the course of the Middle Ages and indeed has never since been. To be sure, it is necessary to read the poem alongside baptismal theological treatises: but not because they provide a historical reference point by which a literary text can be made more fully legible. It is necessary because, as the *Erkenwald*-poet well knew, baptismal theology itself already shelters and transmits a form of literature, the very form of literature that *Erkenwald* itself consists in.

It is now possible to turn finally to the fourth kind of reading of the poem, or of failure to read it: the ventriloquizing interpretation. Bishop Erkenwald, before the mysterious tomb, sets aside illiterate ignorance, textual interpretation, and historical research. He calls upon the mute corpse to speak; he relies on invocation. If the poem ever tricks anyone into offering an interpretation that would correspond to the Bishop's, that interpretation could be recognized by the way it would force the poem to speak, in a voice not its own, words it has never yet said. It would force it finally to give up its secrets. But to take seriously the allegory of reading that the poem elaborates is to be forewarned against anything that passes itself off as a solution. If any such reading is ever offered, the poem already makes clear that it will prove the worst failure of all: its fanfare will do no more than conceal, imperfectly, the fact that despite everything all of the poem's primary obscurities remain intact.

This is the time to say that this chapter claims to offer a solution to *Erkenwald*. It is also the time to insist that a solution is in fact what it demands. For if the poem has managed to conceal the fact that it is a riddle, this is simply part of its design. As D. Vance Smith has made plain, it is, through and through, a "cryptic writing," or enigma.⁹ The riddle is posed, first of all, on the level of form. The poem is structured according to certain numerical patterns, some of which are more immediately evident than others.¹⁰ Among the various principles that determine its formal disposition, one is the most conspicuous by far. As it appears in the single manuscript in which it survives, the poem is divided into two exactly even halves. The two halves are separated by a break, and each begins with a rubricated capital. It is not even necessary to read a single word of the poem to know that it disposes itself into two equal parts, maintaining both a separation and a correspondence between them. But the question that arises, once the poem begins to be read, is what this jointing accomplishes: what the subject matter of the first half of the poem has to do with that of the second. That is, what the indecipherable inscriptions that appear at the beginning have to do with the improbable baptism that takes place at the end. This is the most fundamental interpretative question of the poem, the question of the relation between illegibility and baptism. Nonetheless, it has never truly been taken up, let alone answered.

The argument of this chapter is as follows. The overall operation of the poem is to suture the problem of unreadable inscriptions with the problem of a certain unresolved question of baptismal theology. What is produced by this operation is neither political opinion nor theological argumentation but a certain kind of thought experiment: a riddle. Everything necessary to the solution of the riddle is given in the poem. The solution is a single word, a word that appears nowhere in the poem, even as it is the only thing that appears. For just as a riddle is constituted by the solution of which it is the enigmatization, *Erkenwald* is generated from a cryptonym, an occluded ornament that is its kernel.¹¹

This, in short, is the riddle of *Erkenwald*: *I am an indecipherable inscription. I am what remains of baptism. I am the scar that joins them. I am the matter of this poem. Say what I am called.*

VIGURES FULLE VERRAY

Masons are excavating the foundations of what was once a pagan temple, called in ancient times by the (undisclosed) name of the devil to whom it was consecrated, and is now St. Paul's cathedral. In the process of digging, they come across a marble tomb, covered in gargoyles. The slab of marble that seals the tomb shut is ornamented with certain "bryȝt golde lettres" that provoke the wonder of the masons, because:

> Roynyshe were þe resones þat þer on row stoden.
> Fulle verray were þe vigures þer auisyde hom mony,
> Bot alle muset hit to mouthe and quat hit mene shulde:
> Mony clerkes in þat clos wyt crownes ful brode

Þer besiet hom a-boute no3t to brynge hom in wordes.
Quen tithynges token to þe þoun of þe toumbe wonder
Mony hundrid hende men highide þider sone.¹²

[The letterforms that stood there in a row were mysterious.
As many confirmed, the figures were entirely distinct.
But everyone was baffled as to how to pronounce it and what it might mean.
Many scholars in that enclosure, with their shaved heads,
Busied themselves to no avail to make words out of them.
As soon as the rumor of the marvelous tomb spread through the town
Many hundreds of people hastened there.]

The passage is thornier than my modernization suggests. It is a description of certain *resounes*, that is, "letters" or "letterforms"—or, perhaps, "meanings," or even "resoundings." These *resounes* appear on the tomb, lined up in a row, and they are *roynyshe*: "rough," "mysterious," or even (perhaps) "runic." What this mysteriousness consists in appears to be that the *vigures*—which means "letterforms" or "characters," and seems to refer to the same thing as the *resounes* just mentioned—are not worn away or otherwise difficult to make out but entirely distinct (*fulle verray*), and yet they present a problem for those who try to read them. Everyone is uncertain about (*muset*) how to pronounce it (the antecedent of this "it" is by no means clear) and about its meaning, or again about what it commemorates or mourns (*quat hit mene shulde*). Many learned men exert themselves to no avail in their efforts to discern words amid the inscriptions—or, alternatively, to find anything at all to say about them (*to brynge hom in wordes*).

But if the inconsistencies and ambiguities of syntax and diction that multiply here replicate the mysteriousness of the inscriptions they describe, there does seem nonetheless to be a way of understanding the passage that hangs together better than others, and I have modernized accordingly. What is established in these lines appears to be that the ornamentation of the tomb is made up of letterforms, or quasi-letterforms. These forms are clearly discernible—the designs would be susceptible of exact reproduction—but they do not allow themselves to be pronounced or understood, that is, they cannot be put together into words. Finally, although they do not communicate anything in particular to the scholars who read them, as such they are far from a matter of indifference. They cause those who study them to "muse," that is, be wonderstruck, and they produce a commotion among the populace. It is this commotion that will lead, in short order, to the opening of the tomb, the summoning of the bishop, and thereby to the poem's dénouement: the baptism of the dead man. In other words, these mysterious inscriptions are not only mute and incomprehensible but also, and for that very reason, efficacious—and what they put in motion is the machinery of the poem as a whole.

Accordingly, in order to make an approach to the poem it is necessary to consider the nature and status of these inscriptions. What, exactly, are they? To answer this question, the presence in the poem of these inscriptions must be restored to the *roynyshe* status that it has for the readers within the poem. It does not suffice to proceed as though they were merely an instance, in a poetic context, of a kind of thing that could also be imagined or known to have existed in some extraliterary reality; or to treat them as an indifferent contrivance seized upon by the *Erkenwald*-poet for the purposes of his "plot"; or to assimilate them, under the heading "literary motif," to other unreadable inscriptions in works of fancy or hagiography. It must be determined whether they have their own consistency as such, that is, as they are described and function in *Erkenwald* itself. Fortunately, the account given of them in the poem is nothing if not precise. In fact, it will be seen to attain to the status of a technical definition. The *roynyshe resounes* answer to the following description: unpronounceable and unrecognizable letterforms, of uncertain provenance and of no discernible meaning, that cause things to happen. And once this description is allowed to emerge in its precision, the nature and status of the inscriptions actually turns out to be self-evident. They are recognizable instances of something that is by no means unfamiliar.

In the course of their major study of a certain neglected form of medieval writing called by various names—*figura*, *signum*, *sigillum*, *nota*, and especially *caracter*—Benoît Grévin and Julien Véronèse undertake to define the object of their research. Their analysis leads them to offer the following account:

> *Character* (or *karacter*) refers to signs written or engraved superficially (thus in two dimensions), which should not or cannot be spoken aloud. . . . They are possessed of an intrinsic efficacy that does not pass through speech; they are thus the visual equivalents of prayers, conjurations, and other exorcisms. As for the question of their signification for the initiated, it remains open . . . these "caracters" are the incarnation of a millennial knowledge . . . whose efficacy does not pass through the understanding of its contemporaries . . . their power is held to be all the greater the further they are removed from any apparent signification.[13]

These *caracteres* were inscribed on the ground, on various parts of the body, on parchment or sheets of metal, on talismans to be worn (for example) around the neck, and in manuscripts of various kinds. These marks can take quite distinct forms: some resemble astrological signs or geometric patterns, others illegible signatures, others still letterforms in known or unknown languages. Their use was magical, ritual, or practical: for protection, to gain knowledge, or to bring about certain events. They were widespread in the Middle Ages—and, indeed, long before and after. It is not possible to point to their earliest appearance in Europe, but certainly by the end of antiquity they were in common use throughout the Mediterranean world.[14] What these various sorts of things have in common, such that they all answer to the description of *caracteres* as formulated by Grévin and Véronèse, is that they are indeterminately foreign or ancient signs that operate without signifying, or indeed that operate insofar as they do not signify.

It is their appearance in the so-called *ars notoria* that has brought *caracteres* the most attention in recent decades. This is, to simplify wildly, an occult technique for learning the seven liberal arts in which *nota ineffabilis* are used in rites whose performance allows a student to acquire disciplinary knowledge by magical means.[15] As they do in most other contexts, the *caracteres* seem to work here by allowing their operator to enlist the services of various non-embodied beings. But despite their inescapable connection with theurgy and, still more, necromancy, such practices were by no means confined to the shadowy corners of the medieval world. *Caracteres* survive in documents otherwise composed in Hebrew, Arabic, Greek, and Latin, apart from the various vernaculars. These manuscripts belong to a great variety of disciplines: as Linda Voigts emphasizes, "carecters are commonly found in late-medieval English texts on magic, alchemy, weights and measurements, astronomy and astrology, and medical remedies."[16] And they survive outside of manuscripts as well, on a variety of objects, talismans above all.[17] They are discussed, in the Latin tradition alone, by Augustine, Isidore, Gratian, Bacon, Aquinas, and Oresme, among very many others. As for English literature in the decades of *Erkenwald*'s composition, it is worth recalling in this connection the *ymages* of Chaucer's physician, the so-called Pentangle of Solomon that features so prominently in *Sir Gawain and the Green Knight*, and the multiple mentions of *caracteres* by that very name in Gower and Lydgate.[18]

None of which is of course to say that medieval *caracteres* somehow eluded the taint of superstition and illicit magic. Augustine fulminates against their use, and his example was by no means ignored: the list just given of thinkers who discuss *caracteres* is, in fact, effectively a list of those who condemned them.[19] Still, conclusions should not be drawn too hastily from this fact. The frequency with which it is denounced only demonstrates the resilience of a practice; the inclusion, for example, of a stricture against the use of *caracteres* in the Condemnations of 1277 indicates nothing so much as that the question of the *caracter* was a live one in the thirteenth-century university.[20] And indeed the ritual inscription of *caracteres* was by no means only a residue of pre-Christian belief, nor a folk as opposed to elite practice. It was part of a complex of practices, no less vocal than graphic, from which it cannot be dissociated: namely, those practices in which incantation and inscription are carried out ritually in order to produce effects in the world.[21]

Verbal charms, divination, prayer, oaths: all of these operate on the basis of *virtus verborum*, the power of words. If the recitation of the first lines of the Gospel of John, or indeed its inscription and use as a talisman, seems different than the inscription of an unknown but presumably devilish mark, the difference is not always easy to locate. A common type of charm for epilepsy, for instance, incorporates the names of the three Magi and the mysterious, quasi-biblical word *ananizapta*, sometimes along with unpronounceable sequences of letters on the order of *pgcpevoxagz*.[22] Here, and elsewhere, the difference between magical *caracteres* and everyday letterforms is not always easy to determine, as in a medical recipe that calls for the sequence "✠ . q . p . x . t . g . y . h ." to be marked on an egg as part of a ritual to see whether someone will live or die.[23] As for charms that allow themselves to be spoken aloud, they are frequently nonsensical,[24] on the order of *abracadabra*: "hon con non ton ron yon zon," to restore lost money;[25] "fliberty, gibberty, flashy flum" for the same purpose;[26] "Amara. tum. taturi. postos. sicalos. sicaluri. / Ely. poli. caritas. polyly. pilinique. linarras," to cure mania;[27] and so forth.[28] The use of such *voces magicae* or *onomata barbara* is impossible to dissociate, as illicit, from such licit activities as making the sign of the cross, taking a juridical oath, and the various rites performed by priests—or bishops. Stephen Wilson makes this point forcefully:

> Though historians, like anthropologists and others, have discriminated clearly between religion and magic in this sphere, and although there are valid distinctions to make between the established official ritual of the Churches and the informal rites of magic, there was in practice an enormous overlap between the two. The ritual of the Catholic Church in particular was brought into play by the clergy to ensure fertility, well-being and health, while magical practitioners used Christian formulae and prayers, and objects and substances blessed by the clergy.[29]

The example of "Amara. tum. taturi. postos. sicalos. sicaluri," in all its hieratic meaninglessness, points emphatically toward the fact that the rites of the church themselves, carried out in a language that would remain a cipher for the majority of people, not excluding the priests administering them, might easily participate in the magic of the incomprehensible.

It is thus no longer possible to avoid giving the *resounes* carved on the tomb in *Erkenwald* their proper name, which is *caracteres*. Indeed, the poet already calls them *vigures*, that is, *figurae*: one of the more common synonyms of *caracter*. They are *roynyshe*, an adjective that points toward the runic alphabets of Northern Europe, which from the earliest times were used as *caracteres* for theurgic purposes, and have of course continued to be used for such purposes ever since.[30] They are discovered on a remnant of a temple that, it is said, used to bear the name of a certain unnamed devil.[31] Most of all, they answer—point for point—to the description given by Grévin and Véronèse: indeterminately foreign or ancient signs that operate without signifying—that operate insofar as they do not signify.

But to give the inscrutable inscriptions in *Erkenwald* the name *caracter*, thereby restoring them to their association with a whole complex of linguistic practices, is not to have "identified" them in the way that you might track down the historical bearer of an obscure proper name. What is important here is not that a cultural practice can be seen to have left traces in a literary context but rather that by including these *caracteres* the poem opens itself to a very particular tradition of theorization. For *caracteres* were not just used ritually by various sorts of people, not just condemned by various others, not just used and condemned by the very same people, though all of this is true. They also served another purpose.

Although the medieval thinkers who turned their attention to the *caracteres* did so, for the most part, in order to distinguish their use from that of licit recourse to the power of words (prayer, for example), they also emerged as an object of interest for another reason. They were studied and speculated about in their own right, over and above the question of whether their use was licit or otherwise. This was because, as the schoolmen well saw, they have properties that allow them to serve as an instructive limit-case in reflections on the sign. For the *caracter* seems to be a kind of sign, and yet it is nothing but a configuration of empty marks, of no discernible signification. It would thus seem possible for there to be a sign that does not signify—which is, on its face, absurd. The paradoxical existence of a sign that does not signify demanded further attention. And it did so in one particular connection especially. The *caracter* would seem to belong to a certain important class of signs, those whose utterance or inscription causes something to happen: that is, performatives. To inscribe a *caracter* is to cure an illness, or acquire knowledge by occult means, or curse an enemy, or whatever it might be. The existence of the *caracter* appears to demonstrate not only that a sign can be devoid of sense, but that nonsense can produce effects. But if linguistic efficacy does not depend on linguistic sense, then the efficacy of meaningful signs as well might turn out to have nothing to do with their meaning. Even an intelligible word might cause things to happen that have no relation to what it names or asks for or commands; and even if it has an effect that seems related to the meaning of the sign, this correspondence might be pure happenstance. The possibility is unsettling, to say the least.

The dominant explanation of the operation of the *caracteres* adopted by the schoolmen managed to reduce this difficulty to almost nothing. According to this model, *caracteres* work because, although one might oneself happen not to know what meaning is invested in them, they are in fact written in a language understood by demons. Their efficacy depends entirely on convention, exactly like that of any other sign: just as humans have agreed among themselves, arbitrarily, that the word *homo* will pick out the rational and mortal animal, so likewise have they agreed with demons that this particular *caracter* will be the name, as it were, of that particular demon or magical operation. It is for this reason that Nicolas Weill-Parot has called the use of such signs *magie destinative*, addressative magic: the seemingly incomprehensible marks are in fact addressed to demons (or angels), who understand them.[32] Thus, according to this model, the *caracteres* are not nonsensical after all: they have been "imposed to signify" some particular thing. This position, for which the authority was no less than Augustine, was adopted by a succession of prominent thinkers.[33] But a second theory was also in circulation.

According to this second theory, *caracteres* do not operate because of any supposed agreement with demons but simply because of a natural force that inheres in them. That is, the very figure itself, thanks solely to its configuration, brings about effects in the world. Without any meaning's having been encoded in it, in accordance solely with the properties of things, the *caracter* itself will make things happen. Béatrice Delaurenti has demonstrated that the idea that words have a natural rather than merely conventional force did not subsist merely in the margins of the Augustinian tradition but in fact constituted a vital and long-standing countertradition.[34] This "naturalist" position, associated with the name of al-Kindi and developed notably by Roger Bacon, came into conflict with the "conventionalist" position in the middle of the thirteenth century and was more or less defeated by it; but its consistency, and attraction, should not be underestimated.[35] Although the importance of this position has sometimes been downplayed, Delaurenti's work has allowed for what she calls a parenthesis of naturalist thinking from 1230–1370 to return to view, and it is again possible to appreciate the viability in the thirteenth and fourteenth centuries of considering performative signs as producing effects in the world by virtue of their physical qualities rather than by arbitrarily signifying. Needless to say, this model holds the attraction, in the present day, of dispensing with the role played by demons—a type of being now rarely discussed by theorists of language. But the question that is at stake in the medieval discussion of demonic or natural operation is not at all whether demons exist but rather whether a mind (of whatever sort, embodied or otherwise) needs to cognize an inscription in order for that inscription to carry out its work. The importance of the naturalist school of thought, for the purposes of our inquiry, is that it represents a sophisticated and long-standing elaboration of a theory according to which meaningless signs can be said to operate without ceasing to be meaningless.

It is these discussions that *Erkenwald* resumes in its depiction of the effects of an encounter with meaningless signs. Without their inscrutability being in any way reduced, the *roynyshe resounes* set in motion a whole series of events. And it is no accident that this series culminates in a baptism. For the scholastic inquiries into the relation between efficacy and signification were undertaken in one field in particular: that of sacramental theology.

SIGNUM EFFICAX

Here is what occurs in the second half of the poem: Erkenwald, the Bishop, having been called in to deal with the corpse in its *caracter*-covered tomb, abandons scholarship and addresses the dead man directly. He performs a kind of invocation or conjuration, pronouncing the name of Jesus in such a way as to compel the body to give up its secrets. The invocation accomplishes what it is meant to do: the corpse begins to speak, or rather to "drive out words." For it speaks not with its own voice, that is, not with the voice of the man it once belonged to, but with that of "sum goste" (a certain spirit) that lends it life:[36]

> "Bisshop," quoþ þis ilke body, "þi bode is me dere.
> I may not bot boghe to þi bone for bothe myne eghen;
> To þe name þat þou neuenyd has and nournet me after
> Al heuen and helle heldes to and erthe bitwene."[37]

> ["Bishop," said this same body, "I respect your command.
> I can only obey your injunction, even if it means losing both my eyes;
> The name that you have named and in which you have entreated me
> Is obeyed by all heaven and hell, and by the earth between."]

The hermeneutic practice enacted by the Bishop operates by means of the *virtus verborum*. It is the force of a certain kind of speaking, the invocation of a name, that causes the corpse to speak. This is the same force that has made the church in which all of this is taking place into a church in the first place: at the beginning of the poem, it is said that long ago Augustine of Canterbury washed the pagan temples of England clean by means of the purifying name of Christ, and transformed them into churches by changing the names to which they were dedicated, Jupiter and Juno giving way to Jesus or James.[38] And it is also the same force whose absence is responsible for the unenviable situation of the corpse that has just begun to speak.

The explanation of the marvel, as elicited by Erkenwald's conjuration, is that it is a matter of christening. As the voice explains, the soul that once animated the corpse is stuck in hell, and this despite the fact that the dead man led an honorable and indeed exemplary life. It is stuck there solely because he lived before the coming of Christ, and thus died without ever having heard the gospel. But it is not a matter merely of his being unfamiliar with the events of salvation history and the doctrines of the church, of course; it is a question of a certain rite, baptism, which washes away sin:

> "ȝe were entouchid wyt his tethe and toke in þe glotte
> Bot mendyd wyt a medecyn ȝe are made for to lyuye
> Þat is, fulloght in fonte wyt faitheful bileue,
> And þat han we myste alle merciles, myselfe and my soule."[39]

> ["You were poisoned by [Adam's] teeth and caught up in that filth,
> But, healed by a medicine, you are made to live:
> Namely, the medicine of baptism in the font with faithful belief,
> Of which we—myself and my soul—have been mercilessly deprived."]

All that is preventing the soul from being in heaven is that a certain rite has never been performed, a rite that consists in the recitation of a verbal formula (*ego te baptizo*, etc.) and the performance of a number of ritual gestures (washing, insufflation). This rite will soon be performed, in slapstick form, when Bishop Erkenwald inadvertently brings about the soul's deliverance from hell. In short, the culminating moment of the poem should not be considered in isolation, for it resumes a preoccupation with efficacious linguistic operations that has been in force in the poem from its very beginning. Or, to put a finer point on it, the baptism of the corpse is set up as the mirror image of the *caracteres* whose inscrutability brings it about. The poem as a whole is a medium in which these two performative linguistic elements are placed side by side.

One might imagine that to consider baptism in terms of necromancy would be to misunderstand sacramental theology altogether. A line would have to be maintained between the magical operations of the *caracteres* and the religious operations of baptism. But it is anyone's guess where this line should be drawn. As we have seen, there was in practice a continuity between licit acts, vocalizations, and inscriptions and their illicit counterparts. Baptism, which as Wilson emphasizes was a "genuinely popular sacrament," was no exception to this rule.⁴⁰ Neither was it in practice alone that the *caracter* and the sacrament of baptism were linked together in the Middle Ages. They were linked theoretically as well, that is, within the realm of scholastic thought. The schoolmen who discuss the sacraments not infrequently make explicit reference to *caracteres*. Indeed, Irène Rosier-Catach has shown how the two were sometimes treated as analogous, notably by William of Auvergne and John Duns Scotus; as she points out, it was in fact "in the context of a reflection on magical signs and practices" that one of the main theories accounting for the operation of the sacraments was elaborated.⁴¹

What allows the sacraments to be considered in the light of *caracteres* is that both were said to be signs. Medieval sacramental theology, as it developed in the aftermath of the eleventh-century eucharistic controversy inflamed by Berengar of Tours, was grounded in the Boethian and Augustinian semiotic doctrines that have been examined throughout this book.⁴² Berengar, attempting to explain how it could be that what looked like a piece of bread was in fact the body of Christ, took recourse to Augustine's definition of the sign as something that brings itself into the senses and something else into the intelligence. Although the senses encounter nothing else than bread, he reasoned, the intelligence understands something beyond that sensation, namely, the body of Christ. Thus, the bread should be understood not as the actual body of Christ but as merely a sign of that body. What this crucial figure in the development of sacramental theology was taking up was the problem of the illegibility of the Eucharist: the way that the body of Christ is nowhere to be seen in the piece of bread on the altar. His proposal is an attempt at reducing this difficulty, of course, by making Christ precisely readable there; but it should be emphasized that the signs Berengar had in mind when he assigned the bread to their number were specifically *roynyshe* signs. The Eucharist would effect a connection with God, he proposed, just as the performative inscription of a rune effects a connection with God. Indeed, the entire Berengarian theory of the sacrament is developed around the quasi-theurgical idea that the bread is nothing else than a "*caracter* of Christ."[43]

Berengar was of course forced to recant. According to the doctrine of transubstantiation, the bread is not merely a sign of Christ's flesh but also becomes that very flesh itself. Nonetheless his influence was enormous, and not only because he provided an occasion for the orthodox view to define itself in opposition to his proposal. By importing the terminology of the linguistic sciences into sacramental theology, Berengar determined the form that would be taken by all subsequent treatments of the question. In the wake of Berengar's discussion of the sacrament as a sign, other thinkers followed suit. Among them was Peter Lombard, in whose *Sentences*—the basic textbook of medieval theology—the sacrament is also defined as a sign in the Augustinian sense, making Berengar's innovation the common ground of sacramental theology for centuries to come. Indeed, so entwined did sacramental theology become with the theory of signification in the Middle Ages that it would be difficult to separate them; everywhere there are what Rosier-Catach calls "explicit connections, made by the theologians themselves, between the signifying force of language and the sanctifying force of the sacrament."[44]

But if baptism and the other sacraments are signs, nonetheless they also seem to differ from other signs in ways that ask to be specified. Over the course of the centuries after Berengar, two characteristics of the sacramental sign emerged as distinctive: unlike other signs, it *resembles* and *produces* what it signifies.[45] In the first place, baptism, for example, takes place in a washing with water that is essentially similar to the washing away of sin that is signified in the rite. In this, it is unlike the word *homo*, which is a sign for the human being even though it bears no resemblance to it. Secondly, the sacramental sign is not only significative but also efficacious. In the formula adopted by the schoolmen, *id efficit quod figurat*: it produces or causes what it signifies. To say "human" is not to make anything happen, but to say "I baptize you in the name of the Father, etc." is to cause a baptism to take place. A sacramental sign is one possessed of a performative force.

But it remained a matter of dispute just how the efficacy of the sacraments was to be understood. The positions adopted were those already seen in the case of *caracteres*. Some theologians argued that the sacramental sign operates because of convention, in this case agreement not with demons but with God: the rite of baptism is "imposed to signify" the washing away of sins, and thus does so. Others, less numerous and less influential, argued instead that the words and gestures of the sacramental rite have a natural or physical power rather than a conventional one. The rite, as they explained it, brings about its effects in a manner that does not depend on its being cognized—not by humans, not by angels or demons, and not by God. This is where the separability of signification and efficacy became a matter of interest and concern: in the possibility that baptism, for example, might take place in the absence of intention and understanding, meaninglessly.

The *Erkenwald*-poet leaves little doubt that anyone trying to understand his poem must take into account the theology of baptism, and modern critics have not failed to do so. The question to which the most sustained attention has been paid is that of whether the poem adopts an orthodox or heterodox position on this matter. A consensus has arisen—quite rightly—that the idea (at one time seriously entertained) that the poem is aligned with "Pelagian" or Lollard tendencies conducing toward the rejection of the necessity of baptism for salvation is a misunderstanding. Thus, Gordon Whatley argued some decades ago that the poem in fact represents a "theologically conservative response to radical, antiecclesiastical interpretations of the Gregory/Trajan legend"; developing this argument further, Christine Chism has suggested that "the poem works to quell assertions of civic and religious agency from London Laity"; drawing on their work, David Coley has recently depicted the poem as a "poetic bulwark against the threat of Lollardy," and indeed a "thoroughly anti-Wycliffite work, a poem with an aggressive, even polemical, orthodox agenda."[46] There is a widespread sense that "the poet's aim is to take sides in one of the major theological debates of the age" and that the poem thus has a "propagandist message."[47]

This may well be. But John Bugbee is right to ask, in this connection, "whether the poet's intentions regarding Pelagianism and salvation are undecidable simply because he has left them undecided, perhaps because his real focus is elsewhere."[48] And this because the narrowly political categories of orthodoxy, dissent, and propaganda do not cover the field that is opened by the poem's undeniable investment in baptismal theology. If *Erkenwald* is to be understood in terms of medieval sacramental theology, this need not mean only situating it with respect to a hypostatized notion of the official teaching of the church and then evaluating its orthodoxy. Given that sacramental theology is inextricable from linguistic theory throughout the Middle Ages, in addressing itself to the question of baptism *Erkenwald* also opens itself to reflection on the sign more generally. The baptismal scenario that it elaborates demands to be situated in the wider context of the theory and practice of the medieval performative utterance. What I have established in the preceding pages is that both as a historical practice and as an object of theorization, baptism was part of a complex that included various kinds of linguistic entities, certain of which (*caracteres*, conjuration by the name of Jesus) appear in the poem itself and thus should be positioned formally with respect to the baptismal event described there. But this is not yet to give the real reason why the question of orthodoxy is not appropriate to *Erkenwald*. This is that certain aspects of what takes place in baptism remained entirely mysterious to the theologians who considered them. There were points of baptismal theology that were impervious to the distinction between orthodoxy and heterodoxy for the very simple reason that no one could decide how they should be settled. And it is squarely to these points of confusion that *Erkenwald* addresses itself.

That the mysteries of baptism remained unfathomed by the doctrines that formed around it can be discerned perhaps most readily in the fact that much of its theorization was carried out in the form of preposterous thought experiments. In a recent study that demonstrates the total lack of unanimity that reigned among medieval theorists of baptism, Marcia Colish has drawn attention to a number of limit-cases that exercised the schoolmen for centuries, including so-called fictive baptisms. What if—they asked themselves—a stage play is put on that involves a scene of baptism, and one actor carries out all the elements of the baptismal rite on another actor. Has the second actor been baptized?[49] The question did not come out of nowhere. Such a thing was said really to have happened, and more than once: it was attested in multiple hagiographies. Other occasions of fictive baptism were put forward as well: what if, the schoolmen proposed, an experienced priest is walking an inexperienced one through the ritual and performs it, strictly for instructional purposes, on someone serving as a kind of stand-in or body-double—is the baptism valid?[50]

Nor did they limit themselves to the question of fictive baptisms. All sorts of scenarios, of varying degrees of probability, were imagined. What if the priest performing the rite has a stutter and stammers his way through the formula of consecration?[51] Or again, what if he otherwise garbles the formula?[52] Or yet again, what if the baptizand happens to be sleepwalking or experiencing a fit of insanity when the rite is performed?[53] The examples could be multiplied. The point of these apparently absurd questions is to provide testing grounds for the various accounts of what takes place in the rite, and notably to establish what part is played by the knowledge and intention of its various participants.[54] As Caroline Walker Bynum has suggested in another context, such stage plays and sleepwalkers should be considered analogous to the desert islands and drowning babies of contemporary analytic philosophy, and indeed to the scenarios of time travel or parallel universes that are the stuff of our science fiction.[55] And the stuff, for that matter, of *St. Erkenwald*. For what is the poem but hagiographical science fiction, in this sense? Its *caracteres* and invocations and marvels consist in more and less familiar technologies that cause time to be collapsed, putrefaction to be halted, and communication to take place with alien realms. These science-fictional developments appear in the course of what is, by every indication, the demonstration of the saintliness of Bishop Erkenwald. And the machinery of this proof produces a baptismal oddity that would not have been out of place in the hagiographies from which the theologians took their thought experiments.

It is now possible to turn at last to the culminating moment of the poem. The ventriloquized corpse has explained that the only reason the soul of the just pagan judge to which it once belonged is suffering the torments of hell is that he has been unable, because of the merest accident of historical sequence, to participate in the rite of baptism. Erkenwald is moved to pity by this news. He is reduced to a state of speechlessness, in which what issues from his mouth are not words but sobs and sighs. At length he regains the faculty of articulate speech. He uses it to exclaim that he will go and fetch water, in order that he might himself, then and there, baptize the corpse. In the course of explaining what he will do once he has the water, he cites the formula that he will recite once he is in a position to perform the baptism; meanwhile, one of the tears his pity has produced happens to fall from his eye and onto the face of the corpse:

> And þe bysshop balefully bere doun his eghen
> Þat hade no space to speke so spakly he ȝoskyd,
> Til he toke hym a tome and to þe toumbe lokyd,
> To þe liche þer hit lay, wyt lauande teres.
> "Oure Lord lene," quoþ þat lede, "þat þou lyfe hades,
> By Goddes leue, as longe as I myȝt lacche water
> And cast vpon þi faire cors and carpe þes wordes,
> 'I folwe þe in þe Fader nome and His fre Childes,
> And of þe gracious Holy Goste' and not one grue lenger;
> Þen þof þou droppyd doun dede hit daungerde me lasse."
> Wyt þat worde þat he warpyd þe wete of eghen
> And teres trillyd adoun and on þe toumbe lighten,
> And one felle on his face and þe freke syked.[56]

> [And the bishop, upset, cast down his eyes
> Who sobbed so frequently that he had no room to speak
> Until he paused and looked toward the tomb,
> Toward the corpse where it lay, with cleansing tears.
> "Let Our Lord grant," said that man, "that you live,
> By God's leave, long enough that I might bring water
> And sprinkle it upon your beautiful corpse and speak these words:
> 'I baptize you in the name of the Father and of His noble Son,
> And of the gracious Holy Spirit,' and not a moment longer—
> In that case, even if you dropped down dead it would bother me little.
> With that word that he uttered, the moisture of his eyes
> And tears poured down and landed on the tomb,
> And one fell on his face and the man sighed.]

All unawares, Erkenwald has provided the elements necessary for a baptism. Between the sufflational sighs, the conditional utterance of the baptismal formula, and the sprinkled water of the tears, the rite is accomplished.[57] The law of historical succession, already suspended by the preservation of the corpse, is violated still further: someone who died an indeterminate number of centuries before Christ walked the earth now proves to have been saved by his name. For the voice issuing from the corpse exclaims that a baptism has been effected and the dead man's soul transported from hell to heaven:

> For þe wordes þat þou werpe and þe water þat þou sheddes—
> Þe bryȝt bourne of þin eghen—my bapteme is worthyn.[58]
>
> [By means of the words that you uttered and the water that you shed—
> The bright stream of your eyes—my baptism has been brought about.]

And thus the *Erkenwald*-author sets up a thought experiment that recalls in self-evident ways those of the schoolmen, themselves taken from hagiographies much like *Erkenwald* itself. The "conditional baptism" he depicts is a variation on the baptism by way of demonstration to an inexperienced priest, or in the fictional context of a stage play. The emphasis on the bishop's inability to speak recalls the discussions of what takes place when the sacramental formula is garbled by stuttering or other vocal infirmity. The baptism of a corpse animated by a spirit not its own is a variation on the baptism of a sleepwalker or lunatic.

But neither should the originality of this scenario be downplayed. Difficulties familiar from theological treatises, and from the hagiographies they draw on, have here been mutated, multiplied, and superimposed. The *Erkenwald*-poet seems to delight in upping the ante: what if the baptizand has already died and yet his corpse has been miraculously preserved in a state of freshness? And what if his declaration of faith is uttered not by him but by a mysterious spirit, more or less identifiable with the Holy Spirit, that is ventriloquizing his corpse? That is, what if it is carried out in a state of postmortem glossolalia? As for the officiating priest, what if he mentions rather than uses the baptismal formula—that is, what if the baptismal formula occurs in a kind of *suppositio materialis*? What if he says it in a conditional mode? What if he carries out the baptism without knowing that he is doing so? What if the water used is his own tears? What if instead of carrying out a proper sufflation, the priest merely sighs deeply and moans? And what if all this is true at once—will an effective sacramental sign have been produced out of all these bizarre materials?

This is the provocation that the poem represents. It combines all the most far-fetched scenarios by means of which theologians wrestled, inconclusively, with their doctrines, and ends up with one still more improbable. The poet gives the impression of offering, not an illustration of a particular point of doctrine, nor even the experimental ground that might allow for such a point to be conclusively demonstrated, but rather a scenario so rebarbative as to be calculated to reduce sacramental theology to dizziness. Still, he is doing something more interesting than either propagandizing on behalf of theology or causing it to collapse on itself. To understand the particular ordeal that the poem submits its readers to, it is necessary to return to the *caracter*.

For what is at issue in the thought experiments by which baptismal theological debate was carried out, and in the thought experiment of *Erkenwald*'s second half, is not just the sacrament in general but something more particular. The improbable scenarios are designed to allow questions to be raised about one entity in particular: a certain mark made in the soul by the rite of baptism. According to the schoolmen, baptism is not only itself a sign, one that signifies, resembles, and produces a washing away of sin; it is also the imprinting of yet another sign, a remnant of its own performance. It is the inscription of a sort of brand or *signaculum* on the soul of the baptizand, marking it as the soul of a Christian. What organizes the baptismal theological debates that *Erkenwald* takes up is the question of what, exactly, is essential to the baptismal rite if it is to leave its mark on the soul of the person baptized, and thus attain to the status of a baptism actually accomplished.

The technical term by which sacramental theologians knew this mark, and still know it, does not appear in *Erkenwald*, nor is the mark of baptism named there by any other. Still, its presence is made known unmistakably. When the voice issuing from the corpse declares that a baptism has been brought about, this can mean nothing else than that this particular mark has been inscribed in the soul. Its presence is apprehensible to the intellect even though it is not described, which makes the baptismal inscription strictly analogous—inversely—to the inscriptions in the poem's first half, which are described in detail but remain incomprehensible. Each of these entities has its name withheld, and in each case what goes unrecorded is the same word; for the mark of baptism is of course itself also known as the "character."

ORNAMENTUM ANIMAE

Erkenwald survives in a single manuscript, where it is split into two equal sections of 176 lines, each beginning with a rubricated initial. A blank line is interposed between the two halves. This diptych structure is the poem's most conspicuous formal characteristic, and it gives rise to what is the first and most pressing hermeneutical question posed to anyone who tries to read it. This is the question of how the two halves are to be read together, of what can be said both to join them and to mark out their permanent distinction from each other. What demands to be read is, finally, just this break at the poem's heart.

In other words, this gap is a formal instantiation of a discontinuity that is also to be found at the level of its subject matter, which can be described in various ways: the first half of the poem is concerned with *caracteres*, and the second with baptism; or again, the answers provided in the second half do not correspond to the questions provoked by the uncovering of the tomb in the first. The fact that the blank line is not only a discontinuity but also the very means by which the two halves of the poem are shown to be halves—and shown to communicate, as halves—in itself points toward the manner in which the apparently inassimilable contents of the poem's two halves might after all be put into communication. The remains of a laceration that knits together, a reconciliation commemorating the wound on whose site it has come into being: the break in the center of *Erkenwald* has exactly the status of a scar, or scarification. Its operation is that of what was called, in Middle English, a *caracte* or *caracter*.[59] For bodily markings of this sort went by the same name as did necromantic inscriptions and the mark of baptism. (For the sake of clarity, I distinguish among the three sorts of character by means of an orthographic expedient: necromantic *caracter*, baptismal character, cicatricial *carecte*. But it should be kept in mind that these three spellings correspond only to current, not medieval, usage; in the latter, to the extent that they are a word, they are the same word.)

The gap at the center of the poem is thus also, in its own way, an encryption of the word that is present but unwritten in both the first and the second halves of the poem. Its function is to put these unwritten words in communication with each other. As long as this scar is illegible, the poem as a whole remains illegible; that is, as long as the very word *caracter* is not discerned in the poem, it has not yet been read. The question remains: what is marked out in this (cicatricial) *caracte* by which the (necromantic) *caracter* and the (baptismal) character are knitted together and kept distinct? The necromantic *caracter* having now been examined at length, what now demands to be considered is the baptismal.

Practically the only thing that is clear about the baptismal character is that no one has ever been able to decide what sort of thing it is.[60] Depending on how the evidence is construed, it was either already known in the apostolic and patristic eras or was, instead, an invention of the Middle Ages.[61] In any case, by the second half of the twelfth century the word *character* had become the technical term for this mark, and already within a matter of decades so many different theories of the character were in circulation that complaints arose.[62] The inclusion, in the *Decretals* of Gregory IX, of some remarks by Innocent III concerning the baptism of children, unbelievers, feigned believers, sleepers, and the insane gave official sanction to the idea of the character.[63] But because it made no appearance in the *Sentences* of Peter Lombard, theologians in the centuries to follow did not have a firm common ground on which to discuss it; and although its existence was universally admitted from the twelfth century onward, the question of its exact nature provoked nothing but confusion and disagreement. It was with evident relief, then, not to mention scorn, that the Protestant reformers would dispense with the doctrine of the character altogether. Memorably summarizing a tradition of outrage with the idea already present in the decades of its first appearance and continuing through the Reformation, George Campbell would write in the eighteenth century of medieval sacramental theologians that "the whole of what they agreed in amounts to this, that in the unreiterable sacraments, as they called them, something, they know not what, is imprinted, they know not how, on something in the soul of the recipient, they know not where, which never can be deleted."[64] John Calvin, for his part, had gone so far as to declare that "it was unknown to the first Christians, and accords more with magical incantations than with the sound teachings of the Gospel."[65]

A few indications about the baptismal character as it came to be understood by the late Middle Ages can nevertheless be made without hesitation. It is something imparted by the rite of baptism. (Confirmation and ordination, though not the other four sacraments, also impart their own characters.) Like circumcision, it is a "distinctive sign" of belonging to a particular community. But unlike circumcision, it is a mark not on the body but directly on the soul. This mark is indelible: it can never be lost, and therefore under no circumstances should anyone ever be baptized more than once. It does not guarantee salvation: even a soul that has been relegated to hell will forever retain the mark of its having been baptized. The character is thus to be distinguished on one hand from "grace" (which would in itself be sufficient for salvation) and on the other hand from the utterances and gestures of the exterior rite of baptism (which pertain to the body, not to the soul). Necessary but not sufficient for salvation, the baptismal character is the precondition for the reception of the other six sacraments.

Beyond this, it is difficult to say. What kind of thing is this *ornamentum* or *ornatus animae* (ornament of the soul), as it came to be called, and if it does not in itself ensure salvation, what exactly *does* it do?[66] The schoolmen could never agree. As they said, it might be a reality in itself, or it might just be a relation between realities. It might be a quality, in which case it might be any one of four—or five—different varieties. It might dispose the baptized person to act well, or it might rather ward off demons. And there is an even more fundamental problem with the idea of the baptismal character. It is by no means obvious that the soul is something in which an inscription could be made in the first place. A body can receive the mark of circumcision, certainly, but how can a mark be made in a soul? Even if it is somehow granted that the very idea of a noncorporeal mark is not essentially absurd, there remains the question of who could ever see it. If (as was often maintained) the baptismal character is a sign addressed to demons or angels, indicating to them that the soul bearing it is the soul of a Christian, how are such beings meant to apprehend this sign, since they themselves have no bodies and thus no faculties of sensation?[67] Still worse, even if an account is provided of how disembodied intelligences will be able to make it out, there is still the question of what sort of configuration, exactly, they will be apprehending—that is, of what the invisible mark will look like, as it were.

Despite the fact that most everything about the baptismal character was to remain a matter of great doubt, there was never any question that it, like the rite that produces it, should be understood as a kind of sign. But this small point of agreement only makes the problems just enumerated more intractable. As we have seen, the authoritative Augustinian definition of the sign, enshrined in the opening pages of book 4 of the *Sentences*, holds that a sign is something that brings one thing into the senses and another into the understanding. A noise is received by the ears, for instance, and an idea is made present to the intelligence; the eyes take in a mark on a page and understand from it some concept. According to this model, the sign is nothing else than a passage from the visible to the invisible, a decryption that allows the immaterial to be discerned in the material. To define the baptismal character as a sign would seem, thus, to be a contradiction in terms: an invisible mark in a nonmaterial support somehow counting as something that is by its very nature both material and perceptible.[68] Much ingenuity was brought to bear in the face of this difficulty. A number of theories were developed to explain how the sacramental character might be a sign after all. Perhaps the most prominent of these theories posits the character as an intermediary entity between the sign itself (*signum tantum*) and the signified thing itself (*res tantum*), a kind of both-sign-and-thing (*res et signum* or *res et sacramentum*). But this attempt does nothing more than make the problem recede slightly. Some thinkers saw that it would not suffice to create an exceptional category for the baptismal character: if something invisible can be said to be a sign, then the definition of the sign itself must be rethought. So much was registered for instance by Richard Fishacre, who responded by limiting the Augustinian definition only to certain kinds of signs; and by Roger Bacon, who opted for a more radical solution: revising the Augustinian definition itself.[69] Not everyone would go so far. But neither was anyone able to come to a lasting agreement about how to solve the problem of the character, a problem for both theology and the theory of signification.

And a problem, no less, for aesthetics, in both the modern and the premodern acceptations of that word. It bears on the way that the character might present itself to the senses; on the relation that it instantiates between sensuous form and spiritual content, especially in the doctrine of *res et sacramentum*; on the response that it elicits in those (angels or demons) who look upon it; on the way that its operation is suspended in a kind of "purposiveness without purpose" (for it is finally grace, and not the character, that accomplishes salvation); and perhaps even on the beauty of this ornament of the soul. Sacramental theology points unhesitatingly in the direction of an aesthetics of the invisible ornament, but, perhaps unsurprisingly, it does not do much more than point. The frustration expressed by later Protestant polemicists, and already by medieval theologians themselves, is one that will be experienced by anyone who tries to sort out the medieval doctrine of the character, which becomes increasingly difficult to conceive of the more it is studied. And the incoherence of the doctrine is crystallized especially in its inability to give any persuasive answer to the question of what, if anything, the mark will look like. It is often suggested that what is inscribed in baptism is a likeness of Christ. But what is this supposed to mean? A portrait? An acheiropoieton, a direct impression of his face or body such as appears on the Veil of Veronica or Shroud of Turin? A cross? A Chi Ro? A *nomen sacrum* on the order of IHS?

Perhaps the most promising indications are given by the fact that this mark bears the name that it does. If it seemed fitting to refer to the mark on the soul as a character, it might be because that mark was thought to have something in common with those marks on the body that have also been known by that name.[70] Outside of the context of sacramental theology, bodily marks of various kinds go by the name *character* (*caracter, carecte*): brands, tattoos, scarifications, and so forth. To be sure, such practices, forbidden by scripture, were not widespread in medieval western Europe, though nonhuman animals were of course frequently marked in these ways. But there is evidence, ambiguous as it may be, that the practice of inscribing human flesh with heat, ink, and blades was not in fact unfamiliar, be it in the form of commemorative religious tattoos of various designs on the skin of crusaders and pilgrims returning from Jerusalem, the stigmata that appeared (by means that do not always go without saying) on Francis of Assisi and others, the monogram that Henry Suso famously carved into his chest, or the brands on the hands or foreheads of prisoners and soldiers that functioned as permanent uniforms or scarlet letters.[71] In any event, the historical practice of tattooing was familiar from references to it in, for example, the Bible and Isidore—the latter declaring that to be thus punctured was a mark of nobility among the pre-Christian inhabitants of the British Isles, as the name "Picts," for its part, commemorates.[72]

Indeed, it has been pointed out more than once that the indelible marking of skin was exemplarily associated, for the medieval English, with their distant ancestors.[73] By virtue of its having belonged to someone who lived in London before the Christian era, the corpse uncovered in *Erkenwald* evokes just such distant ancestry, and no leap would be required to imagine it as "pict" in this fashion. Indeed, there is an echo, in the description of the "fresh red" (*ronke rode*) that mysteriously marks the corpse's complexion, of another possibility: that his face bears a "conspicuous cross" (*ronke rode*) that has been tattooed or scarified there.[74] However this may be, it was indeed the cruciform mark that was perhaps the most notable *caracte* to appear on human bodies in the Middle Ages. A great number of images and descriptions survive of the crucifix's branding itself on the skin and in the heart, most prominently in the case of Francis.[75] It is tempting to take such bodily inscriptions as a template for imagining the form of the character impressed in the soul, and to conclude that what the rite of baptism inscribes there is a kind of cross. But there are reasons to hesitate before coming to such a conclusion. Nicholas Häring, who has looked into these matters as deeply as anyone, is insistent that there can be no certainty as to whether the use of the term *character* for the baptismal mark has anything whatsoever to do with the use of that term for bodily markings.[76] Moreover, he argues that, even if it does, the military and juridical markings that went by the name of *character* in the late Roman era consisted in a "name in abbreviated form or a letter" rather than a "symbol," so that it might be better to imagine the baptismal character as taking the form of, say, "IHS" rather than that of a crucifix.

But this distinction between a letter or name and a symbol is by no means absolute. There are inscriptions that are both or neither: and namely, inscriptions on the order of the *roynyshe resounes* of which the *Erkenwald*-poet provides a description. Marks of this sort can as easily be tattooed or scarified on the skin as any others. Indeed, two early witnesses to the practice of tattooing as it was known in Western Europe after late antiquity concern precisely this sort of inscription. Both are early modern, rather than medieval, but they participate in traditions that recede into an unfixable past. In a tattoo stereotype (or "flash") that survives from a Coptic studio in Jerusalem catering to pilgrims, there is a depiction of the Resurrection. The design is surrounded by an ornamental border of Latin letters and quasi-letters arranged in a line, letters that do not form any known or even pronounceable words.[77] The image could almost serve as an illustration for *Erkenwald*. Or consider the celebrated case of an alchemical commonplace book of 1611, in which a certain Simon Forman recounts his having given himself tattoos of various astral *caracteres* on his left arm and right breast. As Jennipher Rosecrans shows in her study of Forman's "inscriptive medicine," this practice has medieval antecedents.[78] Such bodily markings—ornamental, as it may be, or necromantic—do not allow themselves to be understood as symbols rather than letters, or letters rather than symbols, because they are, precisely, *roynyshe*.

If the attempt to picture the baptismal character on the model of the scarified or tattooed image of the cross proves inconclusive, in short, there remains the possibility of imagining it on the model of the necromantic *caracter*, itself sometimes tattooed. And this is the possibility offered by the *Erkenwald*-poet: of thinking the character as *caracter*.

VOYDE

It is now possible to take the measure of the paronomasia from which the poem is generated. *Erkenwald* is indeed, in a certain sense, a proposal about a matter of controversy, or rather total uncertainty, in the field of sacramental theology. That proposal consists in a riddling evocation of the word *caracter* that draws attention from every direction to its homonymy. It might be imagined that the schoolmen who discussed both of these things would themselves have noticed this homonymy, that they would have considered the baptismal and necromantic characters in each other's light. There is reason to believe that they did. As Grévin and Véronèse point out, a William of Auvergne will give the very same examples in his discussions of the two sorts of mark, and thus "the link is all but established" between them. The discussions of the theologians, they go on to suggest, can only have contributed to a sense in the "collective imaginary" that there existed an inverted version of the sacramental rites of the church, in which *caracteres* served nefarious aims.[79] But, for reasons that can perhaps be guessed at, the connection between the character and the *caracter* remain merely implicit within the field of sacramental theology. So, too, does it remain in *Erkenwald*. But the poet is discreet for his own reasons. If he keeps the connection obscure, it is as a move in a larger game: a game in which what is withheld is withheld conspicuously, as a means of trapping the attention. *Erkenwald* is set up so as to provoke, by a kind of mystification, the revelation of its mysteries—as mysteries.

Another way of putting this same point would be to say that the poem's theological concerns are a matter of form. In the first place, its contribution to baptismal theory bears on the formal design of the character. The poet's suggestion runs counter to the notion that the inscription in the soul would allow its bearer to be recognized as belonging to a particular community, the number of the saved. If it were to appear, he suggests, it would appear as a *caracter*: not as an imprinted proper name or meaningful brand, but as a kind of cipher. Permanently illegible, impossible to pronounce, let alone interpret, if any demons or angels were to find themselves before it they would not receive any information from it but, rather, be reduced to a state of mental failure. This is how the promise of salvation—permanent, necessary, effective, and finally insufficient—would make itself known: in the way that the beings who encounter it would "muse it to mouth," fall back fruitlessly on inquiry and erudition, indeed enact any of the hermeneutic failures allegorized in *Erkenwald*. The appearance of the invisible baptismal character is that of what remains merely, and maddeningly, form. In the second place, this proposal about the appearance of the character is put forward by formal means. No programmatic statement can be found in the poem, to this or any other effect; nor do the events that it relates or even its manner of relating them somehow point a moral the poet might have wished to promulgate. All that he does is place the two characters together in formal space. That is, all he does is dispose—around the *carecte* that bisects the poem—the *caracter* and the character in such a way that their relation appears of its own accord.

That relation is one of inversion. What is crucial is that the *caracter* and the character are equivalent not as such but *per speculum in aenigmate*. The blank in the middle of the poem functions as a mirror that inverts each into the form of the other. Without this enigmatization, without the riddling that establishes their formal relation, the two would have nothing whatsoever to do with one another. What this means is that, despite everything, the poem cannot be said to assimilate the character to the *caracter*, or baptism to theurgy: its purposes run in quite a different direction than those of a Calvin, who will relegate the baptismal character to the level of a mere magical charm. For, as the poet saw clearly, in truth the character and the *caracter* can be distinguished with precision. If an analogy obtains between them it is an inverse analogy, or chiasmus. So much can be gathered by placing side by side the problems that they pose for the theory of signification. A sign is a certain conjugation of sensibility and intelligibility: something that, presenting itself to a faculty of sensation, allows something beyond itself to be understood. And thus neither the character nor the *caracter* should qualify as a sign—but not for the same reason. The baptismal character, for its part, would be a sign that is intelligible but not sensible. Whereas the necromantic *caracter* would be something equally absurd: a sign that is sensible but not intelligible. And, again, this is how they make themselves known in the poem: the necromantic *caracteres* are described but cannot be understood, whereas the baptismal character goes unmentioned but can be understood to have been imprinted.

Erkenwald is constructed in such a way as to bring about this juxtaposition, and thus to reveal the formal relation—chiasmus—between character and *caracter*. And it is constructed in this way in order to put forward a further suggestion: an unsuspected, and frankly beautiful, way out of the theological and semiological incoherency of considering these entities to be signs. The solution lies in their relation itself, in the cicatricial *caracte* that both joins and separates them. Each can operate as a sign to the extent that it is supplemented by the other. The phantom visibility of the invisible baptismal mark is that of the necromantic *caracter*; the withheld intelligibility of the nonsensical inscription is that of the sacramental character. It is only by virtue of their bearing the mark of the scar interposed between them—an invisible gap that marks out the impossibility of intention, commemoration, signification, or any other sort of *menying*—that these two defective signs are signs at all. The semiology of *Erkenwald* is thus in the fullest sense a caracterology, in the sense that it points toward the enigmatic residue, the break between its halves, as the basic domain of the sign.

It is in short their having been marked out by the *caracte* that allows the character and the *caracter* to be signs in the absence of any signification whatsoever. It is also what allows them to operate. For *Erkenwald* contains not only a theory of signification but also a theory of linguistic performativity. And that theory is neither conventionalist nor naturalist—to refer again to the two positions that medieval theorists of performativity staked out—but, again, caracterological. In the universe of the poem, these two familiar limit-cases in medieval semiotics, the baptismal character and the necromantic *caracter*, bring about effects not because they signify some encoded meaning (conventionalism) and not because there inheres in them a kind of asemiological physical force (naturalism) but rather because of the way that each precisely fails to signify. The *caracteres* in the first half of the poem bring about the events recounted in the poem as a whole not because of some pact with demons or magical force but simply because in their uninterpretability they open up a terrible gap in the minds of the people who see them. Inversely, the mark made in the dead man's soul brings about his salvation precisely insofar as there is no trace of it. Its operation is indistinguishable, in fact, from the withdrawal of every sensible trace of the man, for it coincides with the undoing of all of the marvelous perceptibility of corpse and voice:

> Wyt this cessyd his sowne, sayd he no more.
> Bot sodenly his swete chere swyndid and faylide
> And alle the blee of his body wos blakke as þe moldes,
> As roten as þe rottok þat rises in powdere.
> For as sone as þe soule was sesyd in blisse
> Corrupt was þat oþir crafte þat couert þe bones,
> For þe ay-lastande life þat lethe shalle neuer
> Deuoydes vche a vayne-glorie þat vayles so litelle.[80]

> [At that point, his sound ceased; he said no more.
> But suddenly his sweet countenance disappeared and went missing,
> And all the color of his body was as black as mold,
> As rotten as the rot that rises in dust.
> For as soon as his soul was brought into bliss
> That other craftwork that covered his bones disintegrated;
> For the eternal life, which will never end,
> Voids all trifles that serve such little purpose.]

No sign remains of the marvel of the corpse's preservation, nor any sign of the miracle that has just been brought about. This passage is not a mere pleasantry about the greater importance of the other world with respect to this one. It marks, more specifically, a voiding or "devoiding" of what can be apprehended by the senses. The emergence of this insensibility is itself the very imprinting of the character in the soul.

Nonetheless this anesthesia is not total. While the disintegration of the corpse is described in great detail, nothing is said about the tomb in which it has rested. Though the poem—now ending on a note of apparent triumph—makes a show of having forgotten about it, there is no avoiding the sense that as it does so the tomb is still there, unmoved, in the foundations of the church. And that the *caracteres* that adorn it remain there, too, entirely unexplained. The imprinting of the baptismal character, by which the soul is liberated into the fullness of heaven and the body brought to nothing, is not the articulation of a final and transcendent signification and commemoration (*menying*). It remains chiefly an enigmatization. What *Erkenwald* offers is an account of the baptismal character as a defective sign, as a sign that signifies and operates in its deficiency, in its caracterological relation to the *caracter*. The poem called *Erkenwald* generates itself from this deficiency. There is nothing to read there but the letters on the page, the written elements that make it up and that are themselves of course nothing else than "characters." These letters do not allow themselves to be distinguished from mere letterforms; they are no more and no less legible than the blank line around which they are disposed. For to follow the logic of the poem is to be faced at every turn with yet another instance of the *caracter*: the scar tissue of the sign, the enigmatic residue in which everything is worked. *Erkenwald* has only ever been a gloss, in ciphered form, of the name of its *prima materia*.

I have attempted in this chapter to rehearse the poem's own gesture as nearly as possible, that is, to provide nothing more than a gloss on the word *caracter*. What results from this exercise can be stated in a few words: *Erkenwald* is a paronomastic riddle whose solution is *caracter*; the poem as a whole is generated from that cryptonym, which appears in it nowhere even as it makes itself known everywhere; it sets up, by formal means, a thought experiment thanks to which it becomes possible to understand in unimagined ways the nature of both the theurgic *caracter* and the baptismal character; and—in sum—its form, content, and interpretation are all a matter, first and foremost, of handing down the enigma of the letter, which is the letter as enigma.

But if any of this were in fact the case, everything would fall apart. To the extent that it were solved, the poem would stop being enigmatic—and to the extent that its solution were a word, that solution would stop being a *caracter*. Fortunately, there is no danger of any of that. To follow the gesture of the poem is to fail to read it, and such a failure is unavoidable. For no reader, perhaps not even the poet himself, has yet laid eyes on the particular *caracter* of which the poem would seem to be a gloss. Nowhere is there included a transcription of the *roynyshe resounes* that appear on the tomb, nor are the particularities of their form described in a way that would allow them to be reconstructed. And yet it is made clear that they are *fulle verray*, that they look quite distinctly like something in particular, so that although in fact they happen not to have been transcribed, they easily might have been. No one knows what the *caracteres* from which the poem is generated might look like; you would not recognize them if you saw them. They remain thinkable only in the form of the scar that marks out their incommensurability with that invisible ornament that the poem shelters, whatever it is that lodges itself in the soul of the work and promises, but does not guarantee, its salvation: at once its miraculous preservation in and as its own form and its instantaneous dissolution into the trackless land that is its only home. It is in this way that the poem maintains, as the *Cloud* does, its self-secrecy. All that you have before you is a little joke, an empty configuration, the name of a gap, the absence of a name. For good or ill, this *amusette* is the kernel—and the shell—of *Erkenwald*, and of literature as such: a cryptonym that resounds at every level, in silence.

It had a most specific function always to be hidden from me. I could therefore puzzle over it endlessly without the least risk. For to know nothing is nothing, not to want to know anything likewise, but to be beyond knowing anything, to know you are beyond knowing anything, that is when peace enters in, to the soul of the incurious seeker. It is then the true division begins, of twenty-two by seven for example, and the pages fill with the true ciphers at last.
—Beckett

ACKNOWLEDGMENTS

With the single exception of its faults, which are my own doing, there is nothing in this book that does not originate in the knowledge, counsel, and forbearance of Daniel Heller-Roazen, Vance Smith, Andrew Cole, Sarah Kay, Rita Copeland, Avital Ronell, Gabriela Basterra, Paul Fleming, Peter Travis, Nicola Masciandaro, Eva Kenny, Emmelyn Butterfield-Rosen, Colleen Rosenfeld, Arden Reed, Kevin Dettmar, Nancy van Deusen, my colleagues in English at Pomona College and in Late Antique and Medieval Studies at the Claremont Colleges, the reviewers and editors of the manuscript, Lopon Barbara Du Bois, my family, and Christopher van Ginhoven Rey. Thank you.

NOTES

THE WIND IN THE SHELL: PROLEGOMENA TO THE STUDY OF MEDIEVAL NONSIGNIFICATION

1. See Manetti, *Theories of the Sign*, chap. 2.

2. See Plato, *Timaeus*, 72b. On the enigmas of the oracle at Delphi, see Fontenrose, *Delphic Oracle*, 79–83.

3. See Plato, *Phaedrus* 275b: "the words of the oak in the holy place of Zeus at Dodona were the first prophetic utterances"; and cf. Barthes, *S/Z*, 14: "The text, in its mass, is comparable to a sky, at once flat and smooth, deep, without edges and without landmarks; like the soothsayer drawing on it with the tip of his staff an imaginary rectangle wherein to consult, according to certain principles, the flight of birds, the commentator traces through the text certain zones of reading, in order to observe therein the migration of meanings, the outcropping of codes, the passage of citations."

4. Woolf, *Pointz Hall*, 48. On this passage, see Apstein, "Chaucer, Virginia Woolf and *Between the Acts*." To be able to recognize what sort of "conversation" Woolf is referring to here, and notwithstanding the fact that her work is inexplicably omitted from many treatments of modernist nonsense, it suffices to recall the illegible skywriting of *Glaxo* and *Kreemo* and the "ee um fah um so/foo swee too eem oo" of *Mrs. Dalloway* (20–21, 80); the "Rattigan Glumphoboo" ("cypher language," "senseless singsong," "nonsense") of *Orlando* (282, 284, 288); the "ron, ron, ron et plon, plon, plon" of the last novel she saw into print, as well as its description of a line of Catullus as "beautiful, yet meaningless," and above all the "hideous," "horrible," "meaningless" dog Greek that occupies ten full lines of its final pages: "Etho passo tanno hai,/Fai donk to tu do," and so forth (*Years*, 91, 394, 429–430); and finally, in the same text whose draft contains the cited remark about Chaucer, the evocation of "words without meaning—wonderful words" (*Between the Acts*, 212).

5. Chaucer, "Summoner's Tale," line 1934; "Parson's Prologue," line 43; "Nun's Priest's Tale," line 3277; "Manciple's Tale," line 243; *Parliament*, line 499; and *House of Fame*, lines 556, 560. These and all further citations of Chaucer's texts are to the named work as it appears in the *Riverside Chaucer*. On the impossibility of deciding whether *cokkow* and *awak* are recognizable English words or uninterpretable avian squawkings, see Koff, "Awak!" and cf., for example, Clanvowe, "Boke of Cupide," lines 123–124.

6. Chaucer, *House of Fame*, lines 7–11. Translations and modernizations in this book are my own except where others' translations are cited.

7. Chaucer, lines 1280–1281.

8. Chaucer, line 663. On the location of the realm of Fame, see Chaucer, lines 845–846. In giving the name *Fame* to language itself, the poet follows Isidore of Seville, who had explained that "Fama autem dicta quia fando, id est loquendo, pervagatur per traduces linguarum et aurium serpens" (fame is so called because by speaking [*fando*], that is, by talking, it wanders around, creeping through the vine-branches of tongues and ears). Isidore, *Etymologies*, 5.27.26. What unites the various senses of *fama*—renown, reputation, infamy, glory, vainglory, rumor, gossip—is the fact that all these things are produced by linguistic means; so that, as Boitani summarizes, "Fame

is language itself." Boitani, *Chaucer and the Imaginary World*, 72 and *passim*. The classic account of fame is Lida de Malkiel, *Idea de la fama*; see also Fenster and Smail, *Fama*; Braudy, *Frenzy of Renown*; Ormrod, "Murmur, Clamour and Noise"; Peters, "Wounded Names"; and Neubauer, *Rumour*. On Chaucerian fame in particular, see the essays in Davis and Nall, *Chaucer and Fame*.

9. There can be little doubt that the poem (and indeed the poet's whole oeuvre) is meant ironically; but any reading that does not dwell on the possibility that Chaucer is offering it as an actual record of a visionary experience—and as an actual intervention into linguistic theory, oneirocriticism, and the physics of sound—entirely misses the joke. On the poet's characteristic irony, see especially the perceptive remarks in Scanlon, "Authority of Fable"; on the neglected but very real question of Chaucer's mysticism, see Masciandaro, *Darkness*, chap. 2. So as to preserve somewhat certain ambiguities that are constitutive of the *House of Fame*, rather than distinguishing artificially among poet, narrator, and dreamer, I will refer to them indiscriminately as "Chaucer."

10. Chaucer, *House of Fame*, lines 1074–1082. On this process, see, for example, Ruggiers, "Words into Images." Boitani's account is precise: "what [the dreamer] contemplates here is not reality as such, as it *exists* in the sublunary world, or as it *is* in the hyperuranian universe of being, but as it is *told*. . . . Reality as told is different from reality as it existed before it was told . . . there is no reality here but only its oral sign." Boitani, *Chaucer and the Imaginary World*, 209–210. On the making visible of sound by shamanic techniques of ecstasy, which are by no means irrelevant here, see Munn, "Mushrooms of Language."

11. Chaucer, *House of Fame*, lines 1277–1281. This largely neglected passage is explicated (to different ends than are pursued here) in Watson, "A Windmill," 2–3. Howard, for his part, asserts without explanation that the image is a "symbol of what artists do," in which "the windmill stands for the cosmos, the walnut shell for the brain." Howard, *Chaucer*, 245. Royster, in 1926, claimed to have discovered the historical corollary of the literary personage "Colin the Tregetour," and his identification has been adopted by subsequent commentators; see his "Chaucer's 'Colle Tregetour.'" In connection with the shell's being that of a walnut in particular, note that Thomas Browne was not the first to discover that "in young Wallnuts cut athwart, it is not hard to apprehend strange characters." Browne, "Garden of Cyrus," 361.

12. That *uncouth* should be understood as a technical term is made clear by its reappearing at a crucial moment in book 3, where the eagle explains that in the wicker house Geoffrey will find solace in the form of "unkouthe syghtes and tydynges" (Chaucer, *House of Fame*, line 2010; *tydynge* is for its part of course the key technical term introduced in the *House of Fame*). Given that what Geoffrey will finally see there ("y saugh a man") is the famously unnamed "man of gret auctorite" with whose apparition the poem breaks off, it also becomes necessary to take the word in an etymological sense.

13. At its first appearance in the poem, *tregetours* is made to rhyme with *jugelours*. Chaucer, lines 1259–1260.

14. On integumental hermeneutics, see de Lubac, *Medieval Exegesis*, 59, 165 with notes; Minnis, *Medieval Theory of Authorship*, 140–141; and Huppé and Robertson, *Fruyt and Chaf*.

15. Jones, "Parodic Sermon," 104, with multiple examples. On the history of windmill technology in medieval England, see Kealey, *Harvesting the Air*.

16. Chaucer, *House of Fame*, lines 1034–1035, 1931–1934 (with 528), 782–783, 675–691. On Chaucer's derivation of the aquiline physics of sound from grammatical and other textbooks, see Irvine, "Grammatical Theory." Note also that if Chaucer is insistent that the sound of language as such is to be understood on the model of the sound of rocks in particular, this is perhaps because the latter was a classical example in the textbooks on the properties of terms. *Collisio lapidum* typifies what the logicians call *sonus non-vox*, a variety of noise to be distinguished from the vocal, writable, and meaningful utterances that they claim will be the sole object of their attention. See, for example, de Rijk, *Logica modernorum*, 2.2.418. But such distinctions do not obtain in the realm of Fame, which is simply that place to which all sounds of every sort whatsoever—be they "speche . . . / Or voys, or noyse, or word, or soun"—are brought by virtue of their sonic nature. For an insightful discussion of Chaucer's doctrine of sonic indistinction, see Zieman, "Chaucer's Voys," 82.

17. Chaucer, *House of Fame*, line 1516. On the memory palace and its vivid images, see Carruthers, *Book of Memory* with Carruthers, "Italy" on the *House of Fame* in particular.

18. *House of Fame*, lines 1365, 351–352 (with 2139).

19. The *House of Fame* would thus answer to Lydgate's famous epithet "Dante in inglissh" in a different manner than we have assumed: that is, insofar as its fundamental gesture would reduplicate that of the *rime petrose*: "la mente mia, ch'è più dura che petra / in tener forte imagine di petra." Lydgate, *Fall of Princes*, line 303; Durling and Martinez, *Time and the Crystal*, 278–279. Needless to say, stone remains a vital figure throughout the poet's oeuvre, not least in the articulation of the very tale-telling contest that organizes the *Canterbury Tales* (Chaucer, "General Prologue," line 774). On stone in the Middle Ages, with frequent reference to Chaucer, see Cohen, *Stone*; on the related healing properties of stones and words in medieval medical and literary text, see Bishop, *Words, Stones, and Herbs*.

20. Chaucer, *Troilus*, 2.1384.

21. Chaucer, *House of Fame*, line 656. On the *récit visionnaire*, see Corbin, *Avicenna and the Visionary Recital*.

22. The word *mantra* means "mind-apparatus"; Chaucer's *engyn of thought* (*House of Fame*, lines 523–528; cf. Dante, *Commedia*, 1.2.7–8) stands to it as a calque. See Padoux, *Vāc*, 373; and Guenther and Trungpa, *Dawn of Tantra*, 392. Note that Chaucer's iconographic attributes are a writing implement in one hand and a rosary in the other; see Loomis, *Mirror*, figs. 3–5 with Davis, "Pendant." On the characteristic nonsignificativity of mantras, see Staal, *Discovering the Vedas*, 194; Staal, "Mantras and Birdsongs," 549; Padoux, "Mantras," 300–301; Padoux, *Vac*, chap. 7; and Trungpa, *Profound Treasury*, 3.72: "They do not make any conventional sense; therefore they are powerful. A mantra changes your psychological state at once, as soon as you hear that particular sound. The closest thing to mantras I have heard is the howling of coyotes."

23. See Agamben, *What is Philosophy?*, chap. 1. Tregetry also serves as a figure of Chaucer's poetics in the *Canterbury Tales*; see Chaucer, "Franklin's Tale," lines 1138–1139.

24. See especially, in addition to the works cited in the following two notes, Zieman, "Chaucer's Voys"; Zieman, "Escaping the Whirling Wicker"; Allen, "Broken Air"; and Ganim, *Chaucerian Theatricality*, chap. 7.

25. Travis, *Disseminal Chaucer*, 202, 209.

26. Smith, "Chaucer as an English Writer," 87–88.
27. Benjamin, *Selected Writings* 1:65; *Gesammelte Schriften* 2.1:140.
28. Benjamin, 1:64; 2.1:141.
29. Benjamin, 1:261; 4.1:19.
30. De Man, *Resistance to Theory*, 92.
31. Benjamin, *On Hashish*, 61; *Über Haschisch*, 110.
32. Jakobson, "Linguistic Glosses," 269; Shklovsky, "On Poetry and Trans-Sense Language," 11.
33. Hamsun, *Hunger*, 87–89.
34. On nonsignification in modernist poetics, see, for example, Perloff and Dworkin, *Sound of Poetry*; Tomiche, "Glossopoïèses."
35. Stein, *Tender Buttons*, 49.
36. Mallarmé, *Oeuvres*, 68; Gide, "Dada," 480: "Le jour où le mot: DADA, fut trouvé, il ne resta plus rien à faire.... Ces deux syllabes avaient atteint le but 'd'inanité sonore,' un insignifiant absolu."
37. "La modernité, c'est le transitoire, le fugitif, le contingent." Baudelaire, *Oeuvres*, 553.
38. Beckett, *Three Novels*, 45.
39. Dolar, *Voice*, 15.
40. Barthes, *S/Z*, 9; Barthes, *Rustle of Language*, 77.
41. Lacan, *Television*, 9 (cf. Lacan, *Seminar XX*, 138–139); Kristeva, *Desire in Language*, 133; Agamben, *Fine del pensiero*.
42. Kittler, *Gramophone*, 86.
43. In addition to the works cited in the following note, see Cole and Smith, *Legitimacy*; and Hollywood, *Sensible Ecstasy*.
44. On Benjamin's medievalism, see Knapp, "Benjamin"; on Lacan's, Labbie, *Lacan's Medievalism*; on Barthes's, Solterer, *Medieval Roles*; and on Kristeva's, Holsinger, *Premodern Condition*.
45. On modernist medievalism generally, see Ullyot, *Medieval Presence*, and Marshall, *Medieval Presence*. On Ball's in particular, see Ball, *Flight out of Time*, 112–113, with White, *Magic Bishop*, 127; on Mallarmé's, Bloch, "Augustine"; on Woolf's, Ellis, "Virginia Woolf's Middle Ages"; on Joyce's, Eco, *Aesthetics*; and on Beckett's, Ullyot, *Medieval Presence*, chap. 5. What would become, ten years later, the first four lines of "Jabberwocky" originally appeared under the title "A Stanza of Anglo-Saxon Poetry" in Carroll's self-published *Mischmasch* in 1855. Neither of course is the medievalizing of *Looking-Glass* restricted to these stanzas: see above all the chapters treating of the "Lion and the Unicorn and those queer Anglo-Saxon Messengers" and of the Red and White Knights. Carroll, *Looking-Glass*, chaps. 7 and 8.
46. Stein, "Lectures in America," 207. On the passage from "Merciles Beaute," and Stein's intention to use it as an epigraph, see Wineapple, *Sister Brother*, 173.
47. Restoring modernist nonsense to a history that includes the Middle Ages would be a different task than the (no less important) one that begins with the recognition that "special languages—meaningless &/or mysterious—are a small but nearly universal aspect of 'primitive-&-archaic' poetry." Rothenburg, *Technicians*, 386.
48. This account of Anselm follows the indications given by Agamben in various places, notably in *Potentialities*, 39–47; and *Language and Death*, 34. See also Sweeney, *Anselm of Canterbury*; Stock, *Implications of Literacy*, 329–361; Colish, *Mirror of Language*, 55–109; Schufreider, *Confessions of a Rational Mystic*; and Logan, *Reading*

Anselm's Proslogion. For Anselm's influence on the experience of prayer in particular, see Fulton, "Praying with Anselm."

49. Anselm of Canterbury, *Opera omnia*, 1.94; *Major Works*, 83.

50. Anselm of Canterbury, 1.100; 87.

51. As Nancy affirms, Anselm is "the bearer of a necessity that defines the modern world of thought, of the existential ordeal of thought. 'God' is for Anselm the name of this ordeal. This name can assuredly be rejected for many reasons. But the ordeal or trial cannot be avoided." Nancy, *Dis-Enclosure*, 11.

52. Anselm of Canterbury, *Opera omnia*, 1.93; *Major Works*, 82.

53. In this, of course, it is utterly different than the argument of Descartes's to which it has too often been assimilated. Descartes thinks that he has proven the existence of both himself and God, when in reality he has merely been taken in by his own grasping at a double illusion of substantial form; Anselm's proof is, by contrast and despite everything, essentially nontheistic—and it is so because Anselmian *fides* consists exactly in the sorrowful willingness not to mistake adventitious thoughts (*cogito*) for actual existence (*sum*).

54. Anselm of Canterbury, *Opera omnia*, 1.101–104; *Major Works*, 87–89.

55. Anselm of Canterbury, 1.126–127; 108.

56. Anselm of Canterbury, 1.130; 111.

57. Heller-Roazen, "Speaking in Tongues," 95.

58. Guglielmo IX, *Poesie*, 92. The translation given of this and the following passage reproduces, with slight alterations, Heller-Roazen's renderings in "The Matter of Language."

59. Agamben, *Idea of Prose*, 43. This observation is developed crucially in Heller-Roazen, "The Matter of Language." Nor of course is the figure confined to this particular exegetical tradition: see for example that *doha* of Milarepa's in which he declares that "My stallion is the prana which consciousness rides." Heruka, *Hundred Thousand Songs*, 213. In the "Manciple's Tale," Chaucer submits the figure to a derangement along the same lines as does William.

60. Guglielmo IX, *Poesie*, 126.

61. For a history of the debates over this passage, see Hilty and Corriente, "Fameuse cobla." On William's "ni bat ni but" and its variants, see Bond, "Philological Comments," 352–353; on the locution generally, see chapter 2 in this book. On William's interest in nonsignification, and that of other troubadours, see Bardin, "Poetics of Nullity."

62. Zumthor, "Fatrasie," 9. Zumthor's terminology is drawn from Garapon, *Fantaisie verbale*, 19–20.

63. Dante, *Inferno*, 31.67. On this passage, see Dronke, *Dante*, 43–49; Guiter, "Sur deux passages"; and Dragonetti, "Dante face à Nemrod." The poet also speaks of Nimrod and the confusion of tongues in *De vulgari eloquentia*, 15.

64. Dante, *Inferno*, 7.1.

65. On barbarolexis, see Zumthor, *Langue et techniques*, 83–111, and Leupin, *Barbarolexis*.

66. "a lui ciascun linguaggio / come l suo ad altrui, ch'a nullo è noto." Dante, *Inferno*, 31.80–81.

67. Dronke, *Dante*, 49. On medieval jargons and invented languages, see Garapon, *Fantaisie verbale*; Renzi, "Aspetto"; Elwert, "Emploi"; and Schnapp, "Between Babel and Pentecost."

68. See chapter 4 in this book.

69. Bodel, *Jeu de saint Nicolas*, 178. A parallel passage can be found in the Middle English *Romaunce of Richard Coer de Lion*, as noted by Akbari, *Idols*, 212n25.

70. Rutebeuf, *Miracolo*, lines 160–168.

71. See Bodel, *Jeu de saint Nicolas*, 275n1512. Zucker explores this phenomenon in the centuries after the end of the Middle Ages in his *"Twelfth Night."*

72. Stevens and Cawley, *Towneley Plays*, 30.249–252. On this passage, see Jennings, "Tutivillus"; and Peterson, "Fragmina Verborum."

73. Eccles, *Mankind*, lines 680–681.

74. This passage is discussed in Dillon, *Language and Stage*, 41.

75. Cited in Jaffe-Berg, "Forays into Grammelot," 3. For a treatment of the prehistory and theory of grammelot, see Pozzo, *Grr . . . grammelot*.

76. For more general historiographical indications about nonsense in the Middle Ages, see Kirk, "Buba, Blictrix, Bufbaf," with bibliography.

77. In music, for example, there are the incomprehensible words of the motet (see Dillon, *Sense of Sound*, 6, 33, 173; Page, *Discarding Images*, 85; and, on a related later phenomenon, Rattray, "In Nomine"); in the liturgy, the braying of the congregation in the so-called asinine masses, in which both Jung and Bakhtin took an interest (Bakhtin, *Rabelais*, 78; Jung, "On the Psychology," 258–259; and, more recently, Harris, *Sacred Folly*); in medicine, the nonsensical syllables of verbal charms against disease (see Orlemanski, "Jargon," and chapter 4 in this book). Outside of the linguistic sphere, that nonrepresentation was a concern of visual art as well is made spectacularly plain in the Rothko-like Color Field abstraction from an eleventh-century manuscript that Herbert Kessler has placed, as a provocation, on the cover of his recent *Seeing Medieval Art*.

78. See Agamben, "What is a Paradigm?," 31: "The paradigmatic case becomes such by suspending and, at the same time, exposing its belonging to the group, so that it is never possible to separate its exemplarity from its singularity."

79. Chaucer, *Parliament*, lines 24–25. Cf. Benjamin, *German Tragic Drama*, 207: "the ancient truth that the authority of a statement depends so little on its comprehensibility that it can actually be increased by obscurity"; Schlegel, "On Incomprehensibility," 144–145: "A classical text must never be entirely comprehensible. But those who are cultivated and who cultivate themselves must always want to learn more from it."

80. Bloch, *Anonymous Marie*, 25. Marie's indications have defied the efforts of modern scholars to come to even the most basic agreement about how they should be construed; the paraphrase offered in the remainder of this paragraph (of *Lais*, Prologue, lines 9–22) is thus altogether tendentious. A detailed and illuminating history of the intertwined editorial and hermeneutic disputes can be found in Burch, "Prologue to Marie's *Lais*." On the central importance of obscurity in Marie's work, see Leupin, "Impossible Task"; on obscurity as a characteristic of twelfth-century French literature generally, see Rider, "Enigmatic Style"; on theories of obscurity in the medieval Latin tradition, Ziolkowski, "Theories of Obscurity"; on the premodern history of obscurity overall, Mehtonen, *Obscure Language*; on the place of allegory in this history, Akbari, *Seeing Through the Veil*.

81. Scholem, "Tradition and Commentary," 49; emphasis in the original.

82. See Agamben, *Infancy and History*, 3.

83. Boynton et al., "Sound Matters"; Kleiman, *Voice and Voicelessness*; Zumthor,

Poésie et la voix and *Introduction à la poésie*; Vance, *Mervelous Signals*; Leach, *Sung Birds*; Allen, *On Farting*; Dillon, *Sense of Sound*; Lawton, *Voice in Later Medieval English Literature*. On medieval "soundscapes," see also Fritz, *Cloche*; on medieval visualizations of voice, Shoaf, "Voice in Relief"; and on dramaturgical discussions of the qualities of voice, Ogden, *Staging of Drama*, 156–158. Outside of medieval studies, the question of the voice is no less prominent: see, for example, Butler, *Ancient Phonograph*; MacKendrick, *Matter of Voice*; Bernhart and Kramer, *On Voice*; Schwartz, *Making Noise*; Mazzio, *Inarticulate Renaissance*; and Cavarero, *For More than One Voice*.

84. For recent work in medieval animal studies, see, for example, Crane, *Animal Encounters*; Kay, *Animal Skins*; Van Dyke, *Rethinking Chaucerian Beasts*; and Kordecki, *Ecofeminist Subjectivities*. The fundamental work on medieval zoosemiotics is Eco and Marmo, *On the Medieval Theory of Signs*; see also Eco, "Latratus Canis." For a consideration of the relation between linguistic diversity and animal sounds in a thirteenth-century English domestic treatise, see Sayers, "Animal Vocalization"; for birdsong in French and Occitan poetry, Zingesser, "Pidgin Poetics"; on Chaucerian birdsong, Gorst, "Interspecies Mimicry." On misogynist, xenophobic, and demonological traditions of classifying, and castigating, "idle talk," and other disorderly varieties of speech, see Le Goff and Schmitt, "Parole nouvelle"; Jennings, "Tutivillus"; Phillips, *Transforming Talk*; Zieman, *Singing the New Song*; Craun, *Lies, Slander, and Obscenity*; and Lochrie, *Covert Operations*, chap. 2.

85. For a salutary caution against the diagnosis of anxiety in medieval authors, see Justice, "Shameless."

86. As McTurk rightly points out, the *House of Fame* should be read within the tradition of the myth of the theft of soma, recorded most prominently in the Rig Veda. See McTurk, *Chaucer and the Norse and Celtic Worlds*, chap. 1; Knipe, "The Heroic Theft"; and Calasso, *Literature and the Gods*, chap. 7. The extent to which the poet's work must be situated within a larger European context is rightly emphasized in Marion Turner's recent *Chaucer*; the necessity of expanding the scope of the context still further is indexed perhaps most patently in the very title of the *Parliament of Fowls* and in the Pardoner's telling of a story from the *Jataka Tales*.

87. On the early history of monasticism, see Dunn, *Emergence*.

88. See Boase, "Arab Influences"; Beech, "Troubadour Contacts," 27–28; and Metlitzki, *Matter of Araby*.

89. See Menocal, *Arabic Role*.

90. See, for example, McEvilley, *Shape of Ancient Thought*.

91. See, for example, Cabezón, *Scholasticism*; and Makdisi, *Rise of Colleges*.

92. On *Barlaam*, see, for example, Lopez and McCracken, *In Search of the Christian Buddha*.

93. Turchin and Hall, "Spatial Synchrony," 37.

94. On Middle English as a specifically postcolonial vernacular, see Bowers, "Chaucer after Smithfield." The possibility of an illustrious vernacular is established most prominently, for the European Middle Ages, by Dante in *De vulgari eloquentia*. For discussions pertaining more particularly to Middle English, see Ebin, "Lydgate's Views," and the important anthology of Wogan-Browne et al., *Idea of the Vernacular*.

95. The term *minor literature* is from Deleuze and Guattari, *Kafka*. On late-medieval xenoglossia, see Cooper-Rompato, *Gift of Tongues*.

96. On the related point that the alchemical process as it appears in the "Canon's Yeoman's Tale" figures Chaucer's poetics, see Ingham, *Medieval New*, chap. 5.

97. Chaucer, "Canon's Yeoman's Tale," line 751. On absolute expenditure, see Bataille, *Accursed Share*; on Bataille's medievalism, Holsinger, *Premodern Condition*, chap. 1.

98. This "literary absolute" is given its classical formulation in the essay on *Unverständlichkeit* (nonunderstanding) by Friedrich Schlegel, written in the midst of his period of closest study of the Middle Ages: "But is nonunderstanding, then, something so evil and objectionable?—It seems to me that the welfare of families and of nations is grounded in it; if I am not mistaken about nations and systems, about the artworks of mankind, often so artful that one cannot enough admire the wisdom of the inventors. An incredibly small portion [of nonunderstanding] suffices, provided it is preserved with unbreakable trust and purity, and no restless intelligence dares to come close to its holy borderline. Yes, even the most precious possession of mankind, inner satisfaction, is suspended, as we all know, on some such point." Schlegel, "Über die Unverständlichkeit," 2:370; de Man, "Concept of Irony," 183 (cf. "On Incomprehensibility," 268). On de Man's account of Schlegelian irony, from which the translation just given is taken, see Ronell, *Stupidity*, chap. 3. On the "literary absolute," see Lacoue-Labarthe and Nancy's book of that title; on Schlegel's medievalism, see Höltenschmidt, *Mittelalterrezeption*.

99. Wind, *Pagan Mysteries*, 15.

1. PRISCIAN, BOETHIUS, AND AUGUSTINE ON *VOX SOLA*

1. On the commentary's date of composition, see de Rijk, "Chronology," 144; on its influence in the Middle Ages, see chapter 2 in this book.

2. The seeming irrelevance of Boethius's opening remark has been noted most forcefully by Hans Arens, whom it appears to have reduced to exasperation. Accusing the commentator of vanity, prolixity, derivativeness, and "gross misunderstanding," Arens does not hesitate to say flatly of Boethius's work that "the start is wrong." *Aristotle's Theory*, 212.

3. Boethius, *Commentarii*, 294. The difficulty of *De interpretatione* was and remains a commonplace. John of Salisbury complains that any of the schoolmen of his own day could teach the subject matter of the treatise both more intelligibly and more succinctly. *Metalogicon*, book 3, chap. 4. Twentieth-century commentators rely on the epithet "elliptical."

4. Boethius, *Commentarii*, 4.

5. Boethius, 4.

6. Aristotle, *De interpretatione*, 16a8; translation modified.

7. Arens, *Aristotle's Theory*, 212.

8. The word *logic* and its derivatives here translates both *logica* and *dialectica*, although these are not, strictly speaking, always identical. On the history of these terms and of their overlapping use, see Michaud-Quantin, "Emploi des termes logica et dialectica." On Boethius's use of *vox*, see Hyman, "Terms for 'Word,'" 155; and Law, *Grammar and Grammarians*, 262–263.

9. On Boethius's project of harmonizing Plato and Aristotle, see notably de Rijk, "On the Chronology of Boethius's Works"; Ebbesen, "Boethius as an Aristotelian Commentator," 375; and Minio-Paluello, "Traductions et commentaires," 328–35.

10. So de Rijk: "while 'Aristotelian' logic is in many respects synonymous with

'Aristotelico-Boethian' logic, the question can be raised whether Aristotle himself was an 'Aristotelian.'" "Boethius on *De Interpretatione*," 207.

11. On the disposition of the medieval sciences, see I. Hadot, *Arts libéraux*; Weisheipl, "Classification of the Sciences"; and Fredborg, "Unity of the Trivium." On the place of *vox* in the various schemata, see Kelly, *Mirror of Grammar*, 11–12; and Rosier-Catach, "Vox and Oratio."

12. Cited in Irvine, *Making of Textual Culture*, 97. On the foundational status of grammar in the medieval curricula, see Chenu, "Grammaire et théologie."

13. "Parmi toutes nos disciplines instituées, nous n'avons pas encore une science de la voix." Zumthor, *Introduction à la poésie*, 11. "Il n'existe pas, en Occident, de savoir classique qui prenne la voix pour objet." Heller-Roazen, "*De voce*," 37.

14. "Si un art ancien rencontre la voix, ce n'est que pour la fracturer, et pour que soient exposés en elle des éléments dont les arts se feront les savoirs." Heller-Roazen, 37; see also his *No One's Ways*, 13–15.

15. On the trivium's foundational role in medieval thought generally, see Copeland, "Trivium and the Classics," 58; Copeland and Sluiter, *Medieval Grammar*, 5; Irvine, *Making of Textual Culture*; Colish, *Mirror of Language*, xi; Cannon, *From Literacy to Literature*; and Stock, *Implications of Literacy*.

16. The best guide to Priscian is Baratin et al., *Priscien*. Priscian's influence on Middle English literature is explored in Irvine, "Grammatical Theory," and Travis, *Disseminal Chaucer*, chap. 5.

17. *Institutiones*, 1.1. Here and in what follows, the translation is that of Copeland and Sluiter, *Medieval Grammar*, with slight modifications.

18. See Hunt, *History of Grammar*; Rosier-Catach, "Vox and Oratio"; Burnett, "Sound and Its Perception"; and Kneepkens, "Priscianic Tradition."

19. On Stoic linguistics, see Colish, *Stoic Tradition*; Sluiter, "Greek Tradition."

20. See, for example, the treatises collected in de Rijk, *Logica modernorum*.

21. Priscian, *Institutiones*, 1.1–2.

22. See Allen, *On Farting*, passim, for instances of the latter usage.

23. On this point, and on the shifting fortunes of the word *articulata* in the grammatical tradition, see Leach, *Sung Birds*.

24. On the ancient thinking of noise, see Gurd, *Dissonance*.

25. Aristophanes, *Frogs*, lines 209–210.

26. Joyce, *Finnegans Wake*, 4.

27. "figmenta poetarum, que ranis loquacibus comparantur." Denifle, *Entstehung*, 1:684, cited in Minnis, *Theory of Authorship*, 11.

28. Priscian, *Institutiones*, 3.14.

29. See Johnson, "Teaching the Children"; Cribiore, *Writing*, 40–42; Cribiore, *Gymnastics* 172–176; and Reynolds, *Medieval Reading*.

30. Cribiore, *Gymnastics*, 173.

31. Quintilian, *Orator's Education*, 1.1.30; cited in Johnson, "Teaching the Children," 447.

32. On the derivation of the locution *neither bu nor ba* from the syllabary and its use in the field of logic, see chapter 2 in this book.

33. For a further example, see chapter 2 in this book.

34. Aristotle, *De interpretatione*, 16a3–8.

138 NOTES TO PAGES 35-39

35. As Isaac writes, "le *Peri hermeneias*,—avec les *Catégories*,—sera le seul ouvrage d'Aristote qu'on lira durant le haut moyen âge, et sa traduction boécienne, très exacte en général, deviendra un texte stéréotypé, à tel point qu'elle ne pourra être détrônée par la version de Guillaume de Moerbeke et qu'elle se maintiendra comme la seule authentique jusqu'à la renaissance." *Peri hermeneias*, 25. The scope of Boethius's influence goes beyond that of the circulation of his own works, for "it was distilled—usually silently—into the texts that were produced by medieval thinkers." Cameron, "Boethius on Utterances," 98.

36. Boethius, *Commentarii*, 20–21.

37. On *orandi ordo*, see Magee, *Boethius on Signification*, chap. 3; and, on its medieval afterlife, Meier-Oeser, "Walter Burley's 'propositio in Re.'"

38. On the extent to which the breakdowns of the *ordo* are integral to its operation, see Sweeney, *Logic*, 12.

39. Aristotle, *On the Soul*, 420b29–421a1.

40. Boethius, *Commentarii*, 21–22.

41. Some modern scholars, having noticed a certain infidelity in his translation of the passage on things, thoughts, and words but without inquiring into the reasons for it, have spoken of a "sad tale of confusion" begun by Boethius and bemoaned his "obscuring" and "obliteration" of Aristotle's actual doctrine. See Eco, "Signification and Denotation," 6; and Kretzmann, "Aristotle on Spoken Sound," 6. However that may be, the truth is that Boethius knows exactly what he is doing. If he departs from Aristotle's teachings on this point, it is not because of negligence but because he is transmitting his own position. On this point, see Magee, *Boethius on Signification*, 53.

42. On this work, see Isaac, *Peri hermeneias*; Magee, "Composition and Sources"; Shiel, "Boethius's Commentaries"; Cameron, "Boethius on Utterances"; Suto, *Boethius on Mind*; and, above all, Magee, *Boethius on Signification*.

43. Boethius, *Commentarii*, 5.

44. Diogenes Laertius, *Lives of Eminent Philosophers*, 7.1.57. "Speech again differs from a sentence or a statement, because the latter always signifies something, whereas a spoken word, as for example *blityri*, may be unintelligible—which a sentence never is."

45. See, for example, the slightly earlier commentary by Ammonius, who indicates that "not every word is a name or verb, for meaningless words like '*blituri*' and '*skindapsos*' are neither of these." *On Aristotle*, 26. See also Artemidorus, *Interpretation of Dreams*, 187; and Galen, *Opera*, 114. On *blityri* and *skindapsos* generally, see Ax, *Laut, Stimme und Sprache*, 195–199; Meier-Oeser and Schröder, "Skindapsos." On the survival of *blityri* in various forms in the Romance languages, see, for example, Spitzer, "Parole Vuote"; and Carabelli, "Blictri."

46. It is the name of an instrument mentioned by Athenaeus and by Pollux. See Mathiesen, *Apollo's Lyre*, 284–285; Maas and Snyder, *Stringed Instruments*, 185–186. See also Aelian, *De natura animalium*, 12.44.

47. Boethius, *Commentarii*, 59.

48. As Ebbesen summarizes, "a fully-fledged word may be devoid of sense," for words "acquire their signification by a human act of will: somebody decides to assign a certain phonetic word to a certain piece of reality of which he has formed a concept." "Boethius on the Metaphysics," 262.

49. Boethius, *Commentarii*, 32.

50. On Cicero's distinct but related use of the term *figura vocis* in a juridical context, see Auerbach, "Figura." On *figura* in medieval musical theory, see van Deusen, *Cultural Context*, chap. 4.

51. Suto, *Boethius on Mind*, 129. As Ebbesen points out, this *figura* cannot be a "complete phonetic shape," because, unlike this specific termination *-lus*, "plenty of morphological structures are not unique to one word-class." It constitutes, rather, a kind of "general stamp, a *typos*" that any word will have insofar as it belongs to a part of speech. Ebbesen, "Boethius on the Metaphysics of Words," 270.

52. As Derrida has made plain, "the absolute precondition for a rigorous difference between grammar and dialectics (or ontology) cannot in principle be fulfilled." *Dissemination*, 166. Colli emphasizes that the verb *proballein* refers in its earliest usage to the proposing of an enigma, and argues that the science of dialectic derives from this practice, so that for him the Greeks would be that people who, practicing divination like all other peoples on the basis of uninterpretable signs, alone made this practice into the very basis of their system of knowledge. Colli, *Nascita della filosofia*.

53. So Arens, with customary pique: "'garalus' would be a unique invention, and I do not believe in it." *Aristotle's Theory of Language*, 217. Others, reading *gargulus* with Migne, think that Boethius is using the word as an adjective to describe some unspecified utterance as "babbling, incomprehensible" rather than mentioning the particular utterance *garalus*: see Henry, *Most Subtle Question*; and Trumper, "Slang and Jargons." But the line of argument set out in the sentence in question strictly rules out any such reading.

54. Holtz, *Donat*.

55. *Garalus* is thus to be considered first of all alongside *nomina sacra* and *nomina divina*. See Heller-Roazen, *Dark Tongues*, chaps. 7 and 8. Or indeed alongside artworks: "a work of art could consist of a *single word* . . . and simply by a skillful alteration of that word the fullness and expressivity of artistic form might be attained." Kruchenykh and Khlebnikov, "Word as Such," 255. Cf. Benjamin, *Selected Writings*, 2:268: "the *Divine Comedy* is nothing but the aura surrounding the name of Beatrice."

56. Sextus Empiricus, *Against the Logicians*, 2.130–135. On this point, see Sinnott, "Peri Phones," 246–247.

57. Boethius, *Commentarii*, 74. That Boethius uses the word *designat* rather than *significat* here has been convincingly ascribed to his habit of alternating between them for the sake of variation. Magee, *Boethius on Signification*, 61.

58. Certeau, "Vocal Utopias," 34. So, too, Lermontov: "There is speech whose meaning / Is dark or without importance, / But to listen to it is impossible / Without agitation." Cited in Shklovsky, "Poetry and Trans-Sense Language," 7.

59. It was used notably by John of Salisbury and Roger Bacon. On Bacon's Augustinian reworking of logic, see chapter 2 in this book.

60. Augustine, *De dialectica*, 88, 90; Jackson's translation.

61. From context, it might seem that they are varieties of *verbum* (word), but *verbum* is also the name of one of the elements being distinguished. This irritating fact has been explained according to the idea that Augustine uses the term in a general as well as a technical sense, which is helpful but ultimately unsatisfying. Baratin, "Origines stoïciennes," 261. Moreover, one of the elements of the schema is *res*, which is explicitly

not a *verbum* at all: it is rather said, altogether opaquely, to be "whatever remains beyond the three that have been mentioned." In short, what is being differentiated into parts here is not at all clear.

62. Todorov, *Theories of the Symbol*, 38.

63. See Augustine, *De dialectica*, 126n9. Augustine appears, among other things, to be anticipating here the theory of material supposition, which I examine in chapter 2. It is of no small significance that Roger Bacon was familiar with *De dialectica*, for he will propose an unusual and recognizably Augustinian theory of material supposition.

64. Pépin, *Augustin et la dialectique*, 80. Pépin is of course quite aware of the point made in this paragraph. As he goes on to write: "Compte tenu du fait que *dictio*, on vient de le voir, traduit *lexis*, on serait tenté de rapprocher la dualité *uerbum-dictio* de la distinction *logos-lexis*, qui est attestée dans le stoïcisme; malheureusement, celle-ci traduit alors l'opposition entre le mot toujour pourvu d'une signification et celui qui peut être insignifiant; en sorte que le *logos* ainsi conçu se trouve entièrement dépourvu de contenu très particulier propre au *uerbum* d'Augustin" (83). Thus, in a certain sense Augustine's *dictio*, he specifies in a footnote, might seem to correspond rather to the Stoic *logos* than to *lexis*—that is, quite the contrary of what he has just proposed; but he decides, for entirely unsatisfying reasons, that this conclusion should be avoided.

65. Todorov, *Theories of the Symbol*; Baratin, "Origines stoïciennes"; and Manetti, *Theories of the Sign*.

66. Baratin, "Origines stoïciennes," 263.

67. Cf. Augustine, *Teacher*, 104–110; *Sermons*, 112.

68. Augustine, *De dialectica*, 86.

69. For example, Markus, "Augustine on Signs," 65.

70. On this point, see Kirwan, *Augustine*, 37; and Jackson, "Theory of Signs."

71. Augustine, *De doctrina*, 1.5.

72. On this point, see Agamben, *Language and Death*. The analogy can already be found in Origen and in Ambrose; see Denecker and Parteons, "De uoce," 108.

73. Augustine, *Sermons*, 112.

74. Augustine, 116. On this point, see Denecker and Partoens, "De uoce," 101.

75. Ando, "Augustine on Language," 45; Phillip Cary, *Outward Signs*.

76. Augustine, *De dialectica*, 88.

77. Augustine, 105.

78. Augustine, *De trinitate*, 10.1; *On the Trinity*, 287.

79. Agamben, *End of the Poem*, 64; see also his *Language and Death*, 33.

80. Augustine, *De magistro*, 1.10.33; *Teacher*, 136. On this passage, see Stock, *Augustine*, 154–155. The precise meaning and form of *sarabarae*, beyond its being a Latinization of an Aramaic word for a kind of head covering, remain obscure.

81. Augustine, *De magistro*, 1.11.36; *Teacher*, 137.

82. Agamben, *End of the Poem*, 67.

83. The task of interpretation, as taught in *De doctrina*, is to discover in a text its point of ultimate incomprehensibility. Twentieth-century "exegetical critics" were of course right to insist that, for Augustine, interpretation consists in discerning how a given text can be understood to refer to the so-called twin commandments to love God and the neighbor. But they did not read Augustine carefully enough to discover that, as he well saw, the twin commandments are themselves a text that stands in need of interpretation. For this reason, they—and their detractors no less—remained unaware of

what occurs when the very principle of intelligibility is referred back upon itself: there opens a permanent gap in the text and in its reader. This gap is the unregistrable differentiation that would obtain between love of God and love of neighbor, which is itself no other than the emptiness of a self-love without object. The famous rule of *caritas*, then, when taken seriously—that is, in accordance with Augustine's own protocols—is finally only an injunction to find in every text that point at which reading will falter in the face of the uninterpretable gap on which it is founded. See Kirk, "What Separates."

84. Augustine, *De doctrina*, 2.51.

85. Augustine's medieval readers did not fail to develop systems involving the memorization of unfamiliar or invented words, notably John of Garland and Thomas Bradwardine. See Dillon, *Sense of Sound*, 145–147; and Carruthers, *Book of Memory*, 221–257.

86. Kittler, *Discourse Networks*, 208.

87. Kittler, 208.

88. Kittler, 210.

2. WALTER BURLEY ON *SUPPOSITIO MATERIALIS*

1. At issue is what he calls a "difficilis dubitatio utrum vox significet species apud animam an res." Bacon, "De Signis," 132.

2. Scotus, *Opera*, 97. The literature on this *magna altercatio* is extensive. See, for example, Mora-Márquez, "Peri hermeneias"; Pini, "Species, Concept, and Thing"; Pini, "Signification of Names"; Perreiah, "Orality and Literacy"; Eco, "Signification and Denotation"; Meier-Oeser, "Meaning of 'Significatio'"; Boehner, "Ockham's Theory of Signification."

3. See Rosier-Catach, "Vox and Oratio"; Burnett, "Sound and Its Perception."

4. *De interpretatione*, in Boethius's translation and accompanied by his commentaries, circulated widely in the Latin-speaking world in the millennium after the Roman senator's death. Known as early as the ninth century, it was studied closely in the eleventh century and began to be commented on again at the beginning of the twelfth. By the thirteenth century, at both Oxford and Paris, anyone wishing to become a *magister artium* would have had to hear *De interpretatione*, along with the other works of the old logic, twice; and explication of the treatise had become, at least at Paris, a requirement of logical study. From the beginning of this period, Boethius's commentaries circulated alongside the treatise itself, and although in the later Middle Ages the copying of these commentaries dropped off, Boethius remained the authority invariably adduced on the many points of difficulty that arose in interpreting Aristotle's *inexplicabilis caligo*. On the survival of Boethian logic through the Middle Ages, see Lewry, "Boethian Logic." On the history of the reception of *De interpretatione* and of the *Organon* more generally, see Isaac, *Le Peri hermeneias*; Cameron and Marenbon, "Aristotelian Logic"; Marenbon, "Medieval Latin Commentaries"; Black, "Aristotle's Peri Hermeneias"; Braakhuis and Kneepkens, *Aristotle's Peri Hermeneias*.

5. Boethius, *Commentarii*, 21. Boethius gives the impression of intervening in what is already a controversy in his own day; he attributes to Alexander of Aphrodisias a view opposing his own. See Mora-Marquez, *Thirteenth-Century Notion*, 36–37.

6. Thomas Aquinas is only the most prominent proponent of a traditionalist view that sometimes refined but did not abandon what is sometimes called the Boethian "semiotic triangle": as Aquinas concludes, "ideo necesse fuit Aristoteli dicere quod

voces significant intellectus conceptiones immediate et eis mediantibus res" (it was therefore necessary for Aristotle to say that *voces* immediately signify the conceptions of the intellect and signify *res* by the mediation of the concepts). Aquinas, *Expositio libri Peryermenias*, 10–11. On Thomas's role in the *magna altercatio*, see especially Pini, "Species, Concept, and Thing."

7. Peter Abelard motions in this direction in the *Logica "Ingredientibus,"* as noted in Jolivet, *Arts du langage*, 112. Cf. the anonymous *De interpretatione* commentary that de Rijk has said "shows many resemblances to" the *Ingredientibus*: *Logica Modernorum*, 2.1:210–212. The *Ars meliduna*, for its part, indicates that a word is "imposed," or assigned as a name, in order not to signify but to appellate, that is, it is given as the name of a thing rather than a thought. See Biard, "Semantique et ontologie"; Braakhuis, "Signification, Appelation and Predication."

8. The history I am tracing here is a specifically English one. The preoccupation with *vox non-significativa* remained constant at Oxford into the fourteenth century in a way that it did not on the continent: for the theory of terms was eclipsed, at Paris, by *grammatica speculativa*, a system whose emphasis on the isomorphism between language and reality left little room for a consideration of meaninglessness. On this point, see Pinborg, "English Contribution," 37; and Ebbesen, "OXYNAT," 1–2. The best guide to speculative grammar is Rosier, *Grammaire speculative*.

9. "Ces manuels ... offrent une particularité remarquable; au lieu de commencer, en effet, en suivant l'ordre habituel, par les questions examinées dans l'*Isagogè* et les *Catégories*, ils n'abordent ordinairement l'étude des prédicables et des prédicaments qu'après un exposé des notions qui font l'objet du *Peri hermeneias*: son, parole, nom, verbe, phrase, proposition, oppositions." Isaac, *Peri hermeneias*, 57–58. Margaret Cameron has referred to the same phenomenon as "a new decision, which is followed by nearly every text-book in the twelfth and thirteenth centuries." Cameron, "What's in a Name," 96. On the necessity of defining *vox*, see Black, "Aristotle's Peri Hermeneias." On the division of old and new more generally, see Dod, "Aristoteles Latinus," 46; Lagerlund, "Assimilation of Aristotelian and Arabic Logic," 283; and de Rijk, *Logica modernorum*, 1:14–15.

10. William of Sherwood, "Introductiones in Logicam," 222–223; *Introduction to Logic*, 22–23; translation modified.

11. On *blityri* and *skindapsos*, see chapter 1 in this book.

12. de Rijk, *Logica modernorum*. It should be noted in this connection that in the *Introductiones montane minores* and *Abbreviatio montana*, rather than some variation of *buba* the example given of *vox non-significativa* is the letter or syllable: insofar as it forms part of the word *sorex* (mouse), the syllable *-rex* (king) does not signify on its own. The question of the syllable will be addressed further in chapter 3. As for the letter as an instance of *vox*, this notion is incoherent according to the received account of the letter as the nonvocalizable element of *vox*; all the same, it points to a millennial apprehension of the letter as the site of linguistic nonsignification. It is also possible that the apparent use of *litterae* as an example in these contexts is simply the result, according to the convincing model proposed by Cameron, of a scribal misreading of *blityri*: a typical medieval form of that word appears, in any case, in the corresponding passage of the associated *Introductiones dialecticae secundum G. Paganellum*, where the examples are *chimaera*, *blictrix*, and *hircocervus*. Cameron, "What's in a Name," 106n39. The *Introductiones* are edited in Iwakuma, "Introductiones dialecticae."

NOTES TO PAGES 55–58   143

13. de Rijk, *Logica modernorum*, 2.1.417. On Burley's adaptation, see de Rijk, 2.1:445–446; and Ebbesen, "OXYNAT," 2–3.

14. This distinction between grammar and logic would remain unstable, in the Middle Ages, both in principle and in fact. "Le *trivium* est en partie mythique. Derrière ce mythe, véhiculé notamment par les classifications des sciences, la réalité montre un lien étroit entre grammaire et logique." Ebbesen and Rosier-Catach, "Trivium," 97. On the relations between logic and grammar in the Middle Ages, see also Fredborg, "Unity of the Trivium"; for a grammarian's use of *biltrix* and *buba*, see Kneepkens, *Judicium Constructionis*, 181.

15. See especially Beylsmit, "Moyen d'exprimer," who adduces examples from Latin, Provencal, Catalan, French, Italian, Dutch, German, Danish, Swedish, English, Irish, and Hungarian, as well as related forms in Spanish and Russian; Maliniemi, "Ensuite, les petits" adds Finnish to the list. Neither these scholars nor the others involved in this inquiry refer to the logical expressions in question here. For their part, historians of logic seem to take these expressions as more or less self-explanatory and do not refer to the research conducted into the expression *neither bu nor ba*.

16. See Maliniemi, "Ensuite, les petits," 68.

17. de Rijk, *Logica modernorum*, 2.1:294.

18. de Rijk, *Logica modernorum* 2.1:139; 152; 561–562. On this passage, see Bos, "Speaking about Signs," 76.

19. See Frege, "Über Sinn und Bedeutung."

20. On imposition, see chapter 1 in this book. *Significatio* never received a clear definition in the Middle Ages, as opposed to *suppositio*, which was minutely described. As Joël Biard remarks, "la signification reste peu thématisée, surtout dans les grands textes du XIIIe siècle, tels que les traités de Lambert de Lagny ou de Pierre d'Espagne à Paris, ceux de Guillaume de Sherwood ou la logique *Cum sit nostra* à Oxford. C'est la supposition . . . qui se trouve au coeur des débats, tandis que la signification semble tenue hors du champ de réflexion ainsi ouvert, simplement posée comme un arrière-fond sur lequel se découpent les variations de référence des termes." *Logique et théorie du signe*, 15.

21. Peter of Spain, *Summule logicales*, 80.

22. As Smith writes, "the rigorous order in which these rules [of supposition theory] were to be applied, and their centrality in the curriculum, meant that every educated reader could be expected to read in the same manner. . . . such rules were a part of the communal experience of educated reading in the English Middle Ages, a reading for form that proceeded out of a common discipline and that ultimately formed the community of readers." "Medieval Forma," 79.

23. de Rijk, *Logica modernorum*, 2.2:446.

24. A series of important articles on material supposition has appeared over the past decades: Karger, "Supposition materielle"; Read, "How Is Material Supposition Possible?"; Panaccio, "Tarski et la suppositio materialis"; Panaccio and Perini-Santos, "Guillaume d'Ockham"; Normore, "Material Supposition"; and above all Rosier-Catach, "Suppositio materialis," on which my discussion closely relies.

25. Definitions of *suppositio materialis* became increasingly complex, largely because it became clear to later writers that the phenomenon could not be explained merely as a reference of the term to itself. Nonetheless, this recursive quality is inseparable from material supposition in all its various definitions. There is a parallel

discussion of autonymy in sacramental theology, where certain thinkers maintained that the distinguishing feature of a sacrament is that it is a sign that signifies itself: Lanfranc of Bec and his followers "soutenaient que le sacrement était à la fois *sacrae rei signum* et *sacrum secretum*, signifiant et signifié, et que c'était précisément la caractéristique du signe eucharistique de signifier non pas autre chose (selon le réquisit de la définition augustinienne), mais soi-même (*non aliud sed ipsum significat*)." Rosier-Catach, *Parole efficace*, 41. I discuss the place of nonsignification in sacramental theology in chapter 4.

26. See Carnap, *Logische Syntax*; and Rey-Debove, *Métalangage*.

27. Petrus Helias, *Summa super Priscianum*, 193.

28. The work, from about 1252, is edited in de Libera, "Summulae dialectices." Pinborg underscores Bacon's dependence there on William of Sherwood as over against Peter of Spain, which is to say, on an English rather than continental model. Pinborg, "English Contribution," 27. The novelty of Bacon's later works with respect to the *Summulae* is remarked by Maloney, "Semiotics of Roger Bacon"; and de Libera, "Roger Bacon et la logique."

29. See Maloney, "Semiotics of Roger Bacon," 151–152.

30. In this and the following paragraphs I rely on the many excellent studies of Bacon's theory of signification, notably de Libera, "Roger Bacon et la logique"; Maloney, "Semiotics of Roger Bacon"; Maloney, "Roger Bacon on the Significatum of Words"; Pinborg, "Roger Bacon on Signs"; and Fredborg, "Roger Bacon." Rosier-Catach in "Suppositio materialis" pays special attention to Bacon's treatment of *buba*.

31. "Signum autem est illud quod oblatum sensui vel intellectui aliquid designat ipsi intellectui." Bacon, *De signis*, 82. On this point, see Maloney, "Semiotics of Roger Bacon," 124.

32. Bacon's doctrine has been slightly simplified for the sake of brevity. For a fuller discussion of this point, see Pinborg, "Roger Bacon on Signs," 408; and Maloney, "Roger Bacon on the Significatum of Words," 191. Notable here is Bacon's opening of logic toward Aristotelian natural science, which, as de Libera notes, is already underway in the early and still overwhelmingly terminist *Summulae dialectices*. "Roger Bacon et la logique," 111.

33. This account of the essentially significative nature of *vox* participates in a larger shift that is perhaps in part a result of the increasing interest in the thirteenth century in Aristotle's *De anima*, where the Philosopher declares explicitly that *vox* is by definition meaningful (see chapter 1 in this book). On the medieval reception of *De anima*, see Lohr, "New Aristotle."

34. See Bacon, *De signis*, 90–91. "Bacon considère que ce transfert revient à 'une nouvelle imposition' du terme, qui 'rénove et élargit sa signification' par rapport à sa signification originelle, puisqu'effectivement elle équivaut à lui donner un second signifié." Rosier-Catach, "Suppositio materialis," 51. See also her *Parole comme acte*, 131–137.

35. Bacon, 66.

36. Bacon, 66.

37. Although Bacon denies the possibility of *voces non-significativae* here, in other contexts his account of the matter is more complicated. His remarks on the *species* of words has been shown to derive in part from passages in al-Kindi's *De radiis* concerning the power of unknown words in the work of enchantment. On this point, see chapter 4.

38. "Il nous semble qu'à la fin du XIIIe siècle Bacon avait déjà proposé une solution

élégante au problème que les logiciens terministes du siècle suivant s'attacheront à résoudre de différentes manières, sans avoir à raisonner dans le cadre de l'alternative rigide dans laquelle ils le traiteront, de faire de l'usage autonyme soit une propriété intrinsèque et originelle du terme soit une propriété purement contextuelle, et en permettant que l'acception autonymique soit un usage *significatif* et volontairement attribué." Rosier-Catach, "Suppositio materialis," 51.

39. See Pinborg, "English Contribution," 27; Courtenay, *Schools and Scholars*, 228.

40. "Another fact pointing toward conservatism in England is that around 1300 the British still care to copy or revise old-fashioned textbooks of logic like *Logica "Cum sit nostra"*—in one manuscript called *Summulae ad modum Oxoniae*. Part of, or at least a regular companion of these *Summulae* is a treatise on fallacies that one manuscript calls *Fallaciae ad modum Oxoniae*.... One teacher who used it as the basic text for a course on fallacies was Burley." Ebbesen, "OXYNAT," 2–3. "The second commentary ... found in this manuscript presents an adaptation by Walther of Burley of our treatise *Cum sit nostra*." de Rijk, *Logica modernorum*, 2.1:445–446.

41. For their influence on Chaucer, see, for example, Kiser, *Truth and Textuality*; for their influence on the *Cloud*, see chapter 3 in this book.

42. The indispensable work on Burley remains Uña Juárez, *Filosofía del siglo XIV*, now to be read with the essays in Conti, *Companion to Walter Burley*. An overview of Burley's life and works can be found in Ottman and Wood, "Walter of Burley." On his influence, see Uña Juárez, *Filosofía del siglo XIV*, 100–115. On his ontological commitments and position within the debate over universals, see Boh, "Walter Burley"; Cesalli, "Réalisme propositionnel"; Conti, "Ontology in Walter Burley's Last Commentary"; Meier-Oeser, "Walter Burley's 'propositio in Re'"; Karger, "Walter Burley's Realism"; and de Libera, *Querelle des universaux*, chap. 6. On the opposition between Burley and Ockham, see Wagner, "Supposition-Theory"; and Karger, "Mental Sentences." Their disagreement on a point of supposition theory, in particular, is the subject of Henry, "Suppositio and Significatio."

43. Burley, "Walter Burleigh's Treatise *De suppositionibus*"; Burley, *De puritate artis logicae*.

44. Edited in Burley, "Middle Commentary." On the dating of the work, see Brown's introductory comments to this edition; and Ottman and Wood, "Walter of Burley"; and on the various timelines, see Conti, *Companion to Walter Burley*.

45. Burley, "Middle Commentary," I.05.

46. Burley, I.06.

47. Burley, I.06.

48. Burley, I.07.

49. Burley, I.07.

50. Cf. the late twelfth-century Priscian commentary described by Fredborg: "His example of the freedom from Latin rules in the case of French words is both humorous and extraordinary, the non-sense word '*buba*' and the pronunciation of this word—'*buuba*,' '*bubaa*,' '*búba*,' '*bùba*' are all admissible, but not '*bubá*'!" Fredborg, "The Priscian Commentary," 65.

51. Burley, I.I4–I6. A perspicuous overview of these sections can be found in Mora-Márquez, "Ontología realista." As Mora-Marquez emphasizes, although Burley appears to support the traditionalist position at various points, these are only moments in a larger argument that decides for the new position.

52. Burley, "Middle Commentary," I.I6.

53. Burley, I.I4.

54. Burley makes use of this precept, actually derived from Averroes, throughout his career; see Spade's note to Burley's ascription of an associated dictum to Boethius in *De puritate*: "The quotation has not been found." Burley, *On the Purity of the Art of Logic*, 88n37.

55. Burley relies here on the distinction between *id quo* and *id quod* made famous by Thomas Aquinas in his discussions of *species intelligibilis*, on which see Spruit, *Species Intelligibilis*; and Pasnau, *Theories of Cognition*.

56. Boethius, *Commentarii*, 74.

57. On Burley's relations to Boethius, see Uña Juárez, *Filosofía del siglo XIV*, 345–347.

58. Burley, *On the Purity of the Art of Logic*, 82–86.

59. Burley, "Walter Burleigh's Treatise *De suppositionibus*."

60. In his *Summa logicae*, Ockham writes that material supposition takes place "quando terminus non supponit significative." *Opera*, 1.1.64. There is an extensive literature on Ockham and supposition. See, for example, Normore, "Material Supposition"; Panaccio, "Tarski et la suppositio materialis"; Biard, "La Redéfinition ockhamiste"; Loux, "Significatio and Suppositio"; and Sirridge, "Grammarians on Language About Language."

61. Smith, "Negative Langland," 58.

62. Courtenay, *Schools and Scholars*, 238. On the history of logic at Oxford in the fourteenth century, see Ashworth and Spade, "Logic in Late Medieval Oxford"; Courtenay, *Ockham and Ockhamism*; and Novaes, "Logic in the Fourteenth Century."

63. Karger, "Supposition materielle"; Read, "How Is Material Supposition Possible?"

64. See Ashworth and Spade, "Logic in Late Medieval Oxford," 60; Novaes, "Logic in the Fourteenth Century," 442; Maierù, *English Logic*; and Courtenay, *Schools and Scholars*, 236.

3. THE *CLOUD OF UNKNOWING* ON THE *LITIL WORDE OF O SILABLE*

1. Anonymous, *Cloud of Unknowing*, passim. The dating of the treatise remains uncertain, as does its authorship. For a summary of the considerations, see Sutherland, "Dating and Authorship," 83.

2. Eleanor Johnson's important recent essay on the *Cloud* contains the fullest and most perceptive discussion of the *litil worde*. See her "Feeling Time."

3. On mantra and nonsignification, see Prolegomena, above.

4. Namely, portions of chaps. 7 and 36–40.

5. On the place of the treatise within the tradition of affective theology, see Lees, *Negative Language*; Minnis, "Sources of the Cloud of Unknowing"; Minnis, "Affection and Imagination"; Turner, *Darkness of God*, chap. 8; Turner, "Dionysius and Some Late Medieval Mystical Theologians"; and Coolman, "Medieval Affective Dionysian Tradition."

6. See, for example, Hugh of Balma, *Théologie mystique*, chaps. 45–47; Hilton, *Scale of Perfection*, 83; and Rolle, *English Writings*, 108. On medieval devotion to the Holy Name, see especially Carsley, "Devotion to the Holy Name"; Bynum, *Christian Materiality*, 343n75; and Coomaraswamy, *Invocation of the Name*, introduction.

7. Too much has been made of the "paradoxical" fact that the *Cloud*-author appears to indulge continually in stylistic flourishes even as he "distrusts language," that he sets himself against the "fleshly tongue" even as he employs "homely metaphors." Accord-

ing to a principle to be found both in the *Celestial Hierarchy* and the *Mystical Theology* of the Pseudo-Dionysius (the latter of which having been translated into Middle English, most likely by the *Cloud*-author himself, under the title *Deonise Hid Diuinite*) it is more fitting to predicate the most apparently unlike thing of God than the most like, given that between God and creatures there is a radical separation in which degrees of likeness hold only in a very tenuous sense. One will be led less astray by the proposition "God is a stick or a stone" than by "God is a spirit," because one will bridle against the former while more or less accepting the latter, when neither is in any case true. Accordingly, the *Cloud*'s "homely" style is no more—and no less—adequate than would be a more refined, spiritual, elevated tone; but its improbability allows its failure to show itself more plainly. It does not betoken a pastoral care for the common folk, who would identify more readily with speech about down-home things. It does not represent a vote in favor of a rustic, authentic, bodily spirit of English commonsense as over against a decadent, Latinate, hierarchical discourse of the Church. To imagine it to do so is to miss the point altogether, which is that such speech is marked in order that its *inappropriateness*, its being apparently—but only apparently—further removed from what it would speak about allows that distance itself to come into view.

8. Burrow, "Fantasy and Language," 143.

9. The most explicit formulation of this point can be found in Taylor, "Paradox upon Paradox." See also Burrow, "Fantasy and Language"; Morris, "Rhetorical Stance"; Lock, "Cloud of Unknowing"; and Boitani, "Reading of the Cloud of Unknowing"

10. On this point, see chapter 1 in this book. As will become clear, the *Cloud*-author's interest is not in the discipline of *grammatica* itself but in the properties of the syllable and the word: properties that were, however, identified and discussed in the realm of grammar. His treatise is not, by any means, a "spiritual grammar," to use the name Dominic Longo has given to such works as Jean Gerson's *Donatus moralizatus*. Nor does it contain the slightest hint of a "grammatical metaphor" as is found in Alain of Lille's *De planctu naturae*, to cite only the best-known example—nor of the theological grammaticizing of that same author's *Regulae theologicae*. Nonetheless the possibility of the spiritual grammar as a genre and the prevalence of the grammatical metaphor in medieval texts speak to my point here: that the *Cloud*-author could simply not have been unaware of the teachings contained in the basic grammar textbooks. Of particular interest in the present connection are the pages John Alford devotes to English *artes praedicandi* in his survey of medieval instances of the grammatical metaphor. See Longo, *Spiritual Grammar*; and Alford, "Grammatical Metaphor."

11. Copeland, *Rhetoric, Hermeneutics, and Translation*, 5. On grammar teaching in the Middle Ages, see Reynolds, *Medieval Reading*; Orme, *Medieval Schools*, chap. 3; and Cannon, *From Literacy to Literature*.

12. An account of the word *werk* in the *Cloud* can be found in Lees, *Negative Language*, 311. On Middle English vocabularies of labor, see Masciandaro, *Voice of the Hammer*.

13. Anonymous, *Cloud of Unknowing*, 70.

14. Aristotle, *Metaphysics*, IX.3.

15. Anonymous, *Cloud of Unknowing*, 69–70.

16. *Cloud of Unknowing*, 17.

17. This temporal atomism of the *Cloud* has been discussed in two recent essays. Johnson considers it in terms both of Augustinian and Boethian distinctions between

time and eternity and of the *Cloud*-author's prose style; Bennett situates the *Cloud*'s advice within a tradition that unfolds under the auspices of the proverb *brevis oratio penetrat celum*. Johnson, "Feeling Time"; Bennett, "*Brevis oratio*."

18. See Johnson, "Feeling Time," 364n15.

19. Anonymous, *Cloud of Unknowing*, 28.

20. *Cloud*, 70.

21. See chapter 1 in this book. The other medieval science in which the term *syllaba* has currency is that of music. There, too, it would indicate an inescapably vocal nature of the prayer. On the relation between grammatical and musical accounts of the utterance, see Leach, *Sung Birds*; and Bower, "Sonus, Vox, Chorda, Nota."

22. Priscian, *Institutiones*, 44.

23. Anonymous, *Cloud of Unknowing*, 70. Zieman has also noted the indispensability of the *litil worde*. As she writes, the *Cloud*-author relies "if not on the voice, then on the idea of vocality and linguistic expression.... The single-syllable is at least an expository, if not an imaginative, necessity." "Perils of Canor," 158.

24. Anonymous, *Cloud of Unknowing*, 78.

25. The supposed silence of the prayer would bring it in line with monastic and, notably, Carthusian devotional practices. But it should be noted that even or especially the monastic acceptation of "silence" does not necessarily involve the absence of vocalization. Many forms of activity falling under the rubric of *vacatio*, *silentium*, and so forth, consist largely in speaking. One has only to imagine the famous apian murmur of the *horae silentii*, on which see Bruce, *Silence and Sign Language*. On monastic silence generally, see Gehl, "Competens Silentium." On Carthusian practices of silence in England, which are of particular importance in the case of the *Cloud*, whose manuscripts are of Carthusian provenance and whose author is assumed, though not without some doubt, to have been a Carthusian himself, see Brantley, *Reading in the Wilderness*.

26. Wogan-Brown et al., *Idea of the Vernacular*, 230; Taylor, "Paradox upon Paradox," 42.

27. Anonymous, *Cloud of Unknowing*, 78.

28. *Cloud of Unknowing*, 28.

29. See, for example, the exhortation at Matthew 6.7–8 *orantes autem nolite multum loqui*, as well as the many regulations of speech found in monastic and pastoral literature, chief among which the formula *multum loqui non amare* in the Benedictine Rule. See Venarde, *Rule of Saint Benedict*. For a discussion of the *Cloud* in this context, see Bennett, "*Brevis oratio*."

30. On Priscian's account, a single syllable can be as long as six letters and as short as one. *Institutiones grammaticorum*, 44. For his part, Donatus defines and discusses the syllable solely in terms of its being short, long, or "common." Indeed, its variable length is of course what matters most about the syllable for the purposes of Latin prosody.

31. Anonymous, *Cloud of Unknowing*, 28.

32. See, for example, Burrow, "Fantasy and Language," 141; Gillespie, "Postcards from the Edge," 153.

33. Anonymous, *Cloud of Unknowing*, 73.

34. *Cloud of Unknowing*, 78.

35. *Cloud of Unknowing*, 76.

36. *Cloud of Unknowing*, 77.
37. *Cloud of Unknowing*, 77.
38. *Cloud of Unknowing*, 77
39. The strangeness of unknown or foreign words has of course sometimes been thought to make them more efficacious. See, for example, Rohrbacher-Sticker, "From Sense to Nonsense." This is precisely not the case with the *Cloud*.
40. Watson, "Censorship and Cultural Change," 837. The category of "vernacular theology" has been enormously productive in the last three decades. Nevertheless, its explanatory capacity is not without limits, as is argued forcefully in Smith, "Application of Thought"; Zieman, "Perils of Canor"; and Gillespie, "Vernacular Theology."
41. As Smith writes, "vernacular theology may constitute daring and original thinking, but to assume that its own aim is to unfold outside institutionalized—among others, 'Latinate'—intellectual formations is to mistake our interests with its own." For him, what is occluded in this focus on our own interests is finally a text's "capacity to respond to something other than its own moment of crisis." "Application of Thought," 89–90.
42. The treatise could have circulated, and did in fact circulate, among readers who had not learned Middle English *cum lacte*—or who had, but who conducted so much of their lives in Latin that its being written in the vernacular would make of it a kind of foreign text. Miles writes of the Carthusians, whose number may well have included the *Cloud*-author himself and in any case included many of his early readers, that "Latin *was* their vernacular—they might have spent more years of their life communicating and thinking in Latin than in their 'mother tongue.'" Miles, "Richard Methley," 454; emphasis in the original. For such readers, to carry out the prayer procedure using the vernacular examples given would itself entail a kind of linguistic estrangement. But my argument is exactly not that the *Cloud*-author is instructing such readers to pray using the particular words *god* and *love*, and thus provoking in them such an estrangement. It is rather the minimal claim that to the extent that it can be assumed that people able to read a Middle English treatise are possessed of a Middle English vocabulary (and no further!), *god* and *love* are adequate examples of words that will be familiar to them. This is true of readers today, and on whatever continent, no less than of readers in the fourteenth or fifteenth century.
43. Methley, *Divina caligo*, 56; see also Anonymous, "Latin Versions."
44. Methley, *Divina caligo*, 20.
45. As Miles affirms in the case of Methley, he "saw nothing inherently 'vernacular' about the *Cloud*'s theology that would not succeed in Latin." "Richard Methley," 455.
46. Anonymous, *Cloud of Unknowing*, 58.
47. *Cloud of Unknowing*, 28–29.
48. Johnson, "Feeling Time," 351.
49. "Differt autem dictio a syllaba, non solum quod syllaba pars est dictionis, sed etiam quod dictio dicendum, hoc est intellegendum, aliquid habet. Syllaba autem non omni modo aliquid significat per se." Priscian, *Institutiones grammaticorum*, 53.
50. On this point, see chapter 1 in this book.
51. "Syllabae enim, cum ex his totum nomen constet, adhuc ipsae nihil omnino significant." Boethius, *Commentarii*, 54.
52. The nonsignificative quality of the syllable is also evidenced in what Zieman, discussing late medieval examinations of clerical literacy, calls a "formulaic expression

regularly used to denote 'minimal ability' in these tests: *legere aut sibilicare*—'read or syllabify.'" *Singing*, 60. The ability to "syllabify" a text is simply to be able to read it aloud correctly, without knowing what it means.

53. "Syllaba autem non omni modo aliquid significat per se: ergo monosyllabae dictiones possunt quodammodo esse et syllabae, non tamen sincere, quia numquam syllaba per se potest aliquid significare: hoc enim proprium est dictionis." Priscian, *Institutiones grammaticorum*, 53.

54. "Vides ergo per se ipsam syllabam deficere praedictorum ratione nec aliter posse examussim tractari, nisi posita sit in dictione." Priscian, 53.

55. Anonymous, *Cloud of Unknowing*, 78.

56. *Cloud of Unknowing*, 78.

57. *Cloud of Unknowing*, 28.

58. Johnson, "Feeling Time," 346; Gillespie, "Postcards from the Edge," 153.

59. "Dictio est pars minima orationis constructae, id est in ordine compositae: pars autem, quantum ad totum intellegendum, id est ad totius sensus intellectum; hoc autem ideo dictum est, ne quis conetur 'vires' in duas partes dividere, hoc est in 'vi' et 'res', vel quaedam huiuscemodi. Non enim ad totum intellegendum haec fit divisio." Priscian, *Institutiones grammaticorum*, 53.

60. Anonymous, *Cloud of Unknowing*, 78.

61. The *Cloud*'s *werk*, of course, is not the only context in which the capacity of repetition to produce mental effects is pressed into service. On repetition of the Holy Name in the *Cloud*-author's time and place, see Carsley, "Devotion to the Holy Name." On repetition in poetry of that same time and place, see Smith, "Medieval Forma," 74; and, outrageously, Chaucer, "Knight's Tale," lines 2321–2337. On repetition and incantation in antiquity, see Dodds, "Ancient Concept of Progress," 199–200; Dodds, *Greeks and the Irrational*, 1232n2; and Boyancé, *Culte des muses*, 76. On shamanic repetition, see, for example, Munn, "Mushrooms of Language."

62. Anonymous, *Cloud of Unknowing*, 74.

63. *Cloud of Unknowing*, 74.

64. *Cloud of Unknowing*, 76.

65. See Rosier-Catach, "Grammar," 212; and cf. Chaucer, *Troilus*, 3.855–859.

66. Anonymous, *Cloud of Unknowing*, 76.

67. *Cloud of Unknowing*, 75–76.

68. See Chaucer, "Nun's Priest's Tale," line 3393; Chaucer's usage will find an echo in Woolf, *Years*, 430.

69. Anonymous, *Cloud of Unknowing*, 90.

70. In Peircean terms, the distinction is between symbol and index. The classic treatment of this distinction in Aristotle is Kretzmann, "Aristotle on Spoken Sound."

71. Anonymous, *Cloud of Unknowing*, 97–98.

72. *Cloud of Unknowing*, 87.

73. *Cloud of Unknowing*, 88.

74. *Cloud of Unknowing*, 125.

75. *Cloud of Unknowing*, 122.

76. Agamben, *Infancy and History*, 4.

77. 1 Cor. 14; on this passage, see Heller-Roazen, "Speaking in Tongues."

78. The final and most difficult to get rid of thought will be the bare thought of

your own existence: the "nakid wetyng and felyng of þi beyng." Anonymous, *Cloud of Unknowing*, 83. On this point, see Masciandaro, "Sorrow of Being," 21–22.

79. Anonymous, *Cloud of Unknowing*, 2.

4. ST. ERKENWALD ON THE CARACTER

1. James, *Turn of the Screw*, 125. The operation of James's trap is laid out in Felman, "Henry James."

2. As Smith has written, the text ornamenting the tomb "remains inscrutable, unknowable, throughout the poem, which recounts a series of failures to decode it." "Crypt and Decryption," 61. As for the years when the man the corpse belonged to was alive, they are revealed in the form of a mathematical problem that is, as far as anyone has been able to discern, thoroughly unsolvable. Thus, in Grady's words, "Bishop Erkenwald is presented in the poem as the 'subject supposed to know,' but it turns out that he really doesn't." Grady, "Looking Awry," 119.

3. Scattergood, who is of the puzzling opinion that "univocality is what the poet aimed for from the beginning," considers that in the matter of its initial obscurities the poem ends by offering an "explanation in full." Scattergood, "*St. Erkenwald*," 194–195. Burrow comes to the same conclusion: "the answers offered by the corpse . . . provide explanations for everything that has been puzzling the Londoners about the marvel they have uncovered." Burrow, *Thinking in Poetry*, 16. So, too, Turville-Petre: "The first half relates the failure of historical enquiry using the standard sources; the second half describes how the questions about the past are miraculously answered." Turville-Petre, "*St. Erkenwald*," 65.

4. A series of articles appeared throughout the 1970s in which scholars faced off over these questions, beginning with Nolan and Farley-Hills, "The Authorship of Pearl." A bibliographical account of the debate can be found in Anonymous, *Saint Erkenwald*, 57n77. For the fruitlessness of the whole approach, see Pearsall, "Alliterative Revival."

5. See most recently Weiskott, *English Alliterative Verse*, for an account of the *status quaestionis*.

6. As Frank Grady has observed, with salutary distance, "*Saint Erkenwald* has always invited historicist readings"—including an earlier essay of his own. "Looking Awry," 105. The most perceptive such readings are Whatley, "Middle English *St. Erkenwald*"; Whatley, "Heathens and Saints"; Chism, *Alliterative Revivals*, chap. 2; and Grady, "*St. Erkenwald*."

7. Thus Burrow can write that the poem is a "pious fraud"; and against this view Turville-Petre can gather evidence that it is rather "a fully developed historical narrative that is not only true, but also. . . ." Burrow, *Thinking in Poetry*, 21; Turville-Petre, "*St. Erkenwald*," 374.

8. An overview of this debate can be found in Coley, *Wheel of Language*, 71–72.

9. Smith, "Crypt and Decryption," 75. On the medieval enigma, see Galloway, "Rhetoric of Riddling"; and Gruenler, *Piers Plowman*. The locus classicus is Augustine, *De trinitate*, 15.9.15. Anglo-Saxon riddles can be found in Williamson, *Feast of Creatures* and are discussed notably in Bitterli, *Say What I Am Called*. For a general history and theory of the enigma, see Cook, *Enigmas and Riddles*; for the enigma as the root of poetry, see Welsh, *Roots of Lyric*; and Tiffany, *Infidel Poetics*.

10. The "number symbolism" at work in the poem, and the way it can be divided up

according to certain numerical patterns, has been the subject of a certain amount of attention. See especially Peck, who discusses the "exact balances and antitheses" in the "gothic structure of the poem." "Number Structure," 10. In a different register, Grady has underscored the poem's resistance to "its own explicit narrative"; the fact that it is "full of doublings, and a certain kind of analysis reveals their pattern to be structural"; and gone so far as to read it as a kind of detective story. Grady, "Looking Awry," 106.

11. On cryptonymy, see Abraham and Torok, *Wolf Man's Magic Word*, and notably Derrida's foreword to that volume.

12. Anonymous, *Saint Erkenwald*, lines 52–58.

13. Grévin and Véronèse, "'Caractères' magiques," 339, 342, 344. The following pages rely extensively on this crucial article. Linda Voigts's essay on *caracteres* is also useful; in her telling, they should be understood as "extra-linguistic representations that lack clear-cut lexical referents." Voigts, "Character of the *Caracter*," 91. See also Flint, *Rise of Magic*, 244–247, 301–310. Reproductions of *caracteres* can be found in Voigts's essay, as well as in Kieckhefer, *Forbidden Rites*, 350–377; Véronèse, Ars notoria *au Moyen Âge*; and Lucentini, "Liber runarum," 431–438.

14. As Gager explains, *caracteres* were omnipresent after the second century. *Curse Tablets*, introduction. See also Dodds, *Greeks and the Irrational*, 291–295; Frankfurter, "Magic of Writing." On Anglo-Saxon use of *caracteres*, see Flint, *Rise of Magic*, 307. Needless to say, such inscriptions also appear with great frequency outside of a narrowly European context, for instance in Haitian veves, Tibetan dakini script, Indian yantras, and so forth.

15. For an edition and discussion, see Véronèse, Ars notoria *au Moyen Âge*. Klaassen reports that he has discovered more than fifty manuscripts in which such materials survive, and he indicates that there no doubt remain many others. Klaassen, "English Manuscripts of Magic," 14. See also Skemer, *Binding Words*, 116–124.

16. Voigts, "Character of the *Caracter*," 91.

17. See Skemer, *Binding Words*.

18. Chaucer, "General Prologue," line 418; Anonymous, *Sir Gawain*, lines 620–621. In the *Speculum astronomie*, "Salomian" magic is that characterized by the presence of *caracteres*; and the pentacle is sometimes considered an unpronounceable name, that is, of God. See Grévin and Véronèse, "'Caractères' magiques," 318, 330.

19. For Augustine's most notable discussion of *caracteres*, see his *De doctrina*, 2.30.75; he also mentions them in the *Enarratio in psalmos* and the *Treatise on Saint John's Gospel*. See Flint, *Forbidden Magic*, 244.

20. Article 167. See Piché, *Condamnation Parisienne*, 130–131 and de Libera, *Penser au moyen âge*, 195–196, 201–205. As Klaniczay notes, in a related context, such a "judgement might have resolved the debate from the theological point of view, but from an anthropological or historical perspective there is need to continue to reflect on the efficacy anthropologically." "Power of Words," 285.

21. The belief in the efficacy of the word is fundamental and, it would seem, universal. A certain technical analysis has been brought to bear on this matter in the field of anthropology; see such influential works as Tambiah, "Magical Power of Words," and Malinowski, *Coral Gardens*. Greene calls this belief the "conjunctive view." Greene, *Poetry, Signs, and Magic*, 30. On its operation in the ancient world, see especially Laín Entralgo, *Therapy of the Word*; for the Middle Ages, in addition to the works cited in the following notes, see Wilson, *Magical Universe*, 427–428; Bever, *Realities of Witch-*

craft, chap. 7; and Delaurenti, *Puissance des mots*, whose analysis forms the basis of my discussion in these paragraphs: "L'idée que les mots disposent d'un certain pouvoir, en particulier un pouvoir curatif, appartient au paysage culturel et intellectuel de l'époque, même si les auteurs ne cherchent pas toujours à en cerner la portée ni à en expliquer les causes" (24).

22. Bozoky, *Charmes et prières*, 61. On *ananizapta*, see Werner, "Ananizapta."
23. Meyer, *Recettes médicales*, 368.
24. See, for example, Thomas Fayreford's inscription "+ bhurnon + bhurini + bhituono" in Harley MS 2558, as cited in Olsan, "Charms in Medieval Memory," 74; and the innumerable instances in Lecouteux, *Dictionary of Ancient Magic Words*.
25. Skemer, *Binding Words*, 80.
26. Roper, *English Verbal Charms*, 20. For additional instances see Kieckhefer, *Magic in the Middle Ages*, 4.
27. See Olsan, "Marginality of Charms," 135. As Olsan notes, a cross is marked above each of these words in the manuscript where it is found.
28. On *onomata barbara*, see Bozoky, *Charmes et prières*; Graf, *Magic in the Ancient World*, 218–219; Gager, *Curse Tablets*; Frankfurter, "Magical Power"; and Miller, "In Praise of Nonsense." For an overview of surviving charms in Middle English, see Keiser, "Charms," 3669–3679, which makes reference to the Chaucerian charms of the "Miller's Tale," "Parson's Tale," and *Troilus*, and notes their "pervasiveness in medieval life." Roper, *English Verbal Charms*, is also useful.
29. Wilson, *Magical Universe*, xviii. In this connection, the use of curses in monastic contexts is of special interest. See Little, *Benedictine Maledictions*.
30. On the efficacy of runes, see Flowers, *Runes and Magic*. For an instance of runes used as *caracteres*, see Lucentini, "Liber Runarum"; and Burnett and Stoklund, "Scandinavian Runes."
31. Anonymous, *Saint Erkenwald*, lines 27–28.
32. Weill-Parot, *Les "images astrologiques,"* 37.
33. The locus classicus is Augustine, *De doctrina*, 2.24.
34. See Delaurenti, *Puissance des mots*. On this point, see also Rosier-Catach, *Parole efficace*, 124–125.
35. On Bacon, see Fanger, "Things Done Wisely," 108–109. The pertinent text of al-Kindi's is edited and discussed in Burnett, "Theory and Practice of Powerful Words"; see also Weill-Parot, *"Images astrologiques,"* 155–174. *Nomina barbara* on the order of *abracadabra* are sometimes held to possess a greater force than known words. Burnett has observed, of a prayer to be found in a twelfth-century work on talismans by Adelard of Bath, that its "words are mostly in the language of the speaker—i.e., fitted to his time and place, but include one word—*elaalem*—which is left in Arabic.... Within a context in which Arabic is not used (i.e., Bath, in the West of England), it becomes a nonsignificative word (a word with no meaning) which acquires its nature and effect directly from the celestial harmony." Burnett, "Theory and Practice," 226.
36. This spirit is not identified explicitly as the Third Person of the Trinity, but there is every reason to think that it is in fact the Holy Spirit. Of particular interest in this connection is the reference to the Pentecostal cenacle or upper room at line 336, which associates the ventriloquy of the corpse with the exemplary instance of speaking in tongues, so that Smith calls it a "mortuary version of the Pentecostal visitation of alien languages." "Crypt and Decryption," 65.

37. Anonymous, *Saint Erkenwald*, lines 193–196.
38. *Saint Erkenwald*, lines 16–22.
39. *Saint Erkenwald*, lines 297–300.
40. Wilson, *Magical Universe*, xx.
41. Rosier-Catach, *Parole efficace*, 115, 119, 288. The following paragraphs take their cue from this important book.
42. On this point, see Rosier-Catach, 36.
43. See Fulton, *From Judgment to Passion*, 41–42; and Chazelle, "Figure, Character, and the Glorified Body."
44. Rosier-Catach, *Parole efficace*, 28.
45. Rosier-Catach, 40.
46. Whatley, "Heathens and Saints," 353; Chism, *Alliterative Revivals*, 42; Coley, *Wheel of Language*, 75, 89. See also Kamowski, "*Saint Erkenwald*"; and Sisk, "Uneasy Orthodoxy."
47. Turville-Petre, "*St. Erkenwald*," 369; Scattergood, "*St. Erkenwald*," 199.
48. Bugbee, "Sight and Sound," 207.
49. See Colish, *Faith, Fiction and Force*, 94–95.
50. See Rosier-Catach, *Parole efficace*, 288–289.
51. See Lombard, *Sentences*, 4.6.4.
52. See Rosier-Catach, *Parole efficace*, 24–25.
53. See Boureau, *Satan the Heretic*, 156–157.
54. As Boureau writes, "the human categories dealt with [in such a discussion] are considered as judicial cases whose value is related precisely to their being extremes." Boureau, 158.
55. Bynum, *Fragmentation and Redemption*, chap. 7.
56. Anonymous, *Saint Erkenwald*, lines 311–323.
57. That the sighs are a part of the rite—the so-called sufflation—does not appear to have been remarked, no doubt for the very good reason that the explanation given in the poem leaves it out. In any event, the preponderance of sighs, wailings, and other inarticulate utterances in the poem should be approached in the light of the regular discussion of such things by medieval theorists of the sign.
58. Anonymous, *Saint Erkenwald*, lines 329–330.
59. Although the Middle English Dictionary treats these words as though they were lexically distinct, the rationale for this decision is murky at best. On this point, see Voigts, "Character of the Caracter," 93–94.
60. The crucial modern accounts of sacramental character are Galot, *La Nature du caractère sacramentel* and a series of articles devoted to the subject by Häring. Pourrat, *Théologie sacramentaire* has been superseded in certain respects but remains useful.
61. Both the concept of an inscription in the soul left by baptism and the word *character* appear to have been familiar to the earliest Christians. This concept and this word do not always correspond to each other, however, and it is not at all clear to what extent these matters were thought through technically before the twelfth century.
62. See Häring, "Berengar's Definitions," 134.
63. Gregory IX, *Decretals*, canon *Majores*, 3.42.3.
64. Campbell, *Lectures on Ecclesiastical History*, 185.
65. "Nam veteribus hoc ignotum fuit, et magis consentaneum est incantationibus

magicis, quam sanae Evangelii doctrinae." *Antidotum concilii Tridentini*, ad sess. VII, can 9, cited in Pourrat, *Théologie sacramentaire*, 187.

66. The locution "ornament of the soul" was used notably by William of Meliton and Alexander of Hales.

67. On this point, see Häring, "Berengar's Definitions," 133; Rosier-Catach, *Parole efficace*, 47; and Boureau, *Satan the Heretic*, 167.

68. See Häring, "Berengar's Definitions," 137; and Rosier-Catach, *Parole efficace*, 47–48.

69. See Rosier-Catach, *Parole efficace*, 47–50.

70. This possibility is pursued by Peper, "On the Mark."

71. On the medieval and early modern history of tattooing in the West, see Oettermann, *Zeichen auf der Haut*, 12–20. On penal *caracteres* in late antiquity and their afterlives in the Middle Ages and early modernity, see Gustafson, "*Inscripta in fronte*"; and Jones, "*Stigma*." Jones claims that penal branding was frequent in the Middle Ages. Reproductions of tattoo clichés ("flash") in the tradition of "crusader's stigmata" can be found in Pigorini-Beri, "Tatouage religieux." On Franciscan stigmata, see Frugoni, *Francesco e l'invenzione delle stimmate*. On Suso's inscription, see Keller, "Kolophon im Herzen"; and Hamburger, *Visual and the Visionary*, chap. 5.

72. See Leviticus 19.28 and 21.5, Deuteronomy 14.1, Revelation 19.16; Isidore, *Etymologies*, 386.

73. The association can be found notably in William of Malmesbury. See Thomas, "Interpretation of the Pictish Symbols"; and MacQuarrie, "Insular Celtic Tattooing." MacQuarrie's discussion of the *Vita S. Brigitae*—which constellates salvation, tattooing, and ambiguously visible or invisible marks in ways that recall *Erkenwald*—is of particular interest here; see 42–43.

74. Anonymous, *Saint Erkenwald*, lines 89–92.

75. See Constable, "Cross of the Crusaders"; and Schmitt, *Corps des images*, 80–81.

76. Häring, "Berengar's Definitions," 81.

77. Carswell, *Coptic Tattoo Designs*, plate 1.

78. Rosecrans, "Wearing the Universe."

79. Grévin and Véronèse "'Caractères' magiques," 361–362.

80. Anonymous, *Saint Erkenwald*, lines 341–348.

BIBLIOGRAPHY

Abelard, Peter. *Philosophische Schriften.* Vol. 1, *Die Logica "Ingredientibus."* Münster: Verlag der Aschendorffschen Verlagsbuchhandlung, 1921.
Abraham, Nicolas, and Maria Torok. *The Wolf Man's Magic Word: A Cryptonymy.* Translated by Nicholas Rand. Minneapolis: University of Minnesota Press, 2005.
Aelian. *De natura animalium.* Bibliotheca Scriptorum Graecorum et Romanorum Teubneriana. Berlin: De Gruyter, 2009.
Agamben, Giorgio. *The End of the Poem: Studies in Poetics.* Translated by Daniel Heller-Roazen. Stanford, CA: Stanford University Press, 1999.
———. *Idea of Prose.* Translated by Michael Sullivan and Sam Whitsitt. Albany: State University of New York Press, 1995.
———. *Infancy and History: The Destruction of Experience.* Translated by Liz Heron. London: Verso, 1993.
———. *La fine del pensiero/La fin de la pensée.* Paris: Le nouveau commerce, 1982.
———. *Language and Death: The Place of Negativity.* Translated by Karen E. Pinkus and Michael Hardt. Minneapolis: University of Minnesota Press, 1991.
———. *Potentialities: Collected Essays in Philosophy.* Edited and translated by Daniel Heller-Roazen. Stanford, CA: Stanford University Press, 1999.
———. "What is a Paradigm?" In *The Signature of All Things*, translated by Luca D'Isanto and Kevin Attell, 9–32. New York: Zone, 2009.
———. *What Is Philosophy?* Translated by Lorenzo Chiesa. Stanford, CA: Stanford University Press, 2017.
Akbari, Suzanne. *Idols in the East: European Representations of Islam and the Orient, 1100–1450.* Ithaca, NY: Cornell University Press, 2012.
———. *Seeing Through the Veil: Optical Theory and Medieval Allegory.* Toronto: University of Toronto Press, 2004.
Alford, John. "The Grammatical Metaphor: A Survey of Its Use in the Middle Ages." *Speculum* 57, no. 4 (1982): 728–760.
Allen, Valerie. "Broken Air." *Exemplaria* 16, no. 2 (2004): 305–322.
———. *On Farting: Language and Laughter in the Middle Ages.* New York: Palgrave Macmillan, 2007.
Ammonius. "On Aristotle On Interpretation 1–8." Edited by David Blank. London: Duckworth, 1996.
Ando, Clifford. "Augustine on Language." *Revue des études augustiniennes* 40 (1994): 45–78.
Anonymous. *The Cloud of Unknowing and the Book of Privy Counselling.* Edited by Phyllis Hodgson. EETS 218. London: Oxford University Press, 1944.
———. *Deonise Hid Diuinite and Other Treatises on Contemplative Prayer Related to the Cloud of Unknowing.* Edited by Phyllis Hodgson. EETS 172. London: Oxford University Press, 1955.
———. *The Latin Versions of* The Cloud of Unknowing. Edited by John Clark. Salzburg: Institut für Anglistik und Amerikanistik, 1989.
———. *Saint Erkenwald.* Edited by Clifford Peterson. Philadelphia: University of Pennsylvania Press, 1977.

———. *Sir Gawain and the Green Knight*. In *The Poems of the Pearl Manuscript: Pearl, Cleanness, Patience, Sir Gawain and the Green Knight*, edited by Malcolm Andrew and Ronald Waldron, 207–300. Exeter: University of Exeter Press, 2007.
Anselm of Canterbury. *The Major Works*. Edited by Brian Davies and Gillian Evans. New York: Oxford University Press, 1998.
———. *Opera omnia*. Edited by F. S. Schmitt. Edinburgh: Thomas Nelson and Sons, 1946.
Apstein, Barbara. "Chaucer, Virginia Woolf, and *Between the Acts*." *Woolf Studies Annual* 2 (1996): 117–133.
Aquinas, Thomas. *Expositio libri Peryermenias*. Opera Omnia. Rome-Paris: J. Vrin/Commissio Leonina, 1989.
Arens, Hans. *Aristotle's Theory of Language and Its Tradition: Texts from 500 to 1750*. Philadelphia: John Benjamins, 1984.
Aristophanes. *Frogs. Assemblywomen. Wealth*. Edited and translated by Jeffrey Henderson. Loeb Classical Library 180. Cambridge, MA: Harvard University Press, 2002.
Aristotle. *Aristoteles latinus*. Vol. 2. Edited by L. Minio-Paluello. Bruges: Desclée, De Brouwer, 1965.
———. *Categories and De Interpretatione*. Translated by J. L. Ackrill. London: Oxford University Press, 1963.
———. *Metaphysics*. Vol. 1, *Books 1–9*. Translated by Hugh Tredennick. Loeb Classical Library 271. Cambridge, MA: Harvard University Press, 1933.
———. *On the Soul. Parva Naturalia. On Breath*. Translated by W. S. Hett. Loeb Classical Library 288. Cambridge, MA: Harvard University Press, 1957.
Artemidorus. *The Interpretation of Dreams*. Translated by Robert White. Park Ridge: Noyes Press, 1975.
Ashworth, E. J., and Paul Vincent Spade. "Logic in Late Medieval Oxford." In *The History of the University of Oxford*, edited by J. I. Catto and Ralph Evans, 35–64. Oxford: Oxford University Press, 1992.
Auerbach, Erich. "Figura." In *Time, History, and Literature: Selected Essays*, edited by James Porter, 65–113. Translated by Jane Newman. Princeton, NJ: Princeton University Press, 2014.
Augustine. *Against the Academicians and The Teacher*. Translated by Peter King. Indianapolis: Hackett, 1995.
———. *Confessions*. Vol. 1, *Books 1–8*. Translated by Carolyn J.-B. Hammond. Loeb Classical Library 26. Cambridge, MA: Harvard University Press, 2014.
———. *De dialectica*. Edited by Jan Pinborg. Dordrecht: Reidel, 1975.
———. *De doctrina christiana*. Edited and translated by R. P. H. Green. New York: Oxford University Press, 1995.
———. *De magistro*. Edited by Jacques-Paul Migne. Patrologia Latina 32. Paris: Garnier, 1877.
———. *On the Trinity*. Edited by John Rotelle. Translated by Edmund Hill. Hyde Park: New City, 1991.
———. *Sermons*. Edited by John Rotelle. Translated by Edmund Hill. Hyde Park: New City, 1994.
Ax, Wolfram. *Laut, Stimme und Sprache: Studien zu Drei Grundbegriffen der Antiken Sprachtheorie*. Göttingen: Vandenhoeck and Ruprecht, 1986.

Bacon, Roger. *Compendium of the Study of Theology*. Studien und Texte zur Geistesgeschichte des Mittelalters. Vol. 20. Leiden: E. J. Brill, 1988.
———. *Compendium studii theologiae*. Translated and edited by Thomas Maloney. Leiden: Brill, 1988.
———. "De signis." Edited by K. M. Fredborg, Lauge Nielsen, and Jan Pinborg. *Traditio* 34 (1978): 75–136.
Bataille, Georges. *The Accursed Share*. Vol. 1. Translated by Robert Hurley. New York: Zone, 1991.
Bakhtin, Mikhail. *Rabelais and His World*. Translated by Hélène Iswolsky. Bloomington: Indiana University Press, 1984.
Ball, Hugo. *Flight out of Time: A Dada Diary*. Edited by John Elderfield. Translated by Ann Raimes. Berkeley: University of California Press, 1996.
Baratin, Marc. "Les Origines stoïciennes de la théorie augustinienne du signe." *Revue des études latines* 59 (1981): 260–268.
Baratin, Marc, Bernard Colombat, and Louis Holtz, eds. *Priscien: Transmission et refondation de la grammaire de l'antiquité aux modernes*. Studia Aristarum 21. Turnhout: Brepols, 2009.
Bardin, Gay. "The Poetics of Nullity: 'Nonsense' Verses of William of Aquitaine, Jaufre Rudel, and Raimbaut d'Orange." *Comitatus* 34 (2003): 1–23.
Barthes, Roland. *The Rustle of Language*. Translated by Richard Howard. New York: Macmillan, 1987.
Barthes, Roland. *S/Z*. Translated by Richard Miller. New York: Hill and Wang, 1974.
Baudelaire, Charles. *Oeuvres complètes*. Paris: Seuil, 1968.
Beckett, Samuel. *Three Novels: Molloy, Malone Dies, The Unnameable*. New York: Grove, 2009.
Beech, George. "Troubadour Contacts with Muslim Spain and Knowledge of Arabic: New Evidence Concerning William IX of Aquitaine." *Romania* 113 (1992): 14–42.
Benjamin, Walter. *Gesammelte Schriften*. Frankfurt: Suhrkamp, 1972.
———. *On Hashish*. Translated by Howard Eiland. Cambridge, MA: Harvard University Press, 2006.
———. "On the Middle Ages." In *Early Writings: 1910–1917*, translated by Howard Eiland, 238–240. Cambridge, MA: Harvard University Press, 2011.
———. *The Origin of German Tragic Drama*. Translated by John Osborne. New York: Verso, 1998.
———. *Selected Writings*. Edited by Marcus Bullock and Michael W. Jennings. Cambridge, MA: Harvard University Press, 2004.
———. *Über Haschisch*. Frankfurt am Main: Suhrkamp, 1972.
Bennett, Alastair. "*Brevis oratio penetrat celum*: Proverbs, Prayers, and Lay Understanding in Late Medieval England." *New Medieval Literatures* 14 (2012): 127–163.
Bernhart, Walter, and Lawrence Kramer, eds. *On Voice*. New York: Rodopi, 2014.
Bever, Edward. *The Realities of Witchcraft and Popular Magic in Early Modern Europe: Culture, Cognition, and Everyday Life*. New York: Palgrave, 2008.
Beylsmit, J. J. "Un Moyen d'exprimer 'ne dire/savoir absolument rien': Pour le commentaire de 'ne bu ne ba.'" *Neuphilologische Mitteilungen* 60, no. 4 (1959): 334–347.
Biard, Joël. *Logique et théorie du signe au XIVe siècle*. Paris: J. Vrin, 1989.
———. "La Redéfinition ockhamiste de la signification." In *Sprache und Erkenntnis im*

Mittelalter, edited by Jan P. Beckmann and Wolfgang Kluxen, 1:451–458. Miscellanea mediaevalia 13. Berlin: Walter de Gruyter, 1981.

———. "Semantique et ontologie dans l'Ars meliduna." In *Gilbert de Poitiers et ses contemporains aux origines de la logica modernorum*, edited by Jean Jolivet and Alain de Libera, 121–144. Naples: Bibliopolis, 1987.

Bishop, Louise M. *Words, Stones, and Herbs: The Healing Word in Medieval and Early Modern England*. Syracuse, NY: Syracuse University Press, 2007.

Bitterli, Dieter. *Say What I Am Called: The Old English Riddles of the Exeter Book and the Anglo-Latin Riddle Tradition*. Toronto: University of Toronto Press, 2009.

Black, Deborah. "Aristotle's Peri Hermeneias in Medieval Latin and Arabic Philosophy: Logic and the Linguistic Arts." In *Aristotle and His Medieval Interpreters*, edited by Richard Bosley and Martin Tweedale, 3–46. Calgary: University of Calgary Press, 1992.

Bloch, R. Howard. *The Anonymous Marie de France*. Chicago: University of Chicago Press, 2003.

———. "Augustine, Mallarmé, and the Medieval Roots of Modernity." *Modern Language Notes* 127 Supplement (2012): S6–S22.

Boase, Roger. "Arab Influences on European Love-Poetry." In *The Legacy of Muslim Spain*, edited by Salma Khadra Jayyusi, 457–482. Leiden: Brill, 1992.

Bodel, Jehan. *Le Jeu de saint Nicolas*. Edited by Albert Henry. Brussels: Presses Universitaires de Bruxelles, 1965.

Boehner, Philotheus. "Ockham's Theory of Signification." *Franciscan Studies* 6 (1946): 145–170.

Boethius. *Boethius: On Aristotle on Interpretation 1–3*. Translated by Andrew Smith. London: Duckworth, 2010.

———. *Commentarii in librum Aristotelis Peri hermeneias, pars posterior, secundam editionem continens*. Edited by Carl Meiser. Leipzig: Teubner, 1880.

Boh, Ivan. "Walter Burley." In *Individuation in Scholasticism: The Later Middle Ages and the Counter-Reformation, 1150–1650*, edited by Jorge J. E. Gracia, 347–372. Albany: State University of New York Press, 1994.

Boitani, Piero. *Chaucer and the Imaginary World of Fame*. Cambridge: Brewer, 1984.

———. "A Reading of the Cloud of Unknowing." In *Thou Sittest at Another Boke . . . : English Studies in Honour of Domenico Pezzini*, edited by Giovanni Iamartino, Maria Luisa Maggioni, and Roberta Facchinetti, 187–208. Milan: Polimetrica, 2008.

Bond, Gerald A. "Philological Comments on a New Edition of the First Troubadour." *Romance Philology* 30, no. 2 (1976): 343–361.

Bos, Egbert. "Speaking about Signs: Fourteenth-Century Views on Suppositio Materialis." In *"Der muoz mir süezer worte jehen": liber amicorum für Norbert Voorwinden*, edited by Sjaak Onderdelinden, 71–86. Amsterdam: Rodopi, 1997.

Boureau, Alain. *Satan the Heretic: The Birth of Demonology in the Medieval West*. Translated by Teresa Lavender Fagan. Chicago: University of Chicago Press, 2006.

Bower, Calvin. "Sonus, Vox, Chorda, Nota: Thing, Name, and Sign in Early Medieval Theory." In *Quellen und Studien zur Musiktheorie des Mittelalters*, 3:47–61. Munich: C. H. Beck, 2001.

Bowers, John M. "Chaucer after Smithfield: From Postcolonial Writer to Imperialist Author." In *The Postcolonial Middle Ages*, edited by Jeffrey Jerome Cohen, 53–66. New York: Palgrave Macmillan, 2000.

Boyancé, Pierre. *Le Culte des muses chez les philosophes grecs*. Paris: Editions de Boccard, 1972.
Boynton, Susan, Sarah Kay, Alison Cornish, and Andrew Albin. "Sound Matters." *Speculum* 91, no. 4 (2016): 998–1039.
Bozoky, Edina. *Charmes et prières apotropaïques*. Turnhout: Brepols, 2003.
Braakhuis, H. A. G. "Signification, Appelation and Predication in the Ars Meliduna." In *Gilbert de Poitiers et ses contemporains aux origines de la Logica modernorum*, edited by Jean Jolivet and Alain de Libera, 107–120. Naples: Bibliopolis, 1987.
Braakhuis, H. A. G., and C. H. Kneepkens. *Aristotle's Peri Hermeneias in the Latin Middle Ages: Essays on the Commentary Tradition*. Groningen: Ingenium, 2003.
Brantley, Jessica. *Reading in the Wilderness: Private Devotion and Public Performance in Late Medieval England*. Chicago: University of Chicago Press, 2007.
Braudy, Leo. *The Frenzy of Renown: Fame and Its History*. New York: Oxford University Press, 1986.
Browne, Thomas. "The Garden of Cyrus." In *The Major Works*, edited by C. A. Patrides, 317–388. New York: Penguin, 1977.
Bruce, Scott. *Silence and Sign Language in Medieval Monasticism: The Cluniac Tradition c. 900–1200*. Cambridge: Cambridge University Press, 2007.
Bugbee, John. "Sight and Sound in *St Erkenwald*: On Theodicy and the Senses." *Medium Ævum* 77, no. 2 (2008): 202–221.
Burch, Sally. "The Prologue to Marie's *Lais*: Back to the Littera." *Journal of the Australasian Universities Language and Literature Association* 89, no. 1 (1998): 15–42.
Burley, Walter. *De puritate artis logicae. Tractus longior*. Edited by Philotheus Boehner. St. Bonaventure, NY: Franciscan Institute, 1955.
———. *On the Purity of the Art of Logic: The Shorter and the Longer Treatises*. Edited by Paul Spade. New Haven, CT: Yale University Press, 2000.
———. "Walter Burleigh's Treatise *De suppositionibus* and Its Influence on William of Ockham." Edited by Stephen Brown. *Franciscan Studies* 32 (1972): 15–64.
———. "Walter Burley's Middle Commentary on Aristotle's Perihermeneias." Edited by Stephen Brown. *Franciscan Studies* 33 (1973): 45–134.
Burnett, Charles. "Sound and Its Perception in the Middle Ages." In *The Second Sense: Studies in Hearing and Musical Judgment from Antiquity to the Seventeeth Century*, edited by Charles Burnett, Michael Fend, and Penelope Gouk, 43–69. London: Warburg Institute, 1991.
———. "The Theory and Practice of Powerful Words in Medieval Magical Texts." In *The Word in Medieval Logic, Theology and Psychology*, edited by Tetsuro Shimizu and Charles Burnett, 215–231. Turnhout: Brepols, 2009.
Burnett, Charles, and Marie Stoklund. "Scandinavian Runes in a Latin Magical Treatise." *Speculum* 58, no. 2 (1983): 419–429.
Burrow, J. A. W. "Fantasy and Language in the Cloud of Unknowing." In *Essays on Medieval Literature*, 132–147. Oxford: Clarendon Press, 1984.
———. *Thinking in Poetry*. London: Birbeck College, 1993.
Butler, Shane. *The Ancient Phonograph*. New York: Zone, 2015.
Bynum, Caroline Walker. *Christian Materiality: An Essay on Religion in Late Medieval Europe*. New York: Zone, 2015.
———. *Fragmentation and Redemption: Essays on Gender and the Human Body in Medieval Religion*. New York: Zone, 1992.

Cabezón, José Ignacio, ed. *Scholasticism: Cross-Cultural and Comparative Perspectives.* Albany: State University of New York Press, 1998.
Calasso, Roberto. *Literature and the Gods.* Translated by Tim Parks. New York: Vintage, 2001.
Cameron, Margaret. "Boethius on Utterances, Understanding and Reality." In *The Cambridge Companion to Boethius*, edited by John Marenbon, 85–104. Cambridge: Cambridge University Press, 2009.
———. "What's in a Name? Students of William of Champeaux on the *vox significativa*." *Bochumer Philosophisches Jahrbuch für Antike und Mittelalter* 9, no. 1 (2004): 93–114.
Cameron, Margaret and John Marenbon. "Aristotelian Logic East and West, 500–1500: On Interpretation and Prior Analytics in Two Traditions." *Vivarium* 48 (2010): 1–6.
Campbell, George. *Lectures on Ecclesiastical History.* Philadelphia: Hopkins, 1807.
Cannon, Christopher. *From Literacy to Literature: England, 1300–1400.* New York: Oxford University Press, 2016.
Carabelli, Giancarlo. "Blictri: una parola per arlecchino." In *Eredità dell'Illuminismo*, edited by Antonio Santucci, 231–257. Bologna: Il Mulino, 1979.
Carnap, Rudolf. *Logische Syntax der Sprache.* Vienna: Springer, 1934.
Carroll, Lewis. *The Annotated Alice: Alice's Adventures in Wonderland and Through the Looking Glass.* New York: Bramhall House, 1960.
Carruthers, Mary. *The Book of Memory.* New York: Cambridge University Press, 1990.
Carsley, Catherine A. "Devotion to the Holy Name: Late Medieval Piety in England." *Princeton University Library Chronicle* 53 (1991–1992): 157–172.
Carswell, John. *Coptic Tattoo Designs.* Beirut: American University of Beirut, 1958.
Cary, Phillip. *Outward Signs: The Powerlessness of External Things in Augustine's Thought.* New York: Oxford University Press, 2008.
Cavarero, Adriana. *For More Than One Voice: Toward a Philosophy of Vocal Expression.* Stanford, CA: Stanford University Press, 2005.
Certeau, Michel de. "Vocal Utopias: Glossolalias." *Representations*, no. 56 (1996): 29–47.
Cesalli, Laurent. "Le Réalisme propositionnel de Walter Burley." *Archives d'histoire doctrinale et littéraire du Moyen Âge* 68, no. 1 (2001): 155–221.
Chaucer, Geoffrey. *The Riverside Chaucer.* Edited by Larry Benson. Boston, MA: Houghton Mifflin, 1987.
Chazelle, Celia. "Figure, Character, and the Glorified Body in the Carolingian Eucharistic Controversy." *Traditio* 47 (1992): 1–36.
Chenu, Marie-Dominique. "Grammaire et théologie aux XIIe et XIII siècles." *Archives d'histoire doctrinale et littéraire du Moyen Âge* 10 (1936): 5–28.
Chism, Christine. *Alliterative Revivals.* Philadelphia: University of Pennsylvania Press, 2012.
Clanvowe, John. "The Boke of Cupide, God of Love." In *Chaucerian Dream Visions and Complaints*, edited by Dana Symons, 43–52. TEAMS. Kalamazoo: Medieval Institute Publications, 2004.
Cohen, Jeffrey Jerome. *Stone: An Ecology of the Inhuman.* Minneapolis: University of Minnesota Press, 2015.
Cole, Andrew, and D. Vance Smith, eds. *The Legitimacy of the Middle Ages.* Durham, NC: Duke University Press, 2010.

Coley, David. *The Wheel of Language: Representing Speech in Middle English Poetry, 1377–1422*. Syracuse, NY: Syracuse University Press, 2012.
Colish, Marcia. *The Mirror of Language*. Lincoln: University of Nebraska Press, 1983.
———. *The Stoic Tradition from Antiquity to the Early Middle Ages*. Leiden: Brill, 1985.
———. *Faith, Fiction and Force in Medieval Baptismal Debates*. Washington, DC: Catholic University of America, 2014.
Colli, Giorgio. *La nascita della filosofia*. Milan: Adelphi, 1975.
Constable, Gilles. "The Cross of the Crusaders." In *Crusaders and Crusading in the Twelfth Century*. Burlington, VT: Ashgate, 2008.
Conti, Alessandro D., ed. *A Companion to Walter Burley: Late Medieval Logician and Metaphysician*. Leiden: Brill, 2013.
Cook, Eleanor. *Enigmas and Riddles in Literature*. New York: Cambridge University Press, 2006.
Coolman, Boyd Taylor. "The Medieval Affective Dionysian Tradition." *Modern Theology* 24, no. 4 (2008): 615–632.
Coomaraswwamy, Rama. *The Invocation of the Name of Jesus as Practiced in the Western Church*. Louisville, KY: Fons Vitae, 1999.
Cooper-Rompato, Christine F. *The Gift of Tongues: Women's Xenoglossia in the Later Middle Ages*. University Park: Pennsylvania State University Press, 2010.
Copeland, Rita. "The Trivium and the Classics." In *The Oxford History of Classical Reception in English Literature*. Vol. 1, *800–1558*. Edited by Rita Copeland, 53–76. New York: Oxford University Press, 2016.
———. *Rhetoric, Hermeneutics, and Translation in the Middle Ages: Academic Traditions and Vernacular Texts*. New York: Cambridge University Press, 1991.
Copeland, Rita, and Ineke Sluiter. *Medieval Grammar and Rhetoric: Language Arts and Literary Theory, AD 300–1475*. New York: Oxford University Press, 2009.
Corbin, Henry. *Avicenna and the Visionary Recital*. Translated by Willard R. Trask. Princeton, NJ: Princeton University Press, 1960.
Courtenay, William. *Ockham and Ockhamism: Studies in the Dissemination and Impact of His Thought*. Leiden: Brill, 2008.
———. *Schools and Scholars in Fourteenth-Century England*. Princeton, NJ: Princeton University Press, 1987.
Crane, Susan. *Animal Encounters: Contacts and Concepts in Medieval Britain*. Philadelphia: University of Pennsylvania Press, 2013.
Craun, Edwin. *Lies, Slander, and Obscenity in Medieval English Literature: Pastoral Rhetoric and the Deviant Speaker*. Cambridge: Cambridge University Press, 1997.
Cribiore, Raffaella. *Gymnastics of the Mind: Greek Education in Hellenistic and Roman Egypt*. Princeton, NJ: Princeton University Press, 2001.
———. *Writing, Teachers, and Students in Graeco-Roman Egypt*. Atlanta: Scholars Press, 1996.
Dante Alighieri. *De vulgari eloquentia*. Edited by Steven Botterill. Cambridge: Cambridge University Press, 2005.
———. *The Divine Comedy*. Vol. 1, *Inferno*. Translated by Charles Singleton. Princeton, NJ: Princeton University Press, 1970.
Davis, Isabel, and Catherine Nall, eds. *Chaucer and Fame: Reputation and Reception*. Cambridge: Brewer, 2015.

Davis, R. Evan. "The Pendant in the Chaucer Portraits." *Chaucer Review* 17, no. 2 (1982): 193–195.
De Libera, Alain. *La Querelle des universaux*. Paris: Seuil, 1996.
———. *Penser au moyen âge*. Paris: Seuil, 1991.
———. "Roger Bacon et la logique." In *Roger Bacon and the Sciences*, edited by Jeremiah Hackett, 103–132. Leiden: Brill, 1997.
———. "Les Summulae dialectices de Roger Bacon I–II. De termino, De enuntiatione." *Archives d'histoire doctrinale et littéraire du Moyen Âge* 53 (1986): 139–289.
De Man, Paul. "The Concept of Irony." In *Aesthetic Ideology*, edited by Andrzej Warminski, 163–184. Minneapolis: University of Minnesota Press, 1996.
———. *The Resistance to Theory*. Minneapolis: University of Minnesota Press, 1986.
De Rijk, Lambert-Marie. "Boethius on De Interpretatione (ch. 3): Is He a Reliable Guide?" In *Boèce ou la chaîne des savoirs*, edited by Alain Galonnier, 207–227. Louvain: Peeters, 2003.
———. *Logica Modernorum: A Contribution to the History of Early Terminist Logic*. Assen: Van Gorcum, 1967.
———. "On the Chronology of Boethius' Works on Logic." *Vivarium* 2 (1964): 1–49.
Delaurenti, Béatrice. *La Puissance des mots. "Virtus verborum": Débats doctrinaux sur le pouvoir des incantations au Moyen Âge*. Paris: Cerf, 2007.
Deleuze, Gilles, and Félix Guattari. *Kafka: Toward a Minor Literature*. Translated by Dana Polan. Minneapolis: University of Minnesota Press, 1986.
Denecker, Tim, and Gert Partoens. "De uoce et uerbo: Augustine's exegesis of John 1:1–3 and 23 in sermons 288 and 293A auct. (Dolbeau 3)." *Annali di storia dell'esegesi* 31 (2014): 95–118.
Denifle, P. Heinrich. *Die Entstehung der Universitäten des Mittelalters bis 1400*. Berlin: Weidmannsche, 1885.
Derrida, Jacques. *Dissemination*. Translated by Barbara Johnson. Chicago: University of Chicago Press, 1981.
Dillon, Emma. *The Sense of Sound: Musical Meaning in France, 1260–1330*. The New Cultural History of Music. New York: Oxford University Press, 2012.
Dillon, Janette. *Language and Stage in Medieval and Renaissance England*. New York: Cambridge University Press, 1998.
Diogenes Laertius. *Lives of Eminent Philosophers*. Translated by M. A. Hicks. Cambridge, MA: Harvard University Press, 1950.
Dod, Bernard. "Aristoteles Latinus." In *The Cambridge History of Later Medieval Philosophy from the Rediscovery of Aristotle to the Disintegration of Scholasticism 1100–1600*, edited by Norman Kretzmann, Anthony Kenny, and Jan Pinborg, 45–79. Cambridge: Cambridge University Press, 1982.
Dodds, E. R. *The Ancient Concept of Progress and Other Essays on Greek Literature and Belief*. New York: Oxford, 1973.
———. *The Greeks and the Irrational*. Berkeley: University of California Press, 1951.
Dolar, Mladen. *A Voice and Nothing More*. Cambridge, MA: MIT Press, 2006.
Dragonetti, Roger. "Dante face à Nemrod: Babel mémoire et miroir de l'Eden." *Critique* 387–388 (1979): 690–706.
Dronke, Peter. *Dante and Medieval Latin Traditions*. London: Cambridge University Press, 1989.

Dunn, Marilyn. *The Emergence of Monasticism: From the Desert Fathers to the Early Middle Ages*. Oxford: Blackwell, 2000.
Duns Scotus, John. *Opera omnia*. Vatican City: Typis Polyglottis Vaticanis, 1950.
Durling, Robert M., and Ronald L. Martinez. *Time and the Crystal: Studies in Dante's Rime Petrose*. Berkeley: University of California Press, 1990.
Ebbesen, Sten. "Boethius as an Aristotelian Commentator." In *Aristotle Transformed*, edited by Richard Sorabji, 373–391. Ithaca, NY: Cornell University Press, 1990.
———. "Boethius on the Metaphysics of Words." In *Boèce ou la chaîne des savoirs*, edited by Alain Galonnier, 257–275. Louvain: Peeters, 2003.
———. "OXYNAT: A Theory about the Origins of British Logic." In *The Rise of British Logic*, edited by Osmund Lewry, 1–17. Toronto: Pontifical Institute of Medieval Studies, 1985.
Ebbesen, Sten, and Irène Rosier-Catach. "Le trivium à la Faculté des arts." In *L'enseignement des disciplines à la Faculté des arts (Paris et Oxford, XIIIe–XVe siècles)*, edited by Olga Weijers and Louis Holtz, 97–128. Studia Artistarum 4. Turnhout: Brepols, 1997.
Ebin, Lois. "Lydgate's Views on Poetry." *Annuale Mediaevale* 18 (1977): 76–105.
Eccles, Mark, ed. *Mankind*. In *The Macro Plays: The Castle of Perseverance, Wisdom, Mankind*, 153–184. EETS 262. London: Oxford University Press, 1969.
Eco, Umberto. "Latratus canis." *Tijdschrift voor Filosofie* 47, no. 1 (1985): 3–14.
———. "Signification and Denotation from Boethius to Ockham." *Franciscan Studies* 44 (1984): 1–29.
———. *The Aesthetics of Chaosmos: The Middle Ages of James Joyce*. Translated by Ellen Esrock. Cambridge, MA: Harvard University Press, 1989.
Eco, Umberto, and Constantino Marmo. *On the Medieval Theory of Signs*. Philadelphia: John Benjamins, 1989.
Ellis, Steve. "Virginia Woolf's Middle Ages." In *Medieval Afterlives in Popular Culture*, edited by Gail Ashton and Daniel T. Kline, 42–55. New York: Palgrave Macmillan, 2012.
Elwert, Theodor. "L'Emploi des langues étrangères comme procédé stylistique." *Revue de littérature comparée* 34 (1960): 409–437.
Fanger, Claire. "Things Done Wisely by a Wise Enchanter: Negotiating the Power of Words in the Thirteenth Century." *Esoterica* I (1999): 97–132.
Felman, Shoshana. "Henry James: Madness and the Risks of Practice (The Uses of Misprision)." In *Writing and Madness (Literature/Philosophy/Psychoanalysis)*, 141–250. Palo Alto, CA: Stanford University Press, 2003.
Fenster, Thelma, and Daniel Lord Smail, eds. *Fama: The Politics of Talk and Reputation in Medieval Europe*. Ithaca, NY: Cornell University Press, 2003.
Flint, Valerie. *The Rise of Magic in Early Medieval Europe*. Princeton, NJ: Princeton University Press, 1991.
Flowers, Stephen E. *Runes and Magic: Magical Formulaic Elements in the Older Runic Tradition*. Bastrop: Lodestar, 2014.
Fontenrose, Joseph. *The Delphic Oracle: Its Responses and Operations with a Catalogue of Responses*. Berkeley: University of California Press, 1978.

Frankfurter, David. "The Magic of Writing and the Writing of Magic: The Power of the Word in Egyptian and Greek Traditions." *Helios* 21 (1994): 189–221.
Fredborg, Karin Margareta. "Roger Bacon on 'Impositio vocis ad significandum.'" In *English Logic and Semantics from the End of the Twelfth Century to the Time of Ockham and Burleigh*, edited by H. A. G. Braakhuis, C. H. Kneepkens, and L. M. de Rijk, 167–191. Artistarium supplementa I. Nijmegen: Ingenium, 1981.
———. "The Priscian Commentary from the Second Half of the Twelfth Century: Ms Leiden BPL 154." *Histoire Épistémologie Langage* 12, no. 2 (1990): 53–68.
———. "The Unity of the Trivium." In *Sprachtheorien in Spätantike und Mittelalter*, edited by Sten Ebbesen, 325–338. Tübingen: Narr, 1995.
Frege, Gottlob. "Über Sinn und Bedeutung." In *Kleine Schriften*, edited by I Angelelli, 143–162. Hildesheim: Georg Olms Verlag, 1990.
Fritz, Jean-Marie. *La Cloche et la lyre. Pour une poétique médiévale du paysage sonore*. Geneva: Droz, 2011.
Frugoni, Chiara. *Francesco e l'invenzione delle stimmate: Una storia per parole e immagini fino a Bonaventura e Giotto*. Turin: Einaudi, 1993.
Fulton, Rachel. "Praying with Anselm at Admont: A Meditation on Practice." *Speculum* 81, no. 3 (2006): 700–733.
———. *From Judgment to Passion: Devotion to Christ and the Virgin Mary, 800–1200*. New York: Columbia University Press, 2002.
Gager, John G. *Curse Tablets and Binding Spells from the Ancient World*. New York: Oxford University Press, 1992.
Galen. *Opera Omnia*. Edited by C. G. Kühn. Vol. 8. Leipzig: C. Cnobloch, 1824.
Galloway, Andrew. "The Rhetoric of Riddling in Late-Medieval England: The 'Oxford' Riddles, the *Secretum philosophorum*, and the Riddles in *Piers Plowman*." *Speculum* 70, no. 1 (1995): 68–105.
Galot, Jean. *La Nature du caractère sacramentel*. Paris: Desclée de Brouwer, 1956.
Garapon, Robert. *La Fantaisie verbale et le comique dans le théâtre français du Moyen Âge à la fin du XVIIe siècle*. Paris: A. Colin, 1957.
Gehl, P. F. "Competens Silentium: Varieties of Monastic Silence in the Medieval West." *Viator* 18, no. 1 (1987): 125–160.
Gide, André. "Dada." *Nouvelle Revue Française* 14 (1920): 477–481.
Gillespie, Vincent. "Postcards from the Edge: Interpreting the Ineffable in the Middle English Mystics." In *Interpretation: Medieval and Modern*, edited by Piero Boitani and Anna Torti, 137–165. Cambridge: Brewer, 1993.
———. "Vernacular Theology." In *Middle English: Oxford Twenty-First Century Approaches to Literature*, edited by Paul Strohm, 401–420. New York: Oxford, 2007.
Gorst, Emma. "Interspecies Mimicry: Birdsong in Chaucer's 'Manciple's Tale' and *The Parlement of Fowles*." *New Medieval Literatures* 12 (2010): 147–154.
Grady, Frank. "Looking Awry at *St Erkenwald*." *Exemplaria* 23, no. 2 (2011): 105–125.
———. "*St. Erkenwald* and the Merciless Parliament." *Studies in the Age of Chaucer* 22 (2000): 179–211.
Graf, Fritz. *Magic in the Ancient World*. Cambridge, MA: Harvard University Press, 1999.
Greene, Thomas M. *Poetry, Signs, and Magic*. Newark: University of Delaware Press, 2005.

Grévin, Benoît, and Julien Véronèse. "Les 'Caractères' magiques au moyen âge (XIIe–XIVe siècle)." *Bibliothèque de l'École des chartes* 162 (2004): 305–379.
Gruenler, Curtis A. *Piers Plowman and the Poetics of Enigma: Riddles, Rhetoric, and Theology*. Notre Dame, IN: University of Notre Dame Press, 2017.
Guenther, Herbert V., and Chögyam Trungpa. *The Dawn of Tantra*. In *The Collected Works of Chögyam Trungpa*, edited by Carolyn Rose Gimian, 4:331–419. Boston, MA: Shambhala, 2003.
Guglielmo IX. *Poesie*. Edited by Nicolò Pasero. Modena: STEM Mucchi, 1973.
Guiter, Henri. "Sur deux passages obscurs de Dante et de Jehan Bodel." *Revue des langues romanes* 77 (1967): 179–186.
Gurd, Sean Alexander. *Dissonance: Auditory Aesthetics in Ancient Greece*. New York: Fordham University Press, 2016.
Gustafson, W. Mark. "*Inscripta in fronte*: Penal Tattooing in Late Antiquity." *Classical Antiquity* 16, no. 1 (1997): 79–105.
Hadot, Ilsetraut. *Arts libéraux et philosophie dans la pensée antique. Contribution à l'histoire de l'éducation et de la culture dans l'Antiquité*. Paris: Vrin, 2005.
Hamburger, Jeffrey F. *The Visual and the Visionary: Art and Female Spirituality in Late Medieval Germany*. New York: Zone, 1998.
Hamsun, Knut. *Hunger*. Translated by George Egerton. New York: Knopf, 1920.
Häring, Nicholas M. "Berengar's Definitions of *Sacramentum* and Their Influence on Mediaeval Sacramentology." *Mediaeval Studies* 10 (1948): 109–146.
———. "Character, Signum, und Signaculum: Der Weg von Petrus Damiani bis zur eigentlichen Aufnahme in die Sakramentenlehre im 12. Jahrhundert." *Scholastik: Vierteljahrschrift für Theologie und Philosophie* 31 (1956): 41–69.
———. "Character, Signum, und Signaculum: Die Einführung in die Sakramententheologie des 12. Jahrhunderts." *Scholastik: Vierteljahrschrift für Theologie und Philosophie* 31 (1956): 182–212.
———. "Character, Signum, und Signaculum: Die Entwicklung bis nach der karolingischen Renaissance." *Scholastik: Vierteljahrschrift für Theologie und Philosophie* 30 (1955): 481–512.
———. "St. Augustine's Use of the Word *Character*." *Mediaeval Studies* 14:1 (1952): 79–97.
Harris, Max. *Sacred Folly: A New History of the Feast of Fools*. Ithaca, NY: Cornell University Press, 2011.
Heller-Roazen, Daniel. *Dark Tongues: The Art of Rogues and Riddlers*. New York: Zone, 2013.
———. "De voce." In *Du bruit à l'oeuvre: Vers une esthétique du désordre*, edited by Juan Rigoli and Christopher Lucken, 37–48. Geneva: Metispresses, 2013.
———. "The Matter of Language: Guilhem de Peitieus and the Platonic Tradition." *MLN* 113, no. 4 (1998): 851–880.
———. *No One's Ways: An Essay on Infinite Naming*. New York: Zone, 2017.
———. "Speaking in Tongues." *Paragraph* 25, no. 2 (2002): 92–115.
Henry, Desmond Paul. "Suppositio and Significatio in English Logic." In *English Logic and Semantics from the End of the Twelfth Century to the Time of Ockham and Burleigh*, edited by Henk A. G. Braakhuis, C. H. J. M. Kneepkens, and L. M. De Rijk, 361–387. Nijmegen: Ingenium, 1981.

———. *That Most Subtle Question (Quaestio Subtilissima): The Metaphysical Bearing of Medieval and Contemporary Linguistic Disciplines*. Manchester: Manchester University Press, 1984.

Heruka, Tsangnyön. *The Hundred Thousand Songs of Milarepa*. Translated by Christopher Stagg. Boulder, CO: Shambhala, 2016.

Hilton, Walter. *The Scale of Perfection*. Edited by Thomas Bestul. Kalamazoo: Medieval Institute Publications, 2000.

Hilty, Gerold, and Federico Corriente. "La fameuse *cobla bilingue* de la Chanson V de Guillaume IX." *Vox Romanica* 65 (2006): 66–71.

Höltenschmidt, Edith. *Die Mittelalterrezeption der Brüder Schlegel*. Paderborn: Schöningh, 2000.

Hollywood, Amy. *Sensible Ecstasy: Mysticism, Sexual Difference, and the Demands of History*. Chicago: University of Chicago Press, 2001.

Holsinger, Bruce. *The Premodern Condition: Medievalism and the Making of Theory*. Chicago: University of Chicago Press, 2005.

Holtz, Louis. *Donat et la tradition de l'Ɛenseignement grammatical: étude et édition critique*. Paris: CNRS, 1981.

Howard, Donald R. *Chaucer: His Life, His Works, His World*. New York: E. P. Dutton, 1987.

Hugh of Balma. *Théologie mystique*. Sources chrétiennes 408. Paris: Cerf, 1995.

Hunt, Richard William. *The History of Grammar in the Middle Ages: Collected Papers*. Edited by G. L. Bursill-Hall. Amsterdam: John Benjamins, 1980.

Huppé, Bernard F., and D. W. Robertson. *Fruyt and Chaf: Studies in Chaucer's Allegories*. Princeton, NJ: Princeton University Press, 1963.

Hyman, Malcolm D. "Terms for 'Word' in Roman Grammar." In *Ancient Technical Texts*, edited by Thorsten Fögen, 155–170. Berlin: de Gruyter, 2005.

Ingham, Patricia. *The Medieval New: Ambivalence in an Age of Innovation*. Philadelphia: University of Pennsylvania Press, 2015.

Irvine, Martin. *The Making of Textual Culture: Grammatica and Literary Theory 350–1100*. New York: Cambridge University Press, 1994.

———. "Medieval Grammatical Theory and Chaucer's House of Fame." *Speculum* 60, no. 4 (1985): 850–876.

Isaac, Jean. *Le Peri hermeneias en Occident de Boèce à saint Thomas: histoire littéraire d'un traité d'Aristote*. Paris: J. Vrin, 1953.

Isidore of Seville. *Etymologies*. Translated by Stephen A. Barney, W. J. Lewis, J. A. Beach, and Oliver Berghof. New York: Cambridge University Press, 2006.

Iwakuma, Yukio. "The Introductiones dialecticae secundum Wilgelmum and secundum magistrum G. Paganellum." *Cahiers de l'Institut du Moyen-Âge Grec et Latin* 63 (1993): 45–114.

Jackson, B. Darrell. "The Theory of Signs in St. Augustine's *De Doctrina Christiana*." *Revue des études augustiniennes* 15 (1969): 9–49.

Jaffe-Berg, Erith. "Forays into Grammelot: The Language of Nonsense." *Journal of Dramatic Theory and Criticism*, no. 2 (2001): 3–16.

Jakobson, Roman. "Linguistic Glosses to Goldstein's 'Wortbegriff.'" In *Selected Writings*. Vol. 2, *Word and Language*, 267–270. The Hague: Mouton, 1971.

James, Henry. *The Turn of the Screw*. Edited by Deborah Esch and Jonathan Warren. New York: Norton, 1999.

Jennings, Margaret. "Tutivillus: The Literary Career of the Recording Demon." *Studies in Philology* 74, no. 5 (1977): 1–95.
John of Salisbury. *Metalogicon*. Edited by J. B. Hall. Turnholt: Brepols, 1991.
Johnson, Eleanor. "Feeling Time, Will, and Words: Vernacular Devotion in the Cloud of Unknowing." *Journal of Medieval and Early Modern Studies* 41, no. 2 (2011): 345–368.
Johnson, William. "Teaching the Children How to Read: The Syllabary." *Classical Journal* 106, no. 4 (2011): 445–463.
Jolivet, Jean. *Arts du langage et théologie chez Abélard*. Paris: J. Vrin, 1969.
Jones, C. P. "*Stigma*: Tattooing and Branding in Graeco-Roman Antiquity." *Journal of Roman Studies* 77 (1987): 139–155.
Jones, Malcolm. "The Parodic Sermon in Medieval and Early Modern England." *Medium Aevum* 66, no. 1 (1997): 94–114.
Joyce, James. *Finnegans Wake*. New York: Penguin, 1999.
Jung, Carl. "On the Psychology of the Trickster Figure." In *The Archetypes and the Collective Unconscious*. Translated by R. F. C. Hull, 255–274. Princeton, NJ: Princeton University Press, 1969.
Justice, Steven. "'Shameless': Augustine, After Augustine, and Way after Augustine." *Journal of Medieval and Early Modern Studies* 44, no. 1 (2014): 17–43.
Kamowski, William. "'Saint Erkenwald' and the Inadvertent Baptism: An Orthodox Response to Heterodox Ecclesiology." *Religion and Literature* 27, no. 3 (1995): 5–27.
Karger, Elizabeth. "La Supposition materielle comme supposition significative: Paul de Venise, Paul de Pergula." In *English Logic in Italy in the Fourteenth and Fifteenth Centuries*, edited by Alfonso Maierù, 331–341. Naples: Bibliopolis, 1982.
———. "Mental Sentences According to Burley and to the Early Ockham." *Vivarium* 34, no. 2 (1996): 192–230.
———. "Walter Burley's Realism." *Vivarium* 37, no. 1 (1999): 24–40.
Kay, Sarah. *Animal Skins and the Reading Self in Medieval Latin and French Bestiaries*. Chicago: University of Chicago Press, 2017.
Kealey, Edward J. *Harvesting the Air: Windmill Pioneers in Twelfth-Century England*. Berkeley: University of California Press, 1987.
Keiser, George. "Charms." In *A Manual of Writings in Middle English 1050–1500*. Vol. 10: *Works of Science and Information*. New Haven, CT: Yale University Press, 1998.
Keller, Hildegard Elisabeth. "Kolophon im Herzen: Von beschrifteten Mönchen an den Rändern der Paläographie." *Das Mittelalter* 7, no. 2 (2002): 157–182.
Kelly, L. G. *The Mirror of Grammar: Theology, Philosophy, and the* Modistae. Philadelphia: John Benjamins, 2002.
Kessler, Herbert L. *Seeing Medieval Art*. Toronto: University of Toronto Press, 2011.
Kieckhefer, Richard. *Forbidden Rites: A Necromancer's Manual of the Fifteenth Century*. Philadelphia: University of Pennsylvania Press, 1998.
———. *Magic in the Middle Ages*. New York: Cambridge University Press, 1989.
Kirwan, Christopher. *Augustine*. New York: Routledge, 1989.
Kiser, Lisa. *Truth and Textuality in Chaucer's Poetry*. Hanover, NH: University Press of New England, 1991.
Kirk, Jordan. "Buba, Blictrix, Bufbaf: Medieval Theory and Practice of Nonsense." In *The Edinburgh Companion to Nonsense*, edited by Anna Barton and James Williams. Edinburgh: Edinburgh University Press, forthcoming.

———. "What Separates the Birth of Twins." *Glossator* 5 (2011): 1–18.
Kittler, Friedrich. *Discourse Networks, 1800/1900*. Translated by Michael Metteer and Chris Cullens. Stanford, CA: Stanford University Press, 1990.
———. *Gramophone, Film, Typewriter*. Translated by Geoffrey Winthrop-Young and Michael Wutz. Stanford, CA: Stanford University Press, 1999.
Klaassen, Frank. "English Manuscripts of Magic, 1300–1500: A Preliminary Survey." In *Conjuring Spirits: Texts and Traditions of Medieval Ritual Magic*, edited by Claire Fanger, 3–31. University Park: Pennsylvania State University Press, 1998.
Klaniczay, Gábor. "The Power of Words in Miracles, Visions, Incantations and Bewitchments." In *The Power of Words: Studies on Charms and Charming in Europe*, edited by James Kapaló and Éva Pócs, 281–304. Budapest: Central European University Press, 2013.
Kleiman, Irit, ed. *Voice and Voicelessness in Medieval Europe*. New York: Palgrave Macmillan, 2015.
Knapp, Ethan. "Benjamin, Dante, and the Modernity of the Middle Ages; or, Allegory as Urban Constellation." *Chaucer Review* 48, no. 4 (2014): 524–541.
———. "Medieval Studies, Historicity, and Heidegger's Early Phenomenology." In Cole and Smith, *Legitimacy of the Middle Ages*, 159–193.
Kneepkens, C. H. *Het iudicium constructionis. Het leerstuk van de constructio in de 2de helft van de 12de eeuw*. Vol. 3. Nijmegen: Ingenium, 1977.
———. "The Priscianic Tradition." In *Sprachtheorien in Spätantike und Mittelalter*, 239–264. Tübingen: Gunter Narr, 1995.
Knipe, David M. "The Heroic Theft: Myths from Ṛgveda IV and the Ancient Near East." *History of Religions* 6, no. 4 (1967): 328–360.
Koff, Leonard Michael. "'Awak!': Chaucer Translates Bird Song." In *The Medieval Translator*, edited by V. Roger Ellis and Rene Tixier, 390–418. Turnhout: Brepols, 1996.
Kordecki, Lesley. *Ecofeminist Subjectivities: Chaucer's Talking Birds*. New York: Palgrave Macmillan, 2011.
Kretzmann, Norman. "Aristotle on Spoken Sound Significant by Convention." In *Ancient Logic and Its Modern Interpretations*, edited by J. Corcoran, 3–21. Dordrecht: Reidel, 1974.
Kristeva, Julia. *Desire in Language: A Semiotic Approach to Literature and Art*. Edited by Leon S. Roudiez. Translated by Thomas Gora, Alice Jardine, and Leon S. Roudiez. New York: Columbia University Press, 1980.
Kruchonykh, Aleksei, and Velimir Khlebnikov. "The Word as Such." In *Collected Works of Velimir Khlebnikov*, edited by Charlotte Douglas and translated by Paul Schmidt, 255–256. Cambridge, MA: Harvard University Press, 1987.
Labbie, Erin Felicia. *Lacan's Medievalism*. Minneapolis: University of Minnesota Press, 2006.
Lacan, Jacques. *Seminar XX*. Edited by Jacques-Alain Miller. Translated by Bruce Fink. New York: Norton, 1998.
———. *Television*. Edited by Joan Copjec. Translated by Denis Hollier, Rosalind Krauss, and Annette Michelson. New York: Norton, 1990.
Lacoue-Labarthe, Philippe, and Jean-Luc Nancy. *The Literary Absolute: The Theory of Literature in German Romanticism*. Translated by Philip Barnard and Cheryl Lester. Albany: State University of New York Press, 1988.

Lagerlund, Henrik. "The Assimilation of Aristotelian and Arabic Logic up to the Later Thirteenth Century." In *Handbook of the History of Logic*. Vol. 2, *Mediaeval and Renaissance Logic*, edited by Dov M. Gabbay and John Woods, 281–346. Amsterdam: North Holland, 2008.
Laín Entralgo, Pedro. *The Therapy of the Word in Classical Antiquity*. Edited and translated by L. J. Rather and John M. Sharp. New Haven, CT: Yale University Press, 1970.
Law, Vivien. *Grammar and Grammarians in the Early Middle Ages*. New York: Longman, 1997.
Lawton, David. *Voice in Later Medieval English Literature*. New York: Oxford, 2017.
Le Goff, Jacques, and Jean-Claude Schmitt. "Une Parole nouvelle." *Histoire vécue du peuple chrétien* 1 (1979): 257–279.
Leach, Elizabeth Eva. *Sung Birds: Music, Nature, and Poetry in the Later Middle Ages*. Ithaca, NY: Cornell University Press, 2007.
Lecouteux, Claude. *Dictionary of Ancient Magic Words and Spells: From Abraxas to Zoar*. Translated by Jon E. Graham. Rochester, NY: Inner Traditions, 2014.
Lees, Rosemary Ann. *The Negative Language of the Dionysian School of Mystical Theology: An Approach to the Cloud of Unknowing*. Salzburg: Institut für Anglistik und Amerikanistik, 1983.
Leupin, Alexandre. *Barbarolexis: Medieval Writing and Sexuality*. Cambridge, MA: Harvard University Press, 1989.
———. "The Impossible Task of Manifesting 'Literature': On Marie de France's Obscurity." *Exemplaria* 3, no. 1 (1991): 221–242.
Lewry, Osmund. "Boethian Logic in the Medieval West." In *Boethius: His Life, Thought, and Influence*, edited by Margaret Gibson, 90–134. Oxford: Blackwell, 1981.
Lida de Malkiel, María Rosa. *La idea de la fama en la Edad Media castellana*. Mexico City: Fondo de Cultura Économica, 1952.
Little, Lester K. *Benedictine Maledictions: Liturgical Cursing in Romanesque France*. Ithaca, NY: Cornell University Press, 1993.
Lochrie, Karma. *Covert Operations: The Medieval Uses of Secrecy*. Philadelphia: University of Pennsylvania Press, 1999.
Lock, Charles. "The Cloud of Unknowing: Apophatic Discourse and Vernacular Anxieties." In *Text and Voice: The Rhetoric of Authority in the Middle Ages*, edited by Marianne Borch, 207–233. Odense: University Press of Southern Denmark, 2004.
Logan, Ian. *Reading Anselm's Proslogion: The History of Anselm's Argument and Its Significance Today*. Burlington, VT: Ashgate, 2009.
Lohr, Charles. "The new Aristotle and 'science' in the Paris arts faculty (1255)." In *L'Enseignement des disciplines à la Faculté des arts (Paris et Oxford, XIIIe–XVe siècles)*. Edited by Olga Weijers and Louis Holtz, 251–269. Studia Artistarum 4. Turnhout: Brepols, 1997.
Longo, Dominic. *Spiritual Grammar: Genre and the Saintly Subject in Islam and Christianity*. New York: Fordham University Press, 2017.
Loomis, Roger Sherman. *A Mirror of Chaucer's World*. Princeton, NJ: Princeton University Press, 1965.
Lopez, Donald S. Jr., and Peggy McCracken. *In Search of the Christian Buddha: How an Asian Sage Became a Medieval Saint*. New York: Norton, 2014.

Loux, Michael. "Significatio and Suppositio: Reflections on Ockham's Semantics." *New Scholasticism* 53, no. 4 (1979): 407–437.
Lubac, Henri de. *Medieval Exegesis II: The Four Senses of Scripture*. Translated by E. M. Macierowski. Grand Rapids, IA: Eerdmans, 2000.
Lucentini, Paolo, ed. "Liber Runarum." In *Hermes Trismegisti astrologica et diuinatoria*, edited by Gerrit Bos. Turnhout: Brepols, 2001.
Lydgate, John. *Fall of Princes*. Edited by Henry Bergen. EETS 121–124. Oxford: Oxford University Press, 1924–1927.
Maas, Martha, and Jane McIntosh Snyder. *Stringed Instruments of Ancient Greece*. New Haven, CT: Yale University Press, 1989.
MacKendrick, Karmen. *The Matter of Voice: Sensual Soundings*. New York: Fordham University Press, 2016.
MacQuarrie, Charles W. "Insular Celtic Tattooing: History, Myth and Metaphor." In *Written on the Body: The Tattoo in European and American History*, edited by Jane Caplan, 32–45. Princeton, NJ: Princeton University Press, 2000.
Magee, John. *Boethius on Signification and Mind*. Leiden: Brill, 1989.
———. "On the Composition and Sources of Boethius' Second Peri Hermeneias Commentary." *Vivarium* 48 (2010): 7–54.
Maierù, Alfonso, ed. *English Logic in Italy in the Fourteenth and Fifteenth Centuries*. History of Logic 1. Naples: Bibliopolis, 1982.
Makdisi, George. *The Rise of Colleges: Institutions of Learning in Islam and the West*. Edinburgh: Edinburgh University Press, 1981.
Maliniemi, Irja. "'Ensuite, les petits chanterent le *ba be bi bo bu*': Pour le commentaire de 'ne bu ne ba.'" *Neuphilologische Mitteilungen* 62, no. 2 (1961): 65–70.
Malinowski, Bronislaw. *Coral Gardens and their Magic*. Vol. 2, *The Language of Magic and Gardening*. London: Allen and Unwin, 1935.
Mallarmé, Stéphane. *Oeuvres completes*. Paris: Gallimard, 1945.
Maloney, Thomas. "Roger Bacon on the Significatum of Words." In *Archéologie du signe*, edited by Lucie Brind'Amour and Eugence Vance, 187–211. Toronto: Institut Pontifical d'Études Médiévales, 1982.
———. "The Semiotics of Roger Bacon." *Mediaeval Studies* 45 (1983): 120–154.
Manetti, Giovanni. *Theories of the Sign in Classical Antiquity*. Bloomington: Indiana University Press, 1993.
Marenbon, John. "Medieval Latin Commentaries and Glosses on Aristotelian Logical Texts, before c.1150 AD." In *Aristotelian Logic, Platonism, and the Context of Early Medieval Philosophy in the West*, 77–127. Aldershot: Ashgate, 2000.
Marie de France. *Lais*. Edited by Jean Rychner. Paris: Champion, 1973.
Markus, R. A. "St. Augustine on Signs." *Phronesis* 2, no. 1 (1957): 60–83.
Marshall, Simone Celine, and Carole M. Cusack. *The Medieval Presence in the Modernist Aesthetic: Unattended Moments*. Leiden: Brill, 2017.
Masciandaro, Nicola. *On the Darkness of the Will*. Milan: Mimesis, 2018.
———. "The Sorrow of Being." *Qui Parle* 19, no. 1 (2010): 9–35.
———. *The Voice of the Hammer: The Meaning of Work in Middle English Literature*. Notre Dame, IN: University of Notre Dame Press, 2006.
Mathiesen, Thomas J. *Apollo's Lyre: Greek Music and Music Theory in Antiquity and the Middle Ages*. Lincoln: University of Nebraska Press, 1999.

Mazzio, Carla. *The Inarticulate Renaissance: Language Trouble in an Age of Eloquence*. Philadelphia: University of Pennsylvania Press, 2009.
McEvilley, Thomas. *The Shape of Ancient Thought: Comparative Studies in Greek and Indian Philosophies*. New York: Allworth, 2002.
McTurk, Rory. *Chaucer and the Norse and Celtic Worlds*. Burlington, VT: Ashgate, 2005.
Mehtonen, Päivi. *Obscure Language, Unclear Literature*. Helsinki: Academia Scientiarum Fennica, 2003.
Meier-Oeser, Stephan. "The Meaning of 'Significatio' in Scholastic Logic." In *Signs and Signification*, edited by Gill Harjeet Singh and Giovanni Manetti, 2:89–107. New Delhi: Bahri Publications, 2000.
———. "Walter Burley's 'propositio in Re' and the Systematization of the 'ordo Significationis.'" In *Philosophical Debates at Paris in the Early Fourteenth Century*, edited by S. Brown, T. Dewender, and T. Kobusch, 483–505. Leiden: Brill, 2009.
Meier-Oeser, Stephan, and W. Schröder. "Skindapsos." *Historisches Wörterbuch der Philosophie*. Basel: Schwabe, 1971–2007.
Menocal, María Rosa. *The Arabic Role in Medieval Literary History: A Forgotten Heritage*. Philadelphia: University of Pennsylvania Press, 1987.
Methley, Richard. *Divina caligo ignorancie: A Latin glossed version of* The Cloud of Unknowing. Analecta Cartusiana 119. Salzburg: Institut für Anglistik und Amerikanistik, 2009.
Metlitzki, Dorothee. *The Matter of Araby in Medieval England*. New Haven, CT: Yale University Press, 1977.
Meyer, Paul. "Recettes médicales en français." *Romania* 37 (1908): 358–373.
Michaud-Quantin, Pierre. "L'Emploi des termes logica et dialectica au moyen âge." In *Études sur le vocabulaire philosophique du Moyen Âge*. Rome: Edizioni dell'Ateneo, 1970.
Miles, Laura Saetveit. "Richard Methley and the Translation of Vernacular Religious Writing into Latin." In *After Arundel: Religious Writing in Fifteenth-Century England*, edited by Vincent Gillespie and Kantik Ghosh, 449–466. Turnhout: Brepols, 2011.
Miller, Patricia Cox. "In Praise of Nonsense." In *Classical Mediterranean Spirituality: Egyptian, Greek, Roman*, edited by A. H. Armstrong, 481–505. New York: Crossroad, 1986.
Minio-Paluello, Lorenzo. "Les Traductions et les commentaires aristotéliciens de Boèce." In *Opuscula: The Latin Aristotle*, 328–335. Amsterdam: Hakkert, 1972.
Minnis, Alastair. "Affection and Imagination in 'The Cloud of Unknowing' and Hilton's 'Scale of Perfection.'" *Traditio* 39 (1983): 323–366.
———. *Medieval Theory of Authorship*. Philadelphia: University of Pennsylvania Press, 1988.
———. "The Sources of the Cloud of Unknowing: A Reconsideration." In *The Medieval Mystical Tradition in England*, 2:63–75. Exeter: University of Exeter Press, 1982.
Mora-Márquez, Ana María. "La ontología realista de Walter Burleigh y su relación con las teorías del significado y de la suposición." In Walter Burleigh, *Sobre la pureza del arte de la lógica: Tratado breve*, translated by Ana María Mora-Márquez, 173–227. Bogota: CESO, 2009.

———. "Peri hermeneias 16a3–8: Histoire d'une rupture de la tradition interprétative dans le bas moyen âge." *Revue philosophique de la France et de l'étranger* (2011): 67–84.

———. *The Thirteenth-Century Notion of Signification: The Discussions and Their Origin and Development*. Leiden: Brill, 2015.

Morgenstern, Christian. *Galgenlieder*. Berlin: Cassirer, 1917.

Morris, T. J. "Rhetorical Stance: An Approach to The Cloud of Unknowing and Its Related Treatises." *Mystics Quarterly* 13, no.1 (1989): 13–20.

Munn, Henry. "The Mushrooms of Language." In *Hallucinogens and Shamanism*, edited by Michael Harner, 86–122. New York: Oxford University Press, 1973.

Nancy, Jean-Luc. *Dis-Enclosure: The Deconstruction of Christianity*. Translated by Bettina Bergo et al. New York: Fordham University Press, 2008.

Neubauer, Hans-Joachim. *The Rumour: A Cultural History*. New York: Free Association Books, 1999.

Nolan, Barbara, and David Farley-Hills. "The Authorship of *Pearl*: Two Notes." *Review of English Studies* 87, no. 1 (1971): 295–302.

Normore, Calvin G. "Material Supposition and the Mental Language of Ockham's Summa Logicae." *Topoi* 16, no. 1 (1997): 27–33.

Novaes, Catarina Dutilh. "Logic in the Fourteenth Century after Ockham." In *Handbook of the History of Logic*, edited by Dov M. Gabbay and John Woods. Vol. 2. Amsterdam: Elsevier, 2008.

Ockham, William. *Ockham's Theory of Terms: Part I of the Summa Logicae*. Translated by Michael Loux. Notre Dame, IN: University of Notre Dame Press, 1974.

Oettermann, Stephan. *Zeichen auf der Haut: Die Geschichte der Tätowierung in Europa*. Hamburg: Europäische Verlagsanstalt, 1994.

Ogden, Dunbar. *The Staging of Drama in the Medieval Church*. Newark: University of Delaware Press, 2003.

Olsan, Lea. "Charms in Medieval Memory." In *Charms and Charming in Europe*, edited by Jonathan Roper, 59–88. New York: Palgrave, 2004.

———. "The Marginality of Charms in Medieval England." In *The Power of Words: Studies on Charms and Charming in Europe*, edited by James Kapaló and Éva Pócs, 135–164. Budapest: Central European University Press, 2013.

Orlemanski, Julie. "Jargon and the Matter of Medicine in Middle English." *Journal of Medieval and Early Modern Studies* 42, no. 2 (2012): 395–420.

Orme, Nicholas. *Medieval Schools: From Roman Britain to Renaissance England*. New Haven, CT: Yale University Press, 2006.

Ormrod, Mark. "Murmur, Clamour and Noise: Voicing Complaint and Remedy in Petitions to the English Crown, c. 1300–c. 1460." In *Medieval Petitions: Grace and Grievance*, edited by Mark Ormrod, G. Dodd, and A. Musson, 135–155. York: York Medieval Press, 2009.

Ottman, Jennifer, and Rega Wood. "Walter of Burley: His Life and Works." *Vivarium* 37, no. 1 (1999): 1–23.

Padoux, André. "Mantras—What Are They?" In *Understanding Mantras*, edited by Harvey P. Alper, 295–318. Delhi: Motilal Banarsidass, 2002.

———. *Vāc: The Concept of the Word in Selected Hindu Tantras*. Translated by Jacques Gontier. Delhi: Sri Satguru, 1992.

Page, Christopher. *Discarding Images: Reflections on Music and Culture in Medieval France*. New York: Oxford University Press, 1997.
Panaccio, Claude. "Tarski et la suppositio materialis." *Philosophiques* 31, no. 2 (2004): 295.
Panaccio, Claude, and Ernesto Perini-Santos. "Guillaume d'Ockham et la suppositio materialis." *Vivarium* 42, no. 2 (2004): 202–224.
Pasnau, Robert. *Theories of Cognition in the Later Middle Ages*. Cambridge: Cambridge University Press, 1997.
Paul of Venice. *Logica magna: prima pars, tractatus de terminis*. Translated and edited by Norman Kretzmann. Oxford: Oxford University Press, 1979.
———. *Logica parva*. Edited by Alan Perreiah. Leiden: Brill, 2002.
Pearsall, David. "The Alliterative Revival: Origins and Social Backgrounds." In *Middle English Alliterative Poetry and Its Literary Background*, edited by David Lawton, 34–53. Cambridge: Brewer, 1982.
Peck, Russel. "Number Structure in *St. Erkenwald*." *Annuale medievale* 14 (1974): 9–21.
Peper, Bradley Mark. "On the Mark: Augustine's Baptismal Analogy of the *Nota Militaris*." *Augustinian Studies* 38, no. 2 (2007): 353–363.
Pépin, Jean. *Saint Augustin et la dialectique*. Villanova, PA: Augustinian Institute, 1976.
Perloff, Marjorie, and Craig Dworkin, eds. *The Sound of Poetry/The Poetry of Sound*. Chicago: University of Chicago Press, 2009.
Perreiah, Alan. "Orality and Literacy in the *De Interpretatione* Tradition." In *Aristotle's Peri Hermeneias in the Latin Middle Ages*, edited by H. A. G. Braakhuis and C. H. Kneepkens, 51–66. Groningen: Ingenium, 2003.
Peter Lombard, *The Sentences. Book Four: On the Doctrine of Signs*. Translated by Giulio Silano. Toronto: Pontifical Institute of Mediaeval Studies, 2010.
Peter of Spain. *Tractatus; called afterwards Summule logicales*. Edited by Lambert-Marie de Rijk. Assen: Van Gorcum, 1972.
Peters, Edward. "Wounded Names: The Medieval Doctrine of Infamy." In *Law in Medieaval Life and Thought*, edited by Edward King and Susan Ridyard, 43–89. Sewanee: Press of the University of the South, 1990.
Peterson, Michael T. "Fragmina Verborum: The Vices' Use of Language in the Macro Plays." *Florilegium* 9 (1987): 155–167.
Petrus Helias. *Summa super Priscianum*. Edited by Leo Reilly. Toronto: Pontifical Institute of Mediaeval Studies, 1993.
Phillips, Susan E. *Transforming Talk: The Problem with Gossip in Late Medieval England*. University Park: Pennsylvania State University Press, 2007.
Piché, David, ed. *La Condamnation parisienne de 1277*. Paris: Vrin, 1999.
Pigorini-Beri, Catherine."Le tatouage religieux et amoureux au pélérinage de N.-D. de Lorette." *Archives de l'anthropologie criminelle et des sciences pénales* 16 (1891): 5–16.
Pinborg, Jan. "The English Contribution to Logic before Ockham." *Synthese* 40 (1979): 19–42.
———. "Roger Bacon on Signs: A Newly Discovered Part of the Opus Maius." In *Sprache und Erkenntnis im Mittelalter*, edited by Jan P. Beckmann and Wolfgang Kluxen, 1:403–412. Miscellanea mediaevalia 13. Berlin: Walter de Gruyter, 1981.
Pini, Giorgio. "Signification of Names in Duns Scotus and Some of His Contemporaries." *Vivarium* 39, no. 1 (2001): 20–51.

———. "Species, Concept, and Thing: Theories of Signification in the Second Half of the Thirteenth Century." *Medieval Philosophy and Theology* 8 (1999): 21–52.
Plato. *Phaedrus*. Translated by Harold North Fowler. Loeb Classical Library 36. Cambridge, MA: Harvard University Press, 1914.
———. *Timaeus*. Translated by R. G. Bury. Loeb Classical Library 234. Cambridge, MA: Harvard University Press, 1929.
Pourrat, Pierre. *La Théologie sacramentaire: étude de théologie positive*. Paris: Lecoffre, 1907.
Pozzo, Alessandra. *Grr . . . grammelot: parlare senza parole, dai primi balbettii al grammelot di Dario Fo*. Lexis 8. Bologna: CLUEB, 1998.
Priscian. *Institutionum grammaticorum libri XVIII*. Edited by Martin Hertz. Leipzig: Teubner, 1855.
Pseudo-Dionysius. *Pseudo-Dionysius: The Complete Works*. Translated by Colm Luibheid and Paul Rorem. New York: Paulist Press, 1987.
Quintilian. *The Orator's Education, Books 1–2*. Edited and translated by Donald A. Russell. Loeb Classical Library 124. Cambridge, MA: Harvard University Press, 2001.
Rattray, David. "In Nomine." In *How I Became One of the Invisible* 263–282. New York: Semiotext(e), 1992.
Read, Stephen. "How Is Material Supposition Possible?" *Medieval Philosophy and Theology* 8, no. 1 (1999): 1–20.
Renzi, Lorenzo. "Un aspetto del plurilinguismo medievale: dalla lingua dei re magi a papè satan aleppe." In *Omaggio a Gianfranco Folena*, edited by Michele da Caprile, 61–73. Padua: Programma, 1993.
Rey-Debove, Josette. *Le Métalangage: étude linguistique du discours sur le langage*. Paris: Le Robert, 1978.
Reynolds, Suzanne. *Medieval Reading: Grammar, Rhetoric, and the Classical Text*. New York: Cambridge University Press, 1996.
Rider, Jeff. "The Enigmatic Style in Twelfth-Century French Literature." In *Obscurity in Medieval Texts*, edited by Lucie Doležalová, Jeff Rider, and Alessandro Zironi. Krems: Medium Aevum Quotidianum, 2013.
Rohrbacher-Sticker, Claudia. "From Sense to Nonsense, From Incantation Prayer to Magical Spell." *Jewish Studies Quarterly* 3, no. 1 (1996): 24–46.
Rolle, Richard. *English Writings of Richard Rolle, Hermit of Hampole*. Edited by Hope Emily Allen. Oxford: Clarendon Press, 1931.
Ronell, Avital. *Stupidity*. Chicago: University of Illinois Press, 2002.
Roper, Jonathan. *English Verbal Charms*. Helsinki: Academia Scientiarum Fennica, 2005.
Rosecrans, Jennipher Allen. "Wearing the Universe: Symbolic Markings in Early Modern England." In *Written on the Body: The Tattoo in European and American History*, edited by Jane Caplan, 46–60. Princeton, NJ: Princeton University Press, 2000.
Rosier-Catach, Irène. "Grammar." In *The Cambridge History of Medieval Philosophy*, edited by Robert Pasnau and Christina Dyke, 1:196–216. Cambridge: Cambridge University Press, 2010.
———. *La Parole comme acte: sur la grammaire et la sémantique au XIIIe siècle*. Paris: J. Vrin, 1994.
———. *La Parole efficace: signe, rituel, sacré*. Paris: Éditions du Seuil, 2004.

———. "La Suppositio materialis et la question de l'autonymie au Moyen Âge." In *Parler des Mots: le fait autonymique en discours*, edited by Jacqueline Authier-Revuz, Marianne Doury, and Sandrine Reboul-Touré, 21–55. Paris: Presses Sorbonne nouvelle, 2003.

———. "Vox and Oratio in Early Twelfth Century Grammar and Dialectics." *Archives d'histoire doctrinale et littéraire du Moyen Âge* 78, no. 1 (2011): 47–129.

———. *La Grammaire spéculative des Modistes*. Lille: Presses Universitaires de Lille, 1983.

Rothenburg, Jerome, ed. *Technicians of the Sacred: A Range of Poetries from Africa, America, Asia, and Oceania*. New York: Anchor, 1969.

Royster, James F. "Chaucer's 'Colle Tregetour.'" *Studies in Philology* 23, no. 3 (1926): 380–384.

Ruggiers, Paul. "Words into Images in Chaucer's Hous of Fame: A Third Suggestion." *Modern Language Notes* 69, no. 1 (1954): 34–37.

Rutebeuf. *Il miracolo di Teofilo*. Alessandria: Edizioni dell'Orso, 2000.

Sayers, William. "Animal Vocalization and Human Polyglossia in Walter of Bibbesworth's Thirteenth-Century Domestic Treatise in Anglo-Norman French and Middle English." *Sign Systems Studies* 37, nos. 3–4 (2012): 525–541.

Scanlon, Larry. "The Authority of Fable: Allegory and Irony in the Nun's Priest's Tale." *Exemplaria* 1, no. 1 (1989): 43–68.

Scattergood, John. "*St Erkenwald* and the Custody of the Past." In *The Lost Tradition: Essays on Middle English Alliterative Poetry*, 179–199. Dublin: Four Courts, 2000.

Schlegel, Friedrich. "On Incomprehensibility." In *"Lucinde" and the Fragments*. Translated by Peter Firchow, 257–271. Minneapolis: University of Minnesota Press, 1971.

———. "Über die Unverständlichkeit." In *Kritische Friedrich Schlegel Ausgabe*, 2:263–72. Paderborn: Verlag Ferdinand Schöningh, 1967.

Schmitt, Jean-Claude. *Le Corps des images. Essais sur la culture visuelle au Moyen Âge*. Paris: Gallimard, 2002.

Schnapp, Jeffrey T. "Between Babel and Pentecost: Imaginary Languages in the Middle Ages." In *Modernité au Moyen Âge: le défi du passé*, edited by Brigitte Cazelles and Charles Méla, 175–206. Geneva: Droz, 1990.

Scholem, Gershom. "Tradition and Commentary." In *Understanding Jewish Theology: Classical Issues and Modern Perspectives*, edited by Jacob Neusner, 45–51. New York: KTAV, 1973.

Schufreider, Gregory. *Confessions of a Rational Mystic: Anselm's Early Writings*. West Lafayette, IN: Purdue University Press, 1994.

Schwartz, Hillel. *Making Noise*. New York: Zone, 2011.

Sextus Empiricus. *Against the Logicians*. Translated by R. G. Bury. Cambridge, MA: Harvard University Press, 1935.

Shiel, James. "Boethius' Commentaries on Aristotle." In *Aristotle Transformed*, edited by Richard Sorabji, 377–402. Ithaca, NY: Cornell University Press, 1990.

Shklovsky, Viktor. "On Poetry and Trans-Sense Language." Translated by Gerald Janacek and Peter Mayer. *October* 34 (1985): 3–24.

Shoaf, Matthew. "The Voice in Relief: Sculpture and Surplus Vocality at the Rise of Naturalism." In *Resounding Images: Medieval Intersections of Art, Music, and Sound*, edited by Susan Boynton and Diane Reilly. Turnhout: Brepols, 2015.

Sinnott, Eduardo. "El Peri phones de Diógenes de Babilonia y sus fuentes aristotélicas." *Stromata* 57 (2001): 237–254.
Sirridge, Mary. "Grammarians on Language About Language." Unpublished essay.
Sisk, Jennifer L. "The Uneasy Orthodoxy of *St. Erkenwald*." *ELH* 74 (2007): 89–115.
Skemer, Don C. *Binding Words: Textual Amulets in the Middle Ages*. University Park: Pennsylvania State University Press, 2006.
Sluiter, Ineke. "The Greek Tradition." In *The Emergence of Semantics in Four Linguistic Traditions: Hebrew, Sanskrit, Greek, Arabic*, edited by Wout Jac. van Bekkum, 148–224. Philadelphia: John Benjamins, 1997.
Smith, D. Vance. "The Application of Thought to Medieval Studies: The Twenty-First Century." *Exemplaria* 22, no. 1 (2010): 85–94.
———. "Chaucer as an English Writer." In *The Yale Companion to Chaucer*, edited by Seth Lerer, 87–121. New Haven, CT: Yale University Press, 2006.
———. "Crypt and Decryption: *Erkenwald* Terminable and Interminable." *New Medieval Literatures* 5 (2002): 59–85.
———. "Medieval Forma: The Logic of the Work." In *Reading for Form*, edited by Susan Wolfson and Marshall Brown, 66–79. Seattle: University of Washington, 2007.
———. "Negative Langland." *Yearbook of Langland Studies* 23 (2009): 33–59.
Solterer, Helen. *Medieval Roles for Modern Times: Theater and the Battle for the French Republic*. University Park: Pennsylvania State University Press, 2010.
Spitzer, Leo. "Parole vuote (a propositio di blittri)." *Lingua Nostra* 16 (1954): 1.
Spruit, Leen. *Species Intelligibilis*. Vol. 1, *Classical Roots and Medieval Discussions*. Leiden: Brill, 1994.
Staal, Fritz. *Discovering the Vedas: Origins, Mantras, Rituals, Insights*. New York: Penguin, 2008.
———. "Mantras and Birdsongs." *Journal of the American Oriental Society* 105, no. 3 (1985): 549–558.
Stein, Gertrude. "Lectures in America." In *Writings: 1932–1946*, edited by Catharine R. Stimpson and Harriet Chessman, 191–336. New York: Library of America, 1998.
———. *Tender Buttons*. New York: Claire Marie, 1914.
Stevens, Martin, and Arthur C. Cawley. *The Towneley Plays*. EETS 13. Oxford: Oxford University Press, 1994.
Stock, Brian. *Augustine the Reader: Meditation, Self-Knowledge, and the Ethics of Interpretation*. Cambridge, MA: Harvard University Press, 1996.
———. *The Implications of Literacy: Written Language and Models of Interpretation in the Eleventh and Twelfth Centuries*. Princeton, NJ: Princeton University Press, 1983.
Sutherland, Annie. "The Dating and Authorship of the Cloud Corpus: A Reassessment of the Evidence." *Medium Aevum* 71 (2002): 82–100.
Suto, Taki. *Boethius on Mind, Grammar and Logic: A Study of Boethius' Commentaries on Peri Hermeneias*. Leiden: Brill, 2011.
Sweeney, Eileen. *Logic, Theology, and Poetry in Boethius, Abelard, and Alan of Lille: Words in the Absence of Things*. New York: Palgrave Macmillan, 2006.
———. *Anselm of Canterbury and the Desire for the Word*. Washington: Catholic University of America Press, 2012.
Tambiah, S. J. "The Magical Power of Words." *Man* 3, no. 2 (1968): 175–208.

Taylor, Cheryl. "Paradox upon Paradox: Using and Abusing Language in The Cloud of Unknowing and Related Texts." *Parergon* 22, no. 2 (2005): 31–51.
Thomas, Charles. "The Interpretation of the Pictish Symbols." *Archeological Journal* 120, no. 1 (1963): 31–97.
Tiffany, Daniel. *Infidel Poetics: Riddles, Nightlife, Substance*. Chicago: University of Chicago Press, 2009.
Todorov, Tzvetan. *Theories of the Symbol*. Translated by Catherine Porter. Ithaca, NY: Cornell University Press, 1982.
Tomiche, Anne. "Glossopoïèses." *L'Esprit createur* 38, no. 4 (1998): 38–51.
Travis, Peter. *Disseminal Chaucer: Rereading the Nun's Priest's Tale*. Notre Dame, IN: University of Notre Dame Press, 2009.
Trumper, John. "Slang and Jargons." In *The Cambridge History of the Romance Languages*, edited by Martin Maiden, 660–681. Cambridge: Cambridge University Press, 2011.
Trungpa, Chögyam. *The Profound Treasury of the Ocean of Dharma*. Vol. 3, *The Tantric Path of Indestructible Wakefulness*. Edited by Judith Lief. Boston, MA: Shambhala, 2013.
Turchin, Peter, and Thomas Hall. "Spatial Synchrony among and within World Systems." *Journal of World-Systems Research* 11, no. 1 (2003): 37–64.
Turner, Denys. *The Darkness of God: Negativity in Christian Mysticism*. New York: Cambridge University Press, 1995.
———. "Dionysius and Some Late Medieval Mystical Theologians of Northern Europe." *Modern Theology* 24, no. 4 (2008): 651–665.
Turner, Marion. *Chaucer: A European Life*. Princeton, NJ: Princeton University Press, 2019.
Turville-Petre, Thorlac. "*St Erkenwald* and the Crafty Chronicles." In *Studies in Late Medieval and Early Renaissance Texts in Honour of John Scattergood*, edited by Anne Marie D'Arcy and Alan J. Fletcher, 362–374. Dublin: Four Courts, 2005.
Ullyot, Jonathan. *The Medieval Presence in Modernist Literature: The Quest to Fail*. New York: Cambridge University Press, 2016.
Uña Juárez, Agustín. *La filosofía del siglo XIV: contexto cultural de Walter Burley*. Madrid: Real Monasterio de Escorial, 1978.
Vance, Eugene. *Mervelous Signals: Poetics and Sign Theory in the Middle Ages*. Lincoln: University of Nebraska Press, 1986.
Van Deusen, Nancy. *The Cultural Context of Medieval Music*. Santa Barbara, CA: Praeger, 2011.
Van Dyke, Carolynn, ed. *Rethinking Chaucerian Beasts*. New York: Palgrave Macmillan, 2012.
Venarde, Bruce, ed. *The Rule of Saint Benedict*. Cambridge, MA: Harvard University Press, 2011.
Véronèse, Julien. *L'Ars notoria au Moyen Âge*. Florence: SISMEL, 2007.
Voigts, Linda Ehrsam. "The Character of the *Caracter*: Ambiguous Sigils in Scientific and Medical Texts." In *Latin and Vernacular: Studies in Late-Medieval Texts and Manuscripts*, edited by Alaistair Minnis, 91–109. Wolfeboro, NH: Brewer, 1989.
Welsh, Andrew. *Roots of Lyric: Primitive Poetry and Modern Poetics*. Princeton, NJ: Princeton University Press, 1978.

Watson, Nicholas. "Censorship and Cultural Change in Late-Medieval England: Vernacular Theology, the Oxford Translation Debate, and Arundel's Constitutions of 1409." *Speculum* 70 (1995): 822–864.
Watson, Robert Allen. "A Windmill Under a Walnut Shell: Chaucer's 'House of Fame' on the Illusionist Rhetoric of Systems." PhD. diss., Stanford University, 1988.
Weill-Parot, Nicolas. *Les "Images astrologiques" au Moyen Âge et à la Renaissance: Spéculations intellectuelles et pratiques magiques (XIIe–XVe siècle)*. Paris: Champion, 2002.
Weisheipl, James. "Classification of the Sciences in Medieval Thought." *Mediaeval Studies* 27 (1965): 54–90.
Weiskott, Eric. *English Alliterative Verse: Poetic Tradition and Literary History*. Cambridge: Cambridge University Press, 2016.
Werner, Karl. "*Ananizapta*: Eine geheimnisvolle Inschrift des Mittelalters." *Sammelblatt des Historischen Vereins Ingolstadt* 105 (1996): 59–90.
Whatley, Gordon. "Heathens and Saints: *St. Erkenwald* in Its Legendary Context." *Speculum* 61, no. 2 (1986): 330–363.
———. "The Middle English *St. Erkenwald* and Its Liturgical Context." *Mediaevalia* 8 (1982): 278–306.
White, Edmund Wenzel. *The Magic Bishop: Hugo Ball, Dada Poet*. Rochester, NY: Camden House, 1998.
William of Sherwood. *Introduction to Logic*. Edited and translated by Norman Kretzmann. Minneapolis: University of Minnesota Press, 1966.
———. "William of Sherwood, 'Introductiones in Logicam,' Critical Text." Edited by Charles Lohr, Peter Kunze, and Bernhard Mussler. *Traditio* 39 (1983): 219–299.
Williamson, Craig. *A Feast of Creatures: Anglo-Saxon Riddle Songs*. Philadelphia: University of Pennsylvania Press, 1982.
Wilson, Stephen. *The Magical Universe: Everyday Ritual and Magic in Pre-Modern Europe*. New York: Hambledon and London, 2000.
Wind, Edgar. *Pagan Mysteries in the Renaissance*. New York: Norton, 1968.
Wineapple, Brenda. *Sister Brother: Gertrude and Leo Stein*. Lincoln: University of Nebraska Press, 1996.
Wogan-Browne, Jocelyn, Nicholas Watson, Andrew Taylor, and Ruth Evans, eds. *The Idea of the Vernacular: An Anthology of Middle English Literary Theory, 1280–1520*. University Park: Pennsylvania State University Press, 1999.
Woolf, Virginia. *Between the Acts*. New York: Harcourt Brace and Company, 1941.
———. *Mrs. Dalloway*. New York: Harcourt Brace and Company, 1925.
———. *Orlando*. New York: Harcourt Brace Jovanovich, 1928.
———. *Pointz Hall: The Earlier and Later Typescripts of Between the Acts*. Edited by Mitchell A. Leaska. New York: University Publishers, 1983.
———. *The Years*. New York: Harcourt Brace and Company, 1937.
Wyclif, John. *Tractatus de logica*. Edited by M. H. Dziewicki. 3 vols. London: Trübner, 1893–1899.
Zieman, Katherine. "Chaucer's Voys." *Representations* 60 (1997): 70–91.
———. "Escaping the Whirling Wicker: Ricardian Poetics and Narrative Voice in *The Canterbury Tales*." In *Answerable Style: The Idea of the Literary in Medieval England*, edited by Frank Grady and Andrew Galloway. Columbus: Ohio State University Press, 2013.

———. "The Perils of Canor: Mystical Authority, Alliteration, and Extragrammatical Meaning in Rolle, the Cloud-Author, and Hilton." *Yearbook of Langland Studies* 22 (2008): 131–163.

———. *Singing the New Song: Literacy and Liturgy in Late Medieval England*. Philadelphia: University of Pennsylvania Press, 2011.

Zingesser, Eliza. "Pidgin Poetics: Bird Talk in Medieval France and Occitania." *New Medieval Literatures* 17 (2017): 62–80.

Ziolkowski, Jan M. "Theories of Obscurity in the Latin Middle Ages." *Mediaevalia* 19 (1996): 101–170.

Zucker, Adam. "*Twelfth Night* and the Philology of Nonsense." *Renaissance Studies* 30, no. 1 (2016): 88–101.

Zumthor, Paul. "Fatrasie et coq-à-l'âne." In *Fin du Moyen Âge et Renaissance: Mélanges de philologie francaise offerts à Robert Guiette*, 5–18. Anvers: Nederlandsche Boekhandel, 1961.

———. *Introduction à la poésie orale*. Paris: Éditions du Seuil, 1983.

———. *La Poésie et la voix dans la civilisation médiévale*. Paris: Presses Universitaires de France, 1984.

———. *Langue et techniques poétiques à l'époque romane*. Paris: Klincksieck, 1969.

INDEX

Agamben, Giorgio, 7, 11, 21, 47, 49, 95
Allen, Valerie, 21
Anselm of Canterbury, Saint: as "first scholastic," reputation of, 13; formulation of proof of God, 14–15, 133n51; Gaunilo's polemics with, 14–15; on object of faith, 13–14, 133n53; *Proslogion,* 13–14; on search of understanding, 13; sources of, 22–23
Aquinas, Thomas, 141n6
Arens, Hans, 28, 136n2
Aristophanes: *Frogs,* 33
Aristotle: *De anima,* 36, 42, 144n33; definition of the noun, 87; *De interpretatione,* 27–28, 35, 37, 52, 87, 136n3, 141n4; logic of, 28, 37; *Metaphysics,* 78; on nature of *vox,* 144n33; Thomistic critique of, 141–42n6
articulata: in the grammatical tradition, meaning of, 31
Augustine of Canterbury, 109
Augustine of Hippo, Saint, 23, 29; account of four linguistic elements, 43–44; *De dialectica,* 44, 45, 49, 60; *De doctrina christiana,* 49, 140n83; definition of the sign, 110, 119; definition of *vox,* 49; *De trinitate,* 46, 47, 48; experience of an unknown word, 46–47, 50; linguistic ideas of, 19, 43–44, 45, 46, 49; on love of God, 47; on obscure word *sarabarae,* 48; schema for utterances, 44–45; on signification of words, 48; on sound of words, 45–46, 48; sources of, 44; on task of interpretation, 140n83; theory of material supposition, 140n63; treatise on logic, 42–43, 46, 140n64; on use of *caracteres,* 105; on *vocabulum emortuum,* 47, 50, 97
aureation of the mother tongue, 23, 24
autonymy, 54, 59, 144n25Bacon, Roger: *Compendium studii theologiae,* 60; "intentionalism," doctrine of, 53, 61; linguistic studies of, 108; on material supposition, 61, 62; on proposition *buba est vox,* 61, 62; on problem of *vox non-significativa,* 54, 144n37; revision of Augustinian definition of sign, 119; semiotics of, 61; on signification of words, 61; sources of, 60; treatment of meaningful utterances, 60–61; works on logic, 52, 60
Ball, Hugo, 11, 12

baptism: conditional, 115; of a corpse, 115; fictive, 113; Papal decrees on, 117; performance of, 109–10, 113; as a sign, 111, 116
baptismal character, 118–19, 122, 123, 124, 125
baptismal theology, 100, 101, 102, 112
Baratin, Marc, 44
barbarisms, 40–41, 47
Barthes, Roland, 11
Beckett, Samuel, 11
Benjamin, Walter, 8–9, 10, 12
Berengar of Tours, 110, 111
Bodel, Jean, 17
bodily marks. *See* tattooing
Boethius, Anicius Manlius Severinus: on Aristotelian logic, 37; authority of, 52, 138n35; commentary on Aristotle's *De interpretatione,* 27, 37–38, 141n4; critics of, 136n2; dialectic of, 28; discussion of *vox,* 27, 28, 30, 41–42, 52; grammatical analysis of *garalus,* 40; linguistic studies of, 19, 29; on meaningless utterances, 73, 87; sources of, 23; theory of imposition, 38–39; theory of *orandi ordo,* 35–36; on wandering of mind, 94; words invented by, 39–40
bread: as sign of the body of Christ, 110, 111
Burley, Walter: account of *terminus,* 69; background of, 63; on cognition of mind, 72, 74; commentary on Aristotle, 19, 53, 63; debate with William Ockham, 63; *De puritate artis logicae,* 63, 74; on direct and reflexive understanding, 72; discussion of *vox,* 69, 70–71; on failure of knowledge, 74, 75; on linguistic nonsignification, 69, 71; logic of, 19, 55–56, 69, 74; on material supposition, 67–68, 74; *Middle Commentary,* 74, 75; on mind coming to knowledge, 94; on nonsense words, 71; on proposition *buba est buba,* 67, 68, 69; on proposition *buba est disyllabum,* 67, 68, 73; on proposition *bu est bu,* 66–67; on propositional knowledge, 68, 73; remarks on the *commune ens,* 65, 67, 69; revision of Bacon, 71–72; on signification of words, 69–70, 71; sources of, 23; on supposition without signification, 69; theory of terms, 63–65, 67; on utterances *bu* and *ba,* 65–66

Burnett, Charles, 153n35
Burrow, J. A., 77
Bynum, Caroline Walker, 113

Calvin, John, 117
Campbell, George, 117
caracter: and the character, relation of, 122–23, 124; demons and, 107, 108; efficacy of, 107, 108; magic of, 106, 107, 152n18; in medieval writing, 104–5; necromantic, 123; nonsensical nature of, 107–8; sacramental theology and, 122; in *St. Erkenwald,* 106–7; studies of, 105, 107, 125, 152nn14–15; tomb covered by, 108
Carroll, Lewis, 11, 25
character: bodily markings and, 120–21; and *caracter,* relation of, 122–23, 124; theories of, 117, 119
charms, 105–6
Chaucer, Geoffrey: "Canon's Yeoman's Tale," 24; *caracteres* in tales of, 105; fascination by noise, 7–8; *House of Fame,* 3–7; irony of, 130n9; linguistic nonsignifications of, 2, 18–19; mysticism of, 130n9; perception of, 12; poetics of, 7, 24; records of dreams, 2; on sound of language, 131n16; sources of, 22
Chism, Christine, 112
classical text: incomprehensibility of, 134n79
Cloud of Unknowing (anonymous treatise), 19, 23, 63; contents of, 77–78; dating and authorship of, 156n1; discussion of prayer, 76, 77–79, 81, 82–84, 90, 93, 149n42; on failure of knowledge, 94; on familiar words, 95–96; genre of, 147n10; on hideous noise of little word, 92, 93; innovation of, 90; instructions on reading of the treatise of, 96–97; on little word of one syllable, 76, 79–80, 81, 82, 87, 148n23; on love-thrust, 86; main theme of, 75; on prayer *vs.* cry for help, 91–92; on principle of vocal brevity, 82; on production of meaningless word, 90; on properties of the syllable, 147n10; readers of, 149n42; reference to astronomy, 79; on repetition of single word, 88–89; sources of, 77; technique of, 86, 94, 95, 147n7; temporal atomism of, 147n17; translations of, 85; vernacularity of, 77; wholeness of, 96–97
Coley, David, 112
Colish, Marcia, 113
Comestor, Peter, 33
concepts, 35–36

Copeland, Rita, 21, 77
Cribiore, Raffaella, 34

Dante, Alighieri: *Inferno,* 16; linguistic incomprehension, 16–17
De anima (Aristotle), 36, 42, 144n33
De dialectica (Augustine), 43, 45, 49, 60
De interpretatione (Aristotle), 27–28, 35, 37, 52, 87, 136n3, 141n4
Delaurenti, Béatrice, 108
demons, 107, 108
Descartes, René, 133n53
dicibile (concept of a word), 43, 46
dictio, 43, 44, 87–88, 92, 140n64
Dillon, Emma, 21
Diogenes Laertius, 38
Dionysius Thrax, 44
Dolar, Mladen, 11
Donatus, Aelius: *Ars maior,* 31, 40; on barbarism, 41; on writable *vs.* nonwritable *voces,* 32
Dronke, Peter, 17
Duns Scotus, John, 52, 110

Ebbinghaus, Hermann, 50, 51
Eucharist, 110–11
experimentum vocis (experience of the bare vocalization), 7

failures of reading, 99–101
fame: classical accounts of, 129n8
figura vocis (sound-shape of the utterance), 39–40, 42, 47, 60, 68, 90, 139n50
Finnegans Wake (Joyce), 33
Fishacre, Richard, 119
Fo, Dario, 18
Forman, Simon, 121
Frege, Gottlob, 57
Frogs (Aristophanes), 33

garalus (invented word), 39–41, 44, 139nn53, 55
Gaunilo of Marmoutiers, 14–15, 94
Gillespie, Vincent, 89
glos (acronym), 96, 97
God: effect of sign on connection with, 111; formulation of ontological proof of, 14–15; knowledge of, 94; love of, 47
grammar, 33, 34, 40–41; *vs.* dialectic, 139n52; linguistic discipline of, 77, 80; *vs.* logic, 46, 56–57, 69, 143n14; *See also* spiritual grammar

INDEX 185

Gregory IX, Pope, 117
Grévin, Benoît, 104, 105, 121

Hamsun, Knut: *Hunger*, 10, 12
Häring, Nicholas, 120
Heller-Roazen, Daniel, 14, 28
homo: signification of the word, 57, 59–60

imposition: theory of, 38–39
index: *vs.* symbol, 150n70
Innocent III, Pope, 117
Institutiones grammaticae (Priscian), 29–30, 32
Isaac, Jean, 54
Isidore of Seville, 129n8

Jackson, B. Darrell, 43
Jakobson, Roman, 10
James, Henry, 98
James, William, 25
jargon absolu, 16, 18, 22, 24
Jesus: power of name of, 108–9
John of Salisbury, 136n3
Johnson, Eleanor, 79
Joyce, James, 11; *Finnegans Wake*, 33

Karger, Elizabeth, 74, 75
al-Kindi, 108, 153n35
Kittler, Friedrich, 11, 51; *Discourse Networks*, 50
knowledge: failure of, 94, 95; of God, 94
Kristeva, Julia, 11, 12

Lacan, Jacques, 11, 12
language: bourgeois conception of, 8–9, 12, 22; experience of ignorance, 48; invented, 17; limit of, 15; medieval models of, 12
Lawton, David, 21
Leach, Elizabeth Eva, 21
lexis, 38, 39, 42, 44, 140n63
linguistic abstraction, 11
linguistic elements, 43–44, 46
linguistic nonsignification, 11, 18, 71, 142n12
linguistic performativity: theory of, 123
literariness, 24–25
literature: definition of, 11; formation of, 25; medieval, 8, 17–18
little word: characteristics of, 85–86; efficacy of, 92; familiarity of, 95–96; hideousness of, 93; lexical indifference of, 82; repetition of, 88–89; syllabic nature of, 90; in translations, 85; utterance of, 86, 88
locutio (writable voice), 37, 38, 92

logic: Aristotelian, 28; discipline of, 28, 56; *vs.* grammar, 56; "great dispute" in the field of, 52, 53; medieval scholars of, 75; of nonsense, 69; science of, 55; terminist, 57; translations of the word, 136n8
Logica "cum sit nostra" (anonymous work), 53, 55, 58
logical term: nature of, 44, 63–64
ludicrousness, 96

Mallarmé, Stéphane, 11, 12
mantra: meaning of the word, 131n22
Marie de France, 20
material supposition: Bacon's solution to the problem of, 62; definition of, 57, 58, 143–44n25; theory of, 69; varieties of, 74; *vox non-significativa* in, 54, 60, 62, 73–74, 75; *vox significativa* in, 60
meaninglessness: theory of, 21, 32, 51
meaningless word, 11, 50–51, 90
medieval education system, 28
Medieval Grammar and Rhetoric (Copeland and Sluiter), 21
medieval linguistic thought, 21, 22
medieval writing: neglected form of, 104
memory, 50–51
mental prayer, 81
Methley, Richard, 85
Middle English: aureation of, 24; vernacular texts, 19, 23–24; as written language, 22
monastic silence, 148n25
monosyllabic prayer, 82–84
monosyllabic word, 86, 87–88
Morgenstern, Christian, 11, 12

noise, 7–8, 68, 92, 93, 95
nonsense, 13, 18, 107
nonunderstanding: study of, 136n98
number symbolism, 151–52n10

orandi ordo (sequence of speech), 19, 20, 35–36

past conversations, 25–26
Paul of Venice, 75
Pépin, Jean, 44
Peter Helias, 59, 60
Peter Lombard: *Sentences*, 111, 117
Peter of Spain, 58
prayer: choice of words in, 83–84, 149n42; *vs.* cry for help, 91–92; idea of silent, 81; inherently vocal, 81; method of, 90, 93;

prayer (*continued*)
   vs. utterance, 82; work of, 77–78; *See also* mental prayer; monosyllabic prayer
Priscian of Caesarea: background of, 23; *Institutiones grammaticae*, 29–30, 32, 77; on meaningfulness, 32; study of voice, 30–31, 32–33, 34; work on art of language, 19
proballein: earliest usage of the word, 139n52
Pseudo-Dionysius, 147n7
pure language (*reine Sprache*), 9, 19

Read, Stephen, 75
Remigius of Auxerre, 28
repetition of utterance, 89–90, 94
res (thing itself), 43, 46
res et sacramentum: doctrine of, 119
rhetoric: medieval discipline of, 28
Rosecrans, Jennipher, 121
Rosier-Catach, Irène, 21, 53, 62, 110
Rutebeuf: *Miracle de Theophile*, 12, 17

sacramental theology, 25, 108, 110–11, 112, 144n25
sarabarae, 48, 49, 140n80
Schlegel, Friedrich, 136n98
Scholem, Gershom, 8, 21
semantics, 45
semiotics, 45, 123
Sextus Empiricus, 41
Shklovsky, Viktor: *Zaum*, 10
sighs: as part of baptismal rite, 154n57
sign: Augustine's definition of, 110, 119; effect on connection with God, 111; origin of the word, 1; sacramental, 111
signification, 1, 61; *vs.* supposition, 57–58, 143n20
sign itself (*signum tantum*), 119
Sir Gawain and the Green Knight, 105
Sluiter, Ineke, 21
Smith, D. Vance, 7, 74, 101
soul, 78, 99, 109–10, 116, 118, 120, 124
sound: of language, 131n16; petrological, 6; signification of, 93; spoken, 35; theories of, 21; varieties of, 30, 55; without meaning, 37; of word *god*, 14; of words, 45–46, 48
speech: act of, 19, 91; elements of, 35–36; *vs.* sentence, 138n44
spiritual grammar, 147n10
Stein, Gertrude, 11, 12–13; "What is English Literature," 12
St. Erkenwald (poem): apologia for orthodoxy, 24; authorship of, 100; celebratory ending of, 99; contribution to baptismal theology, 109–10, 112, 114–16, 121–22; culminating moment of, 110, 113–14; disintegration of the corpse, 124; encounter of Bishop and the corpse, 108–9; encounter with meaningless signs, 108; excavation of the tomb, 102–3; figure of uncorrupted corpse, 100–1; gap in the middle of, 117, 122; genre of, 23, 25, 98–99; goal of, 122–23; historicist reading of, 99, 100, 151n6; historico-theological commitments of, 101; illiterate reading of, 99, 100; inarticulate utterances in, 109, 154n57; manuscript of, 116; mysteriousness of indecipherable inscriptions in, 99–101, 102–4, 106–7, 117; noncontemporaneity of, 100; obscurities of, 151n3; Pelagianism of, 112; pronouncement of the name of Jesus, 108–9; reference to sighs, 114; reference to spirit, 109, 153n36; scholarly studies of, 19, 100, 112; size of, 98; soul's deliverance from hell, 110; structure of, 102, 116–17, 152n10; summary of, 98, 99; textual interpretation of, 100, 101; theory of linguistic performativity in, 123; unwritten words of, 117; ventriloquizing interpretation of, 101
Stoic linguistics, 28, 30, 38–39, 44
stone in the Middle Ages, 131n19
supposition: *vs.* signification, 57–58, 143n20; theory of, 58, 143n22; without signification, 69, 75
Suso, Henry, 120
Suto, Taki, 40
syllable: distinction between *dictio* and, 87–88; grammatical definition of, 80–81; length of a single, 148n30; meaninglessness of isolated, 87; memorization of meaningless, 34, 50–51; *vs.* monosyllabic word, 88
syllable-word: hideous noise of, 92, 93; power of, 91–92; repetition of, 88, 94
symbol: *vs.* index, 150n70

tattooing, 120, 121, 155n73
Taylor, Cheryl, 81
temetum (antiquated word for wine), 46–47, 48, 49
terms: made out of a *commune ens* (vocal iterability), 69; theory of, 63–65
text: authority of, 20; reader and, 98; uninterpretable gap in, 141n83
things, 35–36

INDEX   187

time: *vs.* eternity, 147–48n17
Todorov, Tzvetan, 43
Towneley plays: linguistic incomprehension in, 17–18
Travis, Peter, 7
tregetour (sleight-of-hand artist), 3, 5, 130n13
tregetrie, 4, 5

unknown with respect to its being discussed, 3–4, 5, 6, 7
unreadable inscriptions, 102, 103–4
utterance: Augustine's schema for, 44–45; definition of, 35–36; inarticulate, 92–93; inherent to the syllable, 81; isolation of the *commune ens* in, 65, 67; meaningful, 60, 73; meaningless, 73, 75; nonsignificative, 40, 66; *vs.* prayer, 82; repetition of, 89–90, 94; significative, 37, 42, 52, 66, 70; of a single word, 81; types of, 41; variability of, 65
utterance *biltrix*, 55, 56, 60
utterance *buba*, 55, 56, 57, 62
utterance *bufbaf*, 57
utterance *hereceddy*, 38, 39–40, 41, 44
utterances *coax* and *cra*, 30–31, 32, 33, 44, 50, 81, 90
utterance *skindapsos*, 38, 39, 41, 55, 138n45

Vance, Eugene, 21
verbum (mentioned word), 43, 45, 46, 139n60
vernacular texts, 19, 23–24
vernacular theology, 84, 149nn40,41
Véronèse, Julien, 104, 105, 121
vocal brevity: principle of, 82
vocal inanity: doctrine of, 75
vocalization, 15–16
voice: extra-linguistic meaning of, 21–22; *vs.* sound, 36–37; theories of, 11, 21; vocal and nonvocal, 31; writable and nonwritable, 32–33
vox: articulate, 30, 31, 37; definitions of, 27, 37, 49; illiterate, 31; inalienable property of, 29; inarticulate, 30; literate, 30–31; literate articulate, 32, 81; literate inarticulate, 33; meaningful, 31, 32, 34; meaningless, 34, 38; as object of study, 28–29; as particular variety of sound, 30; philosophical definition of, 30; problem of spelling of, 31; signification of, 37, 39, 42, 52, 53; as syllabic, 33–34;

taxonomy of, 30–31, 39; *verbum* and, 45; writability of, 31, 32, 37
vox communis, 65, 67, 74
vox non-significativa (nonsignificative utterance): apprehension of, 95; definition of, 55, 56; history of use of, 53–54, 75, 142n8; logic and, 56–57; in material supposition, 54, 60, 62, 73–74; mental effect of, 95; signification of, 61; *vs. vox significativa*, 66
vox significativa (significative utterance), 60, 66, 67
vox singularis (singular utterance), 65, 67, 68, 69, 73
vox sola (bare utterance), 19, 29

walnut shell: interpretations of meaning of, 130n11
Watson, Nicholas, 84
Weill-Parot, Nicolas, 107
Whatley, Gordon, 112
William of Auvergne, 110, 121
William of Ockham, 63, 74, 146n60
William of Sherwood, 53, 54, 55–56
William the Ninth, Duke of Aquitaine, 15–16, 23
Wilson, Stephen, 106, 110
Wind, Edgar, 25
windmill placed under a walnut shell metaphor, 3–4, 5, 6, 7, 130n11
Wogan-Browne, Jocelyn, 81
Woolf, Virginia, 2, 11, 12, 129n4
word(s): experience of hearing, 48–49; expressionless, 9–10; hideous noise of, 95; imposition of, 39; as index, 70; in its kenotic form, 97; in material supposition, 59–60; meaningful, 37–38, 39, 48; meaningless, 38; memorization of unfamiliar, 141n85; as names of themselves, 59; non-identifiable, 48–49; nonsignificative, 40, 153n35; of one syllable, 86, 87; power of, 105, 108; Priscianic definition of, 89; referred to itself, 54; repetition of, 88–89, 94–95, 96; signification of, 40, 52–53, 57, 61–62, 69, 138n48; *vs.* syllable, 89; syllable count, 80; *See also* little word; monosyllabic word
Wyclif, John: *Tractatus de logica*, 75

Zumthor, Paul, 16, 21

Jordan Kirk is associate professor of English at Pomona College.

FORDHAM SERIES IN MEDIEVAL STUDIES

Ronald B. Begley and Joseph W. Koterski, S.J. (eds.), *Medieval Education*
Teodolinda Barolini and H. Wayne Storey (eds.), *Dante for the New Millennium*
Richard F. Gyug (ed.), *Medieval Cultures in Contact*
Seeta Chaganti (ed.), *Medieval Poetics and Social Practice: Responding to the Work of Penn R. Szittya*
Devorah Schoenfeld, *Isaac on Jewish and Christian Altars: Polemic and Exegesis in Rashi and the "Glossa Ordinaria"*
Martin Chase, S.J. (ed.), *Eddic, Skaldic, and Beyond: Poetic Variety in Medieval Iceland and Norway*
Felice Lifshitz, *Religious Women in Early Carolingian Francia: A Study of Manuscript Transmission and Monastic Culture*
Sam Zeno Conedera, S.J., *Ecclesiastical Knights: The Military Orders in Castile, 1150–1330*
J. Patrick Hornbeck II and Michael van Dussen (eds.), *Europe After Wyclif*
Laura K. Morreale and Nicholas L. Paul (eds.), *The French of Outremer: Communities and Communications in the Crusading Mediterranean*
Miguel Gómez, Damian Smith, and Kyle C. Lincoln (eds.), *King Alfonso VIII of Castile: Government, Family, and War*
Jordan Kirk, *Medieval Nonsense: Signifying Nothing in Fourteenth-Century England*

www.ingramcontent.com/pod-product-compliance
Lightning Source LLC
Chambersburg PA
CBHW030442300426
44112CB00009B/1118